Policy and Politics in
Britain

Policy and Politics in Industrial States

A series edited by Douglas E. Ashford, Peter Katzenstein, and T. J. Pempel

Douglas E. Ashford

Policy and Politics in
Britain

The Limits of Consensus

Temple University Press

Philadelphia

Temple University Press, Philadelphia 19122
© 1981 by Temple University
Published 1981
Printed in the United States of America

Library of Congress Cataloging in Publication Data

Ashford, Douglas Elliott.
    Policy and politics in Britain.

    (Policy and politics in industrial states)
    Bibliography: p.
    Includes index.
    1. Great Britain—Politics and government—1945–
2. Great Britain—Economic policy—1945–
3. Great Britain—Social policy. I. Title.
II. Series.
JN425.A83   320.941   80–19771
ISBN 0-87722-194-4
ISBN 0-87722-195-2 (pbk.)

Contents

Editors' Preface

All industrial states face a tension between bureaucracy and democracy. Modern governments have found it increasingly difficult to formulate policies adequate to the complex tasks they undertake. At the same time the growing specialization and widening scope of government have led many to question whether it can still be controlled democratically. Policy and Politics in Industrial States explores how some of the major democracies have dealt with this dilemma.

Policy is a pattern of purposive action by which political institutions shape society. It typically involves a wide variety of efforts to address certain societal problems. Politics is also a much broader concept, involving the conflict and choices linking individuals and social forces to the political institutions that make policy. Comparative analysis of the interaction between policy and politics is an essential beginning in understanding how and why industrial states differ or converge in their responses to common problems.

The fact that the advanced industrial states are pursuing many similar aims such as increasing social well-being, reducing social conflict, and achieving higher levels of employment and economic productivity means neither that they will all do so in the same way nor that the relevance of politics to such behavior will always be the same. In looking at an array of problems common to all industrial states, the books in this series argue that policies are shaped primarily by the manner in which power is organized within each country. Thus, Britain, Japan, the United States, West Germany, Sweden, and France set distinctive priorities and follow distinctive policies designed to achieve them. In this respect, the series dissents from the view that the nature of the problem faced is the most important feature in determining the politics surrounding efforts at its resolution. Taken to its logical extreme, this view supports the expectation that all states will pursue broadly similar goals in politically similar ways. Though this series will illustrate some important similarities among the policies of different countries, one of the key conclusions to which it points is the distinctive approach that each state takes in managing the problems it confronts.

A second important feature of the series is its sensitivity to the difficulties involved in evaluating policy success or failure. Goals are ambiguous and often contradictory from one area of policy to another; past precedents often shape present options. Conversely, adhering to choices made at an earlier time is often impossible or undesirable at a later period. Hence evaluation must transcend the application of simple economic or managerial criteria of rationality, efficiency, or effectiveness. What appears from such perspectives as irrational, inefficient, or ineffective is often, from a political standpoint, quite intelligible.

To facilitate comparison, the books in the series follow a common format. In each book, the first chapter introduces the reader to the country's political institutions and social forces, spells out how these are linked to form that country's distinctive configuration of power, and explores how that configuration can be expected to influence policy. A concluding chapter seeks to integrate the country argument developed in the first chapter with the subsequent policy analysis and provides more general observations about the ways in which the specific country findings fit into current debates about policy and politics.

The intervening six chapters provide policy cases designed to illustrate, extend, and refine the country argument. Each of the six policy analyses follows a common format. The first section analyzes the *context* of the policy problem: its historical roots, competing perceptions of the problem by major political and social groups, and its interdependence with other problems facing the country. The second section deals with the *agenda* set out for the problem: the pressures generating action and the explicit and implicit motives of important political actors, including the government's objectives. The third section deals with *process*: the formulation of the issue, its attempted resolution, and the instruments involved in policy implementation. The fourth and final section of analysis traces the *consequences* of policy for official objectives, for the power distribution in the issue area, for other policies, and for the country's capacity to make policy choices in the future. The element of arbitrariness such a schema introduces into the discussion of policy and politics is a price the series gladly pays in the interest of facilitating comparative analysis of policy and politics.

An important feature of these cases is the inclusion, for each policy problem, of selected readings drawn primarily from official policy documents, interpretations, or critiques of policy by different actors, and politically informed analysis. We have become persuaded that the actual language used in policy debates within each country provides an important clue to the relationship between that country's policy and its politics. Since appropriate readings are more widely available for Britain and the United States than for the non-English–speaking countries in the series, we have included somewhat more policy materials for these countries. In all instances, the readings are selected as illustration, rather than confirmation, of each book's argument.

Also distinctive of the series, and essential to its comparative approach, is the selection of common policy cases. Each volume analyzes at least one case involving intergovernmental problems: reform of the national bureaucracy or the interaction among national, regional, and local governments. Each also includes two cases dealing with economic problems: economic policy and labor-management relations. Lastly, each book includes at least two cases focusing on the relationship of individual citizens to the state, among them social welfare. Our choice is designed to provide a basis for cross-national and cross-issue comparison while being sufficiently flexible to make allowance for the idiosyncracies of the countries (and the authors). By using such a framework, we hope that these books will convey the richness and diversity of each country's efforts to solve major problems, as well as the similarities of the interaction between policy and politics in industrial states.

D. E. A.
P. J. K.
T. J. P.

Preface

The remarkably long and relatively consistent history of British politics and policy raises problems for anyone concerned with differentiating the political significance of policymaking. As I have dug more deeply into the origins of British democracy, I have been repeatedly impressed with how much the underlying pattern of interaction between politics and policy today is consistent with decisions made a century or more ago, even though the scope and scale of government activity in Britain, as elsewhere, has multiplied many times over. In many respects, Victorian politics have been imprinted more firmly on twentieth-century Britain than could be said for nineteenth-century politics in most other European countries. Because the force of British institutions and values looms so large in the evolution of British policies, tracing the interaction of politics and policy is not only an ambitious historical task, but raises particularly difficult analytical problems. Politics always seems to prevail, and policy often seems secondary to political stability and continuity. Conversely, to the extent that one takes a critical stance toward British performance over the past two decades, one almost necessarily condemns institutions and values that are deeply imbedded in British society.

My hope is that the more facile inferences that might be drawn from a simplified juxtaposition of how politics and policy interact have been avoided, or at least suitably qualified, in the analyses to follow. Studying the politics of policymaking in order to better understand political systems does not mean that we must reject the system if we find the policies wanting. Indeed, most persons admire the stability and success of British parties, participation, and political competition. As Professor Beer has so admirably written, Britain fashioned a rare compromise between ideology and participation that few other modern democracies have been able to duplicate.

But viewed in terms of the "outputs" of the political system, the British experience has been more critically assessed. Though limited by its size, this study addresses the relationship between policy and politics: the performance of the system, the accommodation between political imperatives and policy needs, and the constitutional and political adjustments to the complexities of the welfare state. If this analysis at times seems overly critical, it is because policy studies focus on performance. But we should not exclude the possibility that excessive (and successful) concentration on democratic politics (inputs) may be the best explanation of why performance often appears of secondary concern to British leaders and even to the British people.

The origins of this project are described in the series preface, but I must also add my thanks to my colleagues T. J. Pempel and Peter Katzenstein, who have been a constant source of helpful criticism and advice throughout the work on this study. Our association has reinvigorated my confidence that scholarly collaboration is fruitful, though I may at times have given them real doubts about its possibilities.

There is no way I can satisfactorily thank the hundreds of British officials and politicians to whom I have talked in recent years. I also imposed on a number of British experts the task of reading and commenting on chapters where their expertise was most appropriate. By listing them, I hope I have spared them the embarrassment of errors or prejudices I may have imposed on their efforts: Nicholas Deakin, George W. Jones, Dennis Kavanagh, Rudolf Klein, Lewis Kushnik, Norman Macrae, Lewis Minkin, Michael Moran, Peter Self, Helen Wallace, R. W. L. Wilding, and Maurice Wright.

A few words should be said about the references and citations in the book. I include in the References only those official papers that directly enter the argument of each analysis, and all official papers are listed under "Great Britain." Readers will also find that some related official papers are noted in the text, should they wish to follow up the policy background in the *Parliamentary Papers*. In a few instances, I have also cited in the text newspapers or periodicals where they provide important data or views that I summarize, but these are also omitted from the references. I hope these notations will encourage students to use the rich array of policy materials readily available in the *Times, Guardian, Economist, New Society*, and many other lively and well-written periodicals.

I have received support and stimulation from my work with the Western Societies Program of Cornell's Center for International Studies. Many of my ideas about politics and policy were set in motion at a conference on comparative policy studies that I organized for the Program. A grant from the Ford Foundation for the preparation of the volumes provided essential help, but of course my work in no way reflects the views of the Foundation. Much of the groundwork for the case studies began when I was a Fellow of the Netherlands Institute of Advanced Studies, and the book was completed while I was Simon Visting Professor at Manchester University in 1979-80. My thanks are also offered the *Times* Publishing Company, *Guardian* Newspapers, the *Economist*, the *Spectator*, and *New Society* for permission to reprint parts of numerous articles and editorials.

A final note may be appropriate at a moment when Britain is immersed in another cycle of highly controversial policymaking. If I appear at times to despair of a system that gives such unrestricted scope to adversarial politics, I hope the reader will remember that this political style is not new in British politics nor has it allowed British democracy to erode through many periods of equal or greater stress.

Douglas E. Ashford

London
March 1980

Policy and Politics in
Britain

1 Policymaking in the British Welfare State

At the turn of the century, Lowell wrote, "In politics the French-man has tended in the past to draw logical conclusions from correct premises, and his results have often been wrong, while the Englishman draws illogical conclusions from incorrect prem-ises, and his results are commonly right" (1908, pp. 14–15). A generation after the Second World War, many British leaders and analysts would not agree with this statement. Since roughly 1960 there has been a constant stream of books and articles on the British *malaise*, meaning everything from low industrial produc-tivity to poorly conceived international adventures (Shonfield, 1958; Shanks, 1961). It is not the purpose of this study to add to these critiques, much less to exploit the sense of failure that can overcome a country. Nonetheless, it is true that Britain has been slow to make some critical decisions, has vacillated when con-sistent and decisive action was needed, and has generally failed to come to grips with some fundamental social and economic problems.

We cannot hope to explore all the dimensions of Britain's social, economic, and political experience over the past two decades. Our concern will be mainly with the politics of policymaking, with how national leaders appear to make decisions that are, in turn, binding on the British people and government. The policy analy-ses that follow will provide general social and economic material to help the reader see the gravity and scale of particular problems, and to gauge how well national policies have responded to a variety of complex choices. But to say that policymaking is overly political is not necessarily a judgment on the entire society or even on an entire political system. No one would pretend that the success or failure of an intended course of action rests solely with national politicians or national administrators. Political analysis, as well as political practice, would be a simpler matter were the observable evidence of success and failure synonymous with political success and failure.

Not the least of the complications in studying the politics of policymaking is that political leaders try hard to claim credit for everything that goes well and to disclaim responsibility for anything that goes badly. There are some complex policy problems, such as public housing, where British accomplishments are impressive, but where there is also considerable evidence that the underlying policies are confused, erratic, and even contradictory (Lansley, 1979). There are other demanding policy problems, such as the reorganization of social security (see Chapter 6), where leaders have cooperated over a number of years to make improvements, though both major parties naturally seek to take credit for such "successes."

Moreover, national leaders are not solely concerned with binding decisions made in legislation or the choices contained in the orders, regulations, and directives emanating from government; national policies provide the guidelines and targets for government, and ultimately for a society, but they do not encompass all of politics. Political leaders must also worry about the condition of their party, the feelings of their constituents, the issues that might influence future elections, and the general support they appear to enjoy as disclosed in the press and by public opinion generally. Much of their time and energy goes toward keeping essential democratic institutions and processes in workable condition, and has relatively little direct connection to the daily choices that government makes. Politicians want above all not to be defeated in elections. The demands made on them by the public, their immediate followers, their parties, and their colleagues may or may not have anything to do with policymaking.

In nearly every modern democracy, one can find those on the extreme left and the extreme right who feel that the connection between popular preferences, tastes, and attitudes must be made more direct and more reliable. The right tends to think that an elected representative should freely exercise his own best judgment. The left prefers the view that representatives should be wholly accountable to their constituents' preferences and needs. We often forget that the politician's policy role was devised in the eighteenth century, when unsuccessful politicians often spent the rest of their lives in prison or exile. As the critics of eighteenth-century monarchial excesses saw, democracy in even its primitive form could not exist if the price of political failure was one's life or career. Since Labour's defeat in 1979 direct forms of representation have been advocated by the leader of the Labour left wing, Anthony Wedgwood Benn, who would like to see MPs (Members of Parliament) regularly reselected by their constituency party.

Because this study will not spend a great deal of time considering how more direct or personalized forms of representation might or might not improve policymaking, a few words should be given to the relationship of participation to policymaking in the modern state. There are undoubtedly a number of ways in which increased participation in lower-level policy formation and execution could improve democratic life. Many experiments have been made, including more community involvement in local government, worker participation or "industrial democracy" in private firms, and numerous ways of injecting consumer advice into public corporations and governmental agencies. Whether direct participation might improve policymaking at the national level is another question, and for many reasons it seems unlikely that policymaking can be easily subordinated to the short-term ebbs and flows of public opinion. As V. O. Key showed some years ago, the longer-term, secular effects of changing opinion do find their way into government. The reasons for the declining importance of direct democratic control are found not so much in individual alienation of citizens or conspiratorial schemes by politicians but in the paradoxical way in which government loses flexibility and constrains choice as it takes on a larger role in society.

Unfortunately, the phrase "welfare state" is often used in a derogatory sense. Our aim is not to cast doubt on a government that tries to do more for the public and that provides an increasing proportion of the goods and services produced in a society. Here, welfare state means simply a government that is responsible for a large share of the decisions affecting the daily lives of its citizens. The most common measure is the proportion of the national product in the hands of the government. For our purposes the threshold need not be defined precisely, but it is commonly taken to be anything from a third to a half of the national product.

In every modern democratic state, past commitments, the scope of services, the range of benefits, and the elaborate machinery of government itself means that decisions are more complex. In Britain, for example, the future of nationalized industries spills over into questions of incomes policy, the conflicts of industrial labor relations raises major problems of national economic policy and industrial development, and individual benefits as enshrined in past legislation mean that new needs and even unquestioned social inequities are hard to reconcile with continuing obligations. There is little evidence that leaders want policy choices to be more remote from the beneficiaries of government or the public generally, but the complexity of decisions, often their unforeseen effects, has made policymaking a more arduous and complicated problem.

Britain is by no means alone in finding government and administration severely strained as the scope and complexity of the welfare state increases. These difficulties have produced a broad and not entirely conclusive discussion about "governability" and the viability of the modern democratic state (Rose and Peters, 1978). Of course, the welfare state is not an entirely new phenomenon in British politics, and its roots can be traced back to early Victorian Britain (Briggs, 1961). But when one speaks of recent problems of governing the welfare state, one usually has more concrete issues in mind.

First, government has become a potent economic force. The sheer quantity of money involved in the public sector means that public spending affects interest rates, savings, profits, wages, and investment in many more ways than in the past. Government is increasingly cast in the role of mediator between public and private economic interests. Since roughly 1960, most governments have realized that public expenditure has had widely dispersed effects on the economy and the society. Unraveling and forecasting these interdependencies has become a major preoccupation of the welfare state.

A second important change has been the multiplication of intergovernmental agencies, public corporations, regulatory bodies, and specialized activities. Both liberal (Smith, 1979) and socialist (Harris, 1972) analysts have noted the rise of "corporate" control in the welfare state. In general, this means that influential groups, which often have their own clients and following, take on a dual policymaking role. They help formulate and define policies and are, in turn, beneficiaries and interpreters of policies. Corporate decisionmaking may be unaccountable to the public and even to political leaders, but, from a policy perspective, they may be crucial to the effective operation of government. As problems multiply and objectives become more ambitious, government requires more organizational support, touches a wider range of interests, requires more information, and needs more careful monitoring of its activities. However one wishes to explain the organizational complexity of modern government in all the welfare states, few persons have pointed to ways that such interdependence can be reduced.

A third general source of complexity in the welfare state is the blurring of hierarchical relationships. Unless one takes into account how much more the modern welfare state is trying to do and how much more complex the entire structure of government has become, it is hard to see how leaders may have less influence than in an age of simpler and more narrowly defined government. Decisions have ways of spilling over into other policy areas in unpredicted and sometimes contradictory ways. Much of the preoccupation with governmental reorganization in the 1960s was a manifestation of confusion in relating the growing functions of government to policymaking. What seem to be clear-cut choices often prove unworkable when implemented; what start out as carefully designed and rational plans often become highly irrational and ambiguous in application; and even where policies achieve their objectives with relative success, unforeseen effects frequently create new burdens, new constraints, and new problems for other parts of government.

The decisional complexity and interdependence of policies that characterize the development of the welfare state take a peculiar form in Britain. All the studies will to some extent show how particular historical, institutional, and political constraints affect policymaking. The unique characteristic of the British political system with which this study will be primarily concerned is the high premium placed on adversarial behavior at the uppermost levels of decisionmaking. Compared to most modern democracies, the Opposition has relatively few ways to intervene in lawmaking and policy choices, the supporters of the governing majority in Parliament are themselves excluded from policymaking to a remarkable degree, and the inner circle of cabinet and ministers operates under conditions of secrecy and other forms of insulation from external political forces that probably exceeds that of most democratic governments. The formulation, implementation, and evaluation of policies are subject to the judgment and priorities of a very small group of top political leaders. Given this concentration of power at the pinnacle of the British political system, why does it seem that policymaking has in some important respects also been ineffective, erratic, and indecisive?

The paradox is unraveled by considering how elite consensus about the inner workings of government interlocks with social acceptance and support for British political institutions. What Eckstein (1961) has called the high congruence among norms and values about politics has two effects that ultimately affect policymaking by curtailing and moderating the effective influence of adversarial behavior. First, strong elite consensus means that the procedures and rules regulating conflict and competition at high levels in the political system are less subject to change than in most democratic systems. Adversarial behavior is pronounced and dramatic, but focused less on the assessment and goals of existing and future choices than on supporting the existing structure. Second, the high level of social agreement about the organization and values of the system, although severely taxed in recent years, means that mobilizing social protest and social needs in ways that more directly impinge on policy is difficult; to a remarkable extent policymaking is also organized in ways that make exclusion comparatively easy. Thus, the two forces that might focus adversarial behavior on performance rather than on inputs are constrained. This relationship is sustained because the elite naturally have little interest in making changes in a system that bestows enormous powers on them; and the society generally has a high degree of confidence in the system.

The result is that, although leaders have enormous powers and strong social support compared to those in many modern democracies, there are few incentives to extend adversarial politics in ways that might threaten the concentrated powers at the highest levels of government. Adversarial behavior is dramatic in relation to voters and parties but marginally effective in defining the goals of policies, in dealing with structural problems, and in articulating intractable social problems and divisive issues. As we shall see in the policy analyses to follow, leaders can often simply ignore public preferences and new social pressures with relatively little risk to their own status and influence. There are few ways to cast doubt on policies without jeopardizing the close association between elite consensus about the operation of government and societal acceptance of the system. The question is not only what the virtues of highly adversarial behavior are in maintaining the system generally, but how well the constraints of elite and societal agreement on the rules and procedures of government have handled complex and interdependent choices.

One can have highly adversarial behavior about policymaking without necessarily making effective and lasting policies. Issues that might trigger social conflicts do not easily fit the adversarial pattern of British government. Problems that might threaten the elite consensus are postponed and possibly neglected. The policy analyses to follow will provide a rough measure of how well Britain has been able to define its long-term goals, to launch consistent and lasting efforts to deal with some of the needs and weaknesses of the country, and to adapt to a changing international and domestic environment. All this is not to say that the comparatively high level of elite and societal agreement about the system does not have other important benefits for the political system, but the particular aim of policy analysis is to judge how the ways of eliciting agreement and defining objectives solve problems and help redefine issues that are clearly important to the society. The articulation and organization of consensus both within the elite and more widely in the society may work well in sustaining confidence in the institutions themselves, while failing to solve widely recognized problems.

The politics of policymaking emphasizes how a political system deals with a changing environment, but stresses the conflicts and dilemmas of finding solutions within the extremely complex setting of governing the welfare state. Unlike the sociological or economic analysis of policy, "objective" political standards for policies are much more difficult to arrive at. There are many reasons for this difficulty, but perhaps the most important is that defining standards presupposes that we can construct an ideal model of society or of some component of society. Put differently, if we could agree on what an ideal political system might be, then the aims and procedures of policymaking would follow, and governments could be assessed according to how well or how poorly they achieved predetermined goals. Many would argue, of course, that under such conditions democratic politics, at least as now understood, would be impossible. In general, democracies are distinguished by agreement about the ways that individual preferences, attitudes, and values should relate to politics (namely, the electoral and party structures), but do not presuppose how such popular control, once expressed, should determine the policies generated by the political system.

Thus, analyzing the politics of policymaking requires that we have some basic understanding of major constraints placed on converting popular demands into official policies. Parties, legislatures, courts, and bureaucracies are involved in deciding on the essential conditions that should be preserved in converting demands into enforceable rules and collectively shared benefits. Indeed, many feel that as the policy environment becomes more complex, organizational and institutional priorities may overcome effective representation of demands and become an obstacle to change. The compromise between ideology and politics has been most often studied in relation to the demands placed on the system, the nature of participation and parties, and the ways that leaders construct agreements in order to elicit public approval. Beer's analysis of British politics (1965) is probably the definitive study of how the British political system has reconciled changing political values to institutions. In some respects our study builds on this peculiarly British accomplishment, but examines how consensual values relate to the performance of the British political system.

Compared to most modern democracies, Britain has enjoyed remarkably strong social agreement about the form and procedures of government. The political history of the past two centuries has hardly been tranquil, but there have not been the crises of legitimacy, the conflicts of political unification, and the tragic relapses into fascist politics that are found among other European countries. In a sense, the British were able to concentrate on restructuring how demands relate to politics ("inputs"), and this, as Beer shows, they did with great success. Strong social approval provided the foundation for strong elite consensus. Except for the final and foolhardy attempt by the House of Lords to control the House of Commons in 1909, political institutions, political actors, and the basic organization of executive and legislative powers changed very little in this century. The aim of this analysis is to see how the high degree of elite and societal consensus relates to policymaking now that the state has gone through a major evolution into the welfare state.

But it is also possible that strong elite consensus may have made adjusting to the needs of the welfare state too easy. Agreement *about* government might mean that British politicians have been spared many of the perplexing questions about consensus *within* government that are commonly found in the raging constitutional debates of France, the turbulent congressional politics of the United States, and the self-conscious efforts to rebuild Japanese and German democracy. Social values and attitudes necessarily affect how government is justified, but there is a second problem of converting social agreement into effective government. As the environment becomes more complex, as it surely has as the scope of government increases, the vital question is less why social support exists than how well leaders can adjust the performance of government to the constraints of old political institutions, to the parliamentary habits of the past, and above all to their increasing dependence on a huge administrative apparatus.

Although this study is not directly concerned with the roots of societal consensus for government, it is important to understand that the policymaking problems of British government in a more complex environment stem from the unusual relationship between societal and elite consensus in British politics. The essential point was made by Lowell (1908, pp. 2–5) when he noted how the separation of "constituent and law-making powers" does not exist in the British political system. Every modern democratic government except Britain's has an elaborate set of rules or written constitutions that define the interrelationship of key political actors, their respective powers and obligations, and their roles in formulating new laws. Other democracies developed through a series of political crises, revolutions, and major social conflicts that produced a body of laws that more clearly distinguish societal consensus from the specific conduct of government. All the modern democracies experience constitutional crises when political leaders exceed their powers. But in Britain the law does not differentiate as clearly between societal and elite consensus as it does in most democracies. As we shall see, were it to do so, the fundamental principles of British constitutional practice (there is no written constitution as such) would be violated. Hence, societal consensus is virtually synonymous with elite consensus, and may conceal or even repress the need to reexamine how well elite consensus affects policymaking.

Electing a government implies acting on certain priorities and programs, but in Britain the citizen has no reserved powers. Rousseau had this in mind when he wrote that Englishmen are only free at the moment they cast their ballots. The policymaking effect is that the elected government has virtually unlimited legal power to pass laws. The British constitution consists of the entire body of statutory law plus an accumulated and evolving set of customs and conventions. There are no laws on the nature of the representative system (these have been evolved from a series of laws on enfranchisement), on the existence of the House of Commons and how governing majorities are formed within it, on the organization of the cabinet or political parties, or on the powers of the prime minister and the relation of the executive to Parliament. The conduct of government, then, is not only concentrated in the hands of elected representatives but also insulated from social pressures to a greater extent than is found in most democracies.

The immense powers concentrated in British government mean that elite consensus is left to the elected leaders and representatives. Quite literally, the greatest risk to British democracy is the totally unrestrained nature of government itself. Such a concentration of power has both an inhibiting and a liberating effect on government. On the one hand, British politicians are intensely aware of the power that they enjoy and the necessity to observe the procedural and customary rules of lawmaking. Were they not, the entire political system, not just policymaking, would be threatened. On the other hand, they operate under no clear constraints in framing laws, organizing government, and amending past legislation. As Blackstone, a leading legal commentator, wrote, Parliament "can do anything that is not naturally impossible." In the absence of constitutional limitations, British lawmakers can exercise their imagination and ingenuity in ways that are foreclosed in other democracies, but they can also make blunders at relatively low risk to their status and authority.

Thus, the central problem with which the following policy analyses will deal is how the delicate balance is maintained between the arbitrary use of power and the innovation needed to advance the welfare state. Except for the limitations they impose upon themselves, politicians have very few guidelines in resolving policy conflicts and crises. For this reason, Chapman wrote, "British government is a rich Byzantine structure through which few can pick their way with any degree of certainty" (1963, p. 18). There are few legal formalities or constitutional limitations that enable us to separate the process of government from government itself. There is no judicial review, definition of executive powers, or binding administrative law that might provide clues as to how politics intervenes in policymaking. In fact, to consider policy-making as a distinct function of British government would no doubt seem strange to most British politicians and political scientists. Some laws are unquestionably more important and would not be changed lightly, but all laws have equal legal significance. Just as social agreement rests on the existence of government in a more fundamental way than in most democracies, so also elite consensus can only be extracted from the daily exchanges and political battles that take place in the House of Commons, the cabinet, and ministerial offices.

The purpose of this chapter is to describe the most important relationships within British government that bear on making critical decisions. Since there are good accounts of the formalities of British policymaking (Brown and Steel, 1979; Smith, 1970), it will contain little on procedural formalities or on those parts of British government, like the House of Lords (upper legislative chamber), that do not have a strong voice in determining and guiding major policies. The three sections to follow deal with the major elements of policy formation and implementation: the prime minister and cabinet, who form the executive arm of government insofar as it can be distinguished in the British political system; the ministers, their departments, and the administrative structure, which provide the framework for policy formation and execution; and the organization of demands on government through parties, pressure groups, and elections. Before outlining these basic political relationships to policymaking, however, some attention should be given to how Britain itself made the transition from a liberal state to the modern welfare state with all its complexities and uncertainties.

Political Implications of the Welfare State

The nineteenth-century development of the liberal state was more painful and more erratic for most of Europe than for the British political system. When the distinguished Victorian constitutionalist Walter Bagehot pronounced that Britain was living in the best of all possible political worlds, there were few who doubted him, and there were indeed few reasons why he should have been doubted. Few other countries enjoyed the stability and prosperity of Victorian England. Most other European countries were going through serious social conflicts and political crises. France needed over two centuries of successive empires, monarchies, and republics to find an acceptable form of democratic government, and most would agree that modern democratic government was not firmly established until the Dreyfus affair early in this century. Germany and Italy went through extended unification crises, and neither managed to form a democratic government that could withstand fascism. Japan was still ruled at the turn of the century by a group of aggressive modernizers who self-consciously and purposefully set out to blend ancient practices with modern needs. In all these cases, political leaders had to think more carefully about the apparatus of government, the compromises to be made between executive and legislative power, and the effective design of government itself.

British leaders tended to look upon most of these nation-building exercises with skepticism, and even suspicion. In nineteenth-century Britain the requirements of modern democracy were simply superimposed on an existing governmental structure. Many saw the modest expansion of the electorate in 1832 as the end of British democracy, but there was a steady, if controversial, flow of legislation expanding the electorate throughout the century. These changes did not seem to disrupt the life of the ruling class; Parliament itself was dominated by the aristocracy until the turn of the century. Likewise, providing a modern administration seemed no major problem even though there was concern that it would diminish the importance of MPs. A modern civil service system was proposed in 1854, and gradually took root until 1871, when all departments were compelled to recruit higher civil servants through a merit system. Even mass political parties did not seem to pose insuperable problems to the stability of British politics. The transition to modern, highly organized parties was by no means painless, but by the end of the century the Liberals and Conservatives represented distinct alternatives and engaged in mass politics, though each could trace its origins back through several hundred years of aristocratic British government. Elite consensus was never seriously jeopardized by the changes that tore many newer democracies apart and often exposed virtually irreconcilable social differences.

The close association between societal and elite consensus was never questioned. There was no crisis of legitimacy like those that forced leaders of other countries to demarcate the unalienable rights of citizens, the limits of executive and legislative powers, and the forms of redress, amendment, and political organization.

The policymaking machinery did not need to be differentiated from the exercise of authority or, in turn, to be more directly exposed to social change and social pressures. Though it is impossible to do justice to the deep historical roots of this apparently uncritical acceptance of modern democratic government, it is essential to know that the fundamental crisis in the evolution of British politics was not about democracy at all, but about the role of the monarch and the exercise of absolute power. There is indeed a definition of elite consensus in British political history, but it is to be found in the crises of seventeenth- and eighteenth-century politics.

Although the assertion of parliamentary power can easily be traced back to the Magna Carta of 1215, the most important institutional developments emerged from controversies with the Stuart and later the Hanoverian monarchs. These crises account for both the basic limitations and the virtually unlimited power of modern cabinet government in Britain. The seventeenth-century advocates of parliamentary government wanted to outlaw the Star Chamber justice and administration of royal absolutism. To do so, they had to establish the common law and statutory law of Parliament as the supreme law of the land. We can say, simplistically, that the concentration of power in the modern British Parliament originated when the absolute powers of the monarch were transferred to Parliament. Like the absolute monarchs, Parliament "can do no wrong," although it was never empowered through a written constitution. To have devised a written constitution at a time when the monarchial threat to nascent democratic government still existed would have put the slow accumulation of parliamentary power in jeopardy. To seventeenth-century parliamentarians, unlike later democratic revolutionaries, a written constitution was a greater threat to British democracy than an unwritten one. Thus, from its origins British democracy required a high level of elite consensus.

An even more important consequence affecting contemporary policymaking is that no tradition of administrative law emerged. The Stuarts were particularly ingenious in devising ways to establish their own courts of justice, raise taxes, and appoint powerful court officials. To have a distinct set of rules and procedures about administration would have also been a threat to the still weak Parliament. In fact, the leading seventeenth-century jurist Edward Coke was against discretionary powers of any kind, distrusting the "uncertain and crooked cord of discretion" (Wade, 1977, p. 22). British constitutionalists are almost unanimous in their dislike of administrative law. The late nineteenth-century constitutionalist Albert V. Dicey wrote that administrative law is "foreign to the fundamental assumptions of our English common law." Suspicion of administrative justice continues to the present. When a leading spokesman of the Labour Party, Richard Crossman, missed a discussion of French administrative law at Oxford, he wrote in his *Diaries* (1976, p. 146), "Fortunately, everyone said it was nonsense."

However well founded these early precedents were historically, they are of enormous importance in understanding the insularity of elite consensus and the ambiguities of policymaking in contemporary British government. There is no official voice outside Parliament that provides a continuing critique of how well government is working. The French Cour des Comptes or the Conseil d'Etat, for example, are not only constitutional guardians, but critics of ministerial decisions, administrative orders, and even individual treatment by government. Despite the seventeenth-century distrust of delegation, modern government could not operate without huge powers of interpretation and implementation being placed in ministers' hands. Within government, conflicting jurisdictions and objectives multiplied, but untangling these policy problems continues to rest almost entirely with the cabinet and higher civil servants. Perhaps the greatest loss is that learning from past errors and experience depends on a remarkably small number of persons who in fact have very little time, and very little incentive, to make the critiques and evaluations of policy effectiveness that are more pronounced in most other democratic political systems.

The odd result is that, in an age of mass politics, British government makes many crucial decisions with relatively little policy guidance. At best, elections help clarify public controversies confronting political leaders. Electoral outcomes may account for shifts in broad areas of policymaking, but they do not tell leaders how to handle investment in nationalized industries, the advisability of separating ("hiving off") large agencies from government to form new public agencies or public corporations, or the way that tax breaks for industry might be adjusted. Party election manifestos provide the outlines of the policies of a future government, but once in office leaders must adjust their priorities to many unforeseen events and crises and can rarely ignore accumulated legislation and precedents. Once elected to office, British MPs and above all the cabinet are not only hard pressed by the daily flow of business but are comparatively free of the continuing political pressures and demands found in less well-disciplined political systems.

Even within Parliament the political cross pressures and bargaining are less intense. The ruling majority presents an opening address to Parliament (the Queen's Speech) setting out the major legislative aims for the session, but political foresight can generally specify no more than about half the government bills to be enacted. The Opposition is most concerned to demonstrate its fitness to replace the governing majority, but this does not involve making detailed critiques of major legislation. The MP is bound by his party group within the House of Commons, and it is not unusual for an MP from the majority to vote against a bill in committee (a more impartial review of bills) and then to vote for a bill in the House of Commons, where party discipline can be more effectively enforced. Party leaders have to be sensitive to backbench opinions (MPs not in the cabinet), but the individual MP has little influence in drafting bills and very little chance of changing bills once the cabinet has formed its policy. Thus, compared to most modern democracies, policymaking is remarkably concentrated in the cabinet and the higher civil service.

In an era of more narrowly conceived government, the political constraints placed on British policymaking were no doubt much less of a handicap. Government was largely concerned with defense, the national debt, and foreign affairs. There were political crises such as the Irish question in late Victorian England, but they did not call for intricate solutions involving hundreds of civil servants, orchestrating an array of governmental agencies, and manipulating massive sums of public money. The welfare state has produced a new setting for government, and it is with these more distinctly domestic complexities of government that we shall be primarily concerned. In some respects, Britain was unarmed for the complexities of modern government even though the welfare state made important early advances in the nineteenth century (Bruce, 1968; Fraser, 1973). Under the impulse of the early utilitarians, the British generated a notion of "social engineering" that predated the readiness of government to take on many of the social and economic tasks we now automatically associate with the welfare state. Though many Victorian party leaders and MPs were suspicious of utilitarian principles, the century witnessed major improvements in factory inspection, public health, education, and housing. Few of these reforms would be considered adequate today, but on the whole the early demands for better services did not produce political stalemate and reconsideration of the relation of elite consensus to policymaking.

The important point in respect to policymaking was that it became widely accepted that new policies or programs be designed and implemented outside Parliament. If the major parties could put forth the main lines of reform, then design and implementation would go forward with little need for localized political adjustment or for sectoral bargaining. No doubt the stability of parliamentary government itself encouraged detachment from the consequences of decisions. If the utilitarians had less direct policy influence than Bentham and his coterie of reformers wanted, they probably succeeded in implanting the idea that the objectives of new policies could be successfully defined at the pinnacle of government and that rational thinking would evoke a rational response among clients and beneficiaries. Letwin (1965) calls this kind of self-confidence, sometimes taking the form of paternalism, "the pursuit of certainty."

For many reasons, the rising Labour Party did not challenge the basic pattern of politics enshrined in cabinet and parliamentary government. The Labour Party, which actually began by sharing power with the Liberal Party in order to get more seats in the House of Commons, wanted to be accepted in the system, not to change the British power structure. The intellectual leaders of the Labour Party saw government as an instrument to be used on behalf of the less privileged, and were content with the concentration of power, which they saw might well be used for more equalitarian purposes. Although there was a higher proportion of working-class MPs in the Parliamentary Labour Party (PLP) in the 1920s than there is today, the trade unions were most concerned to dismantle oppressive legislation, not to create a social revolution. At the turn of the century a second round of "social engineering" proposals came forth from the Fabians, led by Sidney and Beatrice Webb. Their aim was to "permeate" government, not to restructure the basis of elite and societal consensus. Thus, the major political development that might have introduced a more complex form of political bargaining into British politics, and might have even questioned the role of elite consensus in the political system, did little to alter the politics of policymaking.

A second major force in simplifying the relation of politics to policymaking was the idea that national legislation should be skeletal. Much of the nineteenth-century social reform in fact devolved on local government. Although the national administration grew, it was effectively subordinated to ministers, and the administration was composed of generalists from roughly the same social class as the MPs. Top civil servants were "to serve their masters," not enter into combat with politicians. The grubby business of making political deals and compromises was left to a relatively small number of party leaders working behind the closed doors of the cabinet, and more often meeting in exclusive clubs. There was not much alarm expressed over the growing number of boards, local agencies, and committees dealing with the growing complexities of the welfare state, nor did most leaders think that these organizational and lower-level political problems were very important.

The policymaking effect is especially important because elite consensus was never challenged by the competition between political and administrative powers that can be found in most democracies. France was always threatened with becoming an "administrative state" because its powerful administrative system predates the rise of democratic government. Late modernizers, such as Japan, had to have powerful administrative agencies if they were to catch up with other industrial powers, and the more dynamic remnants of the Tokugawa bureaucracy became the agents of modernization. In Germany there was the deep notion of the Rechtsstaat that made administrative theory, if not practice, central to German political thinking. In the United States the federal system could pit state and national bureaucracies against each other, and the administration was often no less immersed in patronage politics than were politicians. The result was that in most other countries politicians developed a keen sense of how politics and administration interlock. The point is not that more open administrative conflict was necessarily more democratic or even more beneficial for these countries, but that achieving high political office also meant understanding a great deal about how to control and direct administration. In contrast, the British higher civil service never challenged elite consensus and the political system never needed to develop more sophisticated methods of subordinating the bureaucracy.

If we know very little about key policy decisions of political leaders, we also know almost nothing about the advice and influence of top-level British administrators. They have no reason to question the elite consensus that insulates policymaking from external actors and the public because they are the main beneficiaries of this isolation. Too much has probably been made of the efforts to democratize British administration, which becomes increasingly difficult to accomplish as the tasks of government become more specialized and diverse. What political leaders of both major parties have consistently agreed on, however, is that more open government would compromise the British policymaking process as it now exists. The immediate and practical effect would be, of course, to diminish ministerial powers. But at the root of the problem is the interdependence of elite and societal consensus with government and policymaking. It is virtually impossible to find a way that administrative influence and performance might be more openly discussed without simultaneously jeopardizing the constitutional principles on which the entire system rests.

A third and more commonly discussed element in the closely knit political circle surrounding British policymaking is the relatively small size of the political elite. "Political elite" is used in the more specific sense adopted by Putnam (1973, p. 12), meaning "those in any society rank toward the top of the (presumably closely inter-correlated) dimensions of interest, involvement, and influence in politics." There is a great deal of evidence that British political leaders come from the same clubs, the same schools, and often the same families, but as Hewitt points out (1974, pp. 61–62) social background does not account for the organization of their political roles, how they may agree on the essentials of politics, or even their response to socially disadvantaged groups. As might be expected, Conservative leadership conforms more closely to the criteria of social distinction in Britain, but the Labour Party leadership has also gravitated toward university graduates and in particular Oxbridge graduates. There is, of course, little evidence in the history of politics that the rewards and blandishments of office would be less were political leaders more socially representative. Even the more ideologically militant leaders of the French and Italian left profess fairly modest aims in restructuring the policy process.

In relation to policymaking, the limitations of the British political elite are fairly concrete and specific. Politicians enter their political careers at a relatively young age (nearly two-thirds of them before they are forty) and they serve long apprenticeships as dutiful backbenchers and junior ministers (fifteen to twenty years). The test of political promise and skill is how well one learns the rules of the game in the House of Commons. Parliamentary questioning and informal consultations with backbenchers mean that MPs' views on legislation are heard, but compared to most legislatures they are not expected to forge political compromises, to devise new solutions, or to help chart future policy strategies. As Butt points out (1969, pp. 327–37), MPs are by no means "yes men," and party leaders are reluctant to use the most severe punishment, expulsion from the parliamentary party. But their independence is most often exercised on moral issues, such as homosexuality, capital punishment, and abortion, which governments are often happy to leave to "free votes" (non-party) or private member bills. The procedures and, to an increasing extent, the information and skills used to frame new legislation and to resolve complex policy problems rest with the cabinet and with ministers and their departments.

Once MPs achieve ministerial status, their capacity to formulate new policies is limited in various ways. First, British ministers remain in charge of their departments for relatively short periods, about two years. This was not always so. In Lord Salisbury's government (1885–92), ministers stayed in the same department for nearly five years (Heady, 1974, p. 96). There is, of course, a delicate balance to be drawn between the infusion of new ideas and energy and the requisites of effective policymaking. Prolonged tenure can lead to negligence. But contrary to the popular view, British ministers have shorter ministerial tenure than most of their counterparts in Europe (Herman, 1975). Short tenure is partially due to reshuffling of cabinets as ministers make errors or as policy reversals shake confidence in the government. Nonetheless, to the extent that the complexities of policymaking in the welfare state need longer-term, continuing effort in order to permit substantial changes, the highest level of political leadership is handicapped.

Policy innovation and experimentation are not the most highly prized qualities of ministers and aspiring MPs. While it is true that a number of recent prime ministers (Churchill, Macmillan, and Wilson) made their mark by rebelling against party policy, the issues were dramatic problems of foreign policy, not the humdrum problems of reorganizing social security or local government. Ministers are highly prized for their ability to deal with the rough and tumble of the House of Commons and their appeal to the electorate. The experience of the top British policymakers is almost uniformly experience within government. When prime ministers have persuaded outsiders to enter the cabinet directly, the results have been discouraging. In 1964, Wilson brought Frank Cousins, a highly respected leader of the Trades Union Congress (TUC), into his cabinet, but in 1966 the labor leader resigned, disillusioned with the ambiguities and compromises essential to government. Again, in 1970, Heath brought in John Davies, former chairman of the Confederation of British Industries (CBI), but the industrial leader had similar problems with the give and take of the Commons and relating his managerial style to cabinet government.

At the turn of the century, Low (1927, p. 203) suggested that, as government became more specialized and complex, the danger to democratic government was "not that the House of Commons may become too zealous, but that it may not be zealous enough." Whether democratic procedures can in fact encompass the complexity of modern government goes beyond the immediate purpose of this study, but compared to many modern democracies the British political system has generated relatively few incentives to innovate in public policy, to articulate underlying social and economic conflicts, and to expose the administration to public criticism and public demands. It is an open question whether any modern democratic legislature can deal with the complexities of policymaking in the welfare state. Even so, the British political elite is remarkably secure. About two-thirds of the MPs are elected from "safe seats," meaning that so long as they meet the requirements of party discipline in the House of Commons and fulfill the general expectations of their constituencies, they are likely to be reelected. Leading members of the government can, of course, be defeated in elections, as Shirley Williams was in 1979, but the policy implications are not clear and, when they are, the issue is rarely one of the perplexing problems facing government.

British politics provides ways of protecting political leaders in much the same way as any other democratic system. By-elections are used to restore a leading figure to the House of Commons, and occasionally an older member of the party will accept a peerage and membership in the House of Lords in order to vacate a constituency for a defeated MP. The more difficult question is whether the security of the governing elite, in turn, detracts or adds to capacities to make policies in the more complex environment of the welfare state. As the scope and complexity of government increases, the juncture between political competition and policy formation becomes more important. For historical reasons, Parliament and the cabinet have enormous power compared to those in any other modern democratic state. The close association of societal and elite consensus was the foundation of what most would regard as the preeminent example of modern democratic government. In turn, the politics of policymaking is simplified by giving extraordinary power to the executive—the cabinet—which is shielded from many of the political pressures common to the politics of other democracies. Concessions and compromises are undoubtedly made, but the politics of policymaking necessarily takes second place to the requirements of cabinet government. Our first task is to outline how politics and policymaking are joined in the British political system. The policy analyses to follow will then provide a basis for judging how the British have tried to blend the peculiar requirements of their political system with the complications of policymaking in the welfare state.

The more general implications of the politics of British policymaking will be left to Chapter 8. The broad lines of the British approach to policymaking have, I hope, been made clear, and the underlying political constraints outlined. The evolution of British democracy made it difficult, possibly hazardous to democratic government itself, to differentiate the basis of social support for government and the rules of the game surrounding the workings of government. To maintain the close association of societal and elite consensus the ruling majority made substantial concessions to the welfare state in the nineteenth century, and has continued to give social needs a high priority in twentieth-century policies. Whether acceptance of the welfare state was an acknowledged price to be paid to preserve the stability of the political system or was the product of political competition is in many ways the theme of the policy analyses to follow in later chapters. Without prejudging the cases, it is hard to avoid the conclusion that policymakers often acted in anticipation of major social and economic changes, at least insofar as new pressures from the policymaking environment could threaten underlying principles of the British constitution and, in turn, the political consensus on which British government depends. The inference is that policymaking in Britain has, at least in political terms, been primarily defensive, possibly more so than might be expected in any democratic country. The result may be that Britain is governed by a "directionless consensus" (Rose, 1974, p. 424). Such a high value is placed on keeping social and political expectations in harmony that the politics of policymaking has been seriously constrained. The British political system may be unable to accommodate what is in many ways its most creative accomplishment, the welfare state itself.

Cabinet and Ministers: Does the Emperor Have Clothes?

The cabinet is the nerve center of British policymaking. As in the case of most critically important executive bodies at the center of British government, it emerged through the gradual accumulation of customs and conventions. Nearly all the rules governing the organization and procedures of the cabinet are part of the unwritten constitution. Formally speaking, the cabinet is a committee of the Privy Council, a group of royal advisors that were once used to circumvent the wishes of Parliament. As Lowell pointed out (1908, pp. 54–55), it became a special kind of committee because it was indirectly elected (by the parliamentary party in control of the House of Commons) and was not representative, but composed of the men "who have forced themselves into the front rank of the party." His definition still stands today: "an informal but permanent caucus of the parliamentary chiefs of the party in power" (p. 56).

Essential to understanding the contemporary status of the cabinet, and, in turn, the dilemmas of compromising its crucial role in policymaking, is the historical struggle that took place to establish its powers. Although many of the fundamental powers of Parliament were established with the revolution of 1688 (in fact, a change of dynasty), the Hanoverian monarchs of the late eighteenth century engaged in "shameless bribery" (Low, 1927, p. 25) to acquire the support of ministers without their decisions being submitted to Parliament. Much of the struggle to achieve the independence of the cabinet involved excluding royal ministers from Parliament. The Act of Settlement of 1701 provided that officers of the Crown could not sit in Parliament and that all acts must be countersigned by Parliament's own officers. Thus, the defenses now used by the cabinet have their origins in a critically important struggle between monarchial and parliamentary power.

Until the First World War the British cabinet had virtually no formal existence, although it had been recognized as the crucible of government for nearly a century. There were no cabinet records, no designated time or place of meeting, no staff, no rules, and no funds for its support. The chairman of the cabinet, the prime minister, had no legal existence. When proposals were made to Parliament in 1851 that cabinet ministers be given precedence for ceremonial occasions, the idea was rejected because it was unknown to the constitution. Low (p. 29) notes that the title "prime minister" was first used in Parliament in 1900, and it was not recognized in law until 1937, when Britain was preparing to deal with the exigencies of war. The prime minister's formal role depended on his appointment as First Lord of the Treasury, a post that he traditionally still holds in order to be able to sign orders and to conduct government in the name of the Crown.

If the proceedings of the cabinet appear cumbersome, it is because the cabinet evolved as a committee to exclude royal ministers from Parliament, which was essential to the development of independent parliamentary power. The conflict between monarch and Parliament was influential in the American decision to define presidential and legislative powers firmly. The reluctance of Parliament to compromise cabinet powers today is rooted in the struggle to make ministers responsible to it and to no one else. Until 1867 ministers could only change posts in the cabinet by submitting to reelection, and until 1926 ministers were expected to stand for reelection when appointed to the cabinet (Low, 1927, p. 16). As parties evolved, the tradition was also established that the prime minister must be from the House of Commons. Ministerial responsibility emerged before the idea of collective responsibility of the cabinet, and is deeply imbedded in the unwritten constitution. However poorly we may feel that cabinet and ministerial responsibilities can be performed in an era of more complex government, it is important to remember how difficult it would be to replace the responsibility of ministers before Parliament in the British political system.

Formally speaking, the cabinet consists of roughly twenty persons selected by the prime minister. But when the British speak of the government (most often capitalized) they mean the entire body of ministers in the cabinet, additional ministers who may be excluded (about thirty persons), and junior ministers or MPs assigned to help ministers (about fifty persons). In addition, ministers are entitled to have a number of parliamentary private secretaries (about thirty) who keep contact with Parliament, sound out reactions to new proposals, and follow bills that ministers may have before Parliament. The total number of MPs involved in the government has steadily risen since the turn of the century. In 1900 there were 42; in 1950, 95; in 1970, 115; and in 1975, 118 (Butler and Sloman, 1975, p. 73). If we take into account that a governing majority in the House of Commons needs to be 318 MPs (a "safe" majority will be larger), about a third of the MPs of the ruling party are committed to the executive, fall within the rules of confidentiality governing cabinet business, and are excluded from open debate of government proposals until legislation is under way. The way in which cabinet requirements monopolize a large number of influential MPs is, of course, one of the most important ways that policymaking power is restricted in the British political system.

The prime minister is not entirely free in selecting his cabinet; there is more room for a choice in selecting how important ministries will be assigned. Perhaps the most important change brought about by the complexity of modern government is the increasing number of "intermediate ministers," ministers assigned to special tasks within the cabinet and given coordinating roles. There are several cabinet posts without departmental responsibilities that the prime minister can fill to meet his own priorities. For example, Wilson used the position of chancellor of the Duchy of Lancaster to appoint a minister to oversee industrial policy. Similar possibilities are presented by the lord privy seal, the paymaster general, and the lord president of the Privy Council. Assigning tasks to these positions allows the prime minister to state his priorities and also helps accomplish interdepartmental coordination for problems that involve several ministries, such as membership in the European Community. Modern government needs careful policy coordination. Willson (1978, p. 48) finds that there were only three such posts in the Attlee government (1945–51) but twenty-six by 1977.

The modern style of cabinet government is most often dated from Lloyd George's reorganization of the cabinet during the First World War. Oddly enough, it is the expanding role of government that drives prime ministers to form a smaller group of advisors so that basic strategy and priorities may be thrashed out with a smaller number of persons. At the turn of the century, Lord Rosebery, prime minister in 1894–95, noted that the expanding role of government made it harder to exercise "decisive authority," and Arthur Balfour, prime minister from 1902 to 1905, was known to consult a close circle of friends (Lowell, 1908, p. 70). But by roughly 1920 the conduct of government had changed radically. Responsibility had been acquired for unemployment, education, labor relations, transportation, commerce, health, and public works. As the pressure of government business increased, prime ministers turned to a more select group of advisors and confidants, some in the cabinet and some outside. Since the "kitchen cabinet" of Lloyd George there have been repeated experiments: "super-ministers" to oversee large, consolidated departments; "inner cabinets" of trusted friends not always in the cabinet itself; "partial cabinets" assembled from interested ministers, which are, in effect, high-level interdepartmental committees.

The growth of the cabinet and the prime minister's reliance on an inner circle of advisors are to some extent a function of the growth of government, and some feel that both trends have reduced the ability of the House of Commons to follow and to criticize the executive. But the primary responsibility for criticizing a government's policies rests with the leader of the Opposition, who has a shadow cabinet of leading MPs with experience in the various departments. Unless one understands the crucial constitutional role of the cabinet in relation to the monarchy, it is hard to see why, unlike nearly every other democratic legislature, the Opposition is excluded from policy formation. The Opposition is Parliament's only link to an alternative government in a political system where not only does the executive have great power but democratic government rests on a cabinet having the confidence of the House of Commons.

The policymaking role of the Opposition is a delicate balance between harassing and at times even obstructing the cabinet and remaining aloof from policy decisions and the preparation of legislation. The shadow cabinet must always look like a viable alternative government, but were it to have a responsibility for policies, democratic politics would be unable to differentiate alternative governments. For this reason, the role of the leader of the Opposition is in many ways more demanding than that of the prime minister. The Opposition leader and his potential government must raise questions, but cannot appear to be unreasonable; they must point out weaknesses in bills, but without disclosing their alternative plans; and they must contribute to the leadership of the country during major crises without appearing compliant. Because their role is so heavily concentrated on making minority opinion known in the House of Commons and on preparing for a coming election, the Opposition becomes the crucible of adversarial politics. The requirements of this role mean that the policymaking experience of the Opposition is largely lost to a government in office and that even debates in the House of Commons are generally much too crude and even too frivolous to contribute substantially to the complexities of policymaking.

Possibly the most important fact of contemporary cabinet government in Britain, as in most modern democracies, is that the executive is hard pressed just to carry on the daily business of government. There is little time for long-term policy discussion, and ministers easily become mired in the details of running large departments. There have been three academic debates about the growing power of ministers and the cabinet, none of which has probably had much effect on the realities of running an enormously expanded government. The first is that the complexity of government reduces Parliament's capacity to follow and to approve important decisions, perhaps most forcefully put forward by Crick (1964). A second and closely related argument, initiated by Mackintosh (1962), concerns the ability of the cabinet to dominate policymaking. The third, and less well defined, controversy involves how ministers can be made responsible and the power of the prime minister controlled. The three disputes are all evidence of the growing awareness in the 1960s that the House of Commons has a minor role in the initiation of policies and a limited capacity to inquire and to evaluate how policies have worked in practice.

The first two of these debates raise important constitutional problems, and it seems unlikely that a major structural change could be made in the relation of the House of Commons to the executive without changing the very nature of British democracy. The more practical issue is perhaps the third, raising the specter of "presidential rule." The clearest response came from Jones (1965), who argued essentially that political and electoral pressures restrain any arbitrary tendencies of the prime minister. The prime minister's multiple role itself suggests that there may be as many conflicting pressures and requirements as there are opportunities to overrule his colleagues. The prime minister is leader of his party, leader of the government in the House of Commons, and chairman of the cabinet. Although he has numerous ways to discipline impetuous ministers, he must also be aware that his own office is the prime target of ambitious and able party spokesmen.

The collective responsibility of the cabinet is of more recent origin than ministerial responsibility but, like ministerial responsibility, originated to exclude the monarch from the Privy Council and thereby establish the power of Parliament. Collective responsibility dates from the early eighteenth century and was probably irreversibly established in 1782, when the cabinet stood united against George III. In 1825 the cabinet refused to offer the monarch individual opinions on the future of the government. In the setting of modern British democracy, both the principle of collective responsibility and that of ministerial responsibility mean that the executive has substantially greater influence over policymaking than in most democratic governments. A major governmental crisis and a vote of no confidence mean that all MPs must stand for election, and in the recent past ruling parties always run close to their full term (five years) unless they have a slim majority in the House of Commons. One could argue that in an age of inescapably big government, the electoral risks of using collective responsibility are greater than the risks of controversial policy proposals.

Ministerial responsibility is a more complex issue. Many would argue that Britain has ministerial government rather than cabinet government. In any event, there is not much evidence that the well-established procedures of questioning ministers actually influence policymaking. Nor is there much evidence that ministerial responsibility serves as an important check on the cabinet. According to Finer (1975), there were only twenty resignations of ministers from 1855 to 1955. Of those resignations, four were for major blunders (for example, leaking the budget in 1947) and six because the minister found himself repudiated in cabinet. The prime minister's power to dismiss ministers is also a tricky matter. Macmillan's abrupt dismissal of seven ministers in 1962 cast a shadow over his ability to rule. There are also distinct political advantages in keeping a restless minister in the cabinet, where he is exposed to his colleagues and responsible for the government. For example, Callaghan (1976–78) kept the left-wing Labour

Party spokesman, Anthony Wedgewood Benn, in the cabinet although it was widely acknowledged that Benn opposed several major policies.

Given the secrecy of cabinet proceedings, it is difficult to judge how the political constraints of selecting, assigning, and dismissing ministers affect policymaking. Although not as clearly defined as the executive branches of other democratic governments, the British cabinet may still contain a relatively fixed body of opinion and policy advice over its term of office. Most prime ministers follow Gladstone's advice that the only thing worse than leaving out an old minister is appointing a new one. The narrower sense of ministerial responsibility, a minister's technical capacity to follow and to account for the work of a department, is certainly diminished when departments are consolidated into super-ministries and government business involves intricate bodies of rules and regulations. In a remarkably candid statement before the House Expenditure Committee (1977, pp. 756–57), the secretary of the Cabinet Office said, "The concept that because somebody whom the Minister never heard of, has made a mistake, means that the Minister should resign, is out of date, and rightly so." But the additional tasks and complexity generated by the development of the welfare state have increased the responsibility of ministers without providing many clear-cut alternatives to check and to question the exercise of these powers. Neustadt's observations (1966) are more appropriate now than when he made them: the critical constraint on executive power in British government is the department and its minister, not the legislature.

The sheer volume and complexity of government business mean that the cabinet must now be more strongly supported than in the past. The Cabinet Office is responsible to the cabinet as a whole, though it is situated behind the prime minister's Downing Street office and few important decisions are made without the secretary of the Cabinet Office consulting the prime minister. The Office is staffed by the civil service, including about fifteen higher-level civil servants (under secretaries and up) and about six hundred supporting staff. It briefs ministers on the cabinet agenda (usually with the help of the department concerned); coordinates cabinet business and plans the agenda with advice from the prime minister; oversees a few general support agencies of government such as the Central Statistical Office; and provides a home for cabinet minutes and a few top-level advisors. As can readily be seen, there is no item on the list that is not extremely politically sensitive, in particular the cabinet minutes, which in effect become directives to ministers. Secrecy prevents our having even the terse accounts that a presumably more autocratic French Council of Ministers releases to the press.

Although Wilson had more unruly colleagues than most prime ministers, there is considerable evidence that he hoped to make the Cabinet Office into a genuine executive department. The prime minister rarely holds departmental office, although he is designated head of the civil service. Like most prime ministers since the 1960s, Wilson (1964–70) felt that he lacked independent leverage on key ministries and was skeptical about the ability of the civil service. Prime ministers do have a Private Office, numbering about six senior officials and seventy supporting staff, to arrange their personal appointments, handle press relations, and channel private political advice to his office. As Wilson found it harder and harder to manage government in the late 1960s, he relied more heavily on his Private Office and particularly his private secretary, Marcia Williams (now Lady Falkenden), which created an intense controversy about his inaccessibility. When Wilson returned to office in 1974, he created a "Policy Unit" with a special advisor to organize independent policy advice and to help coordinate government business. There was, again, bitter resistance from ministers and Parliament to this effort to take policy initiatives outside the normal framework, which suggests the difficulties of constructing a more elaborate policymaking structure in British government.

Wilson's effort to provide overall policy guidance is put into perspective by very similar efforts under the Conservative government of Heath (1970–74). He organized the Central Policy Review Staff (CPRS), or "Think Tank," to act as a troubleshooter within government and to evaluate some of the more complex problems facing government. As will be described in more detail in Chapter 2, his general strategy was to overturn the basic pattern of departmental policymaking that prevails in British government. The first chairman of the CPRS was Lord Rothschild, one of the more irreverent and outspoken persons to reach the inner sanctum of British policymaking. He assembled a staff of about forty promising young civil servants and outsiders and had direct access to the prime minister. His own description of the CPRS denotes its strengths and weakness: "sabotaging the over-smooth functioning of the machinery of government" (Rothschild, 1977).

A final device to increase the policymaking capacity of ministers and the cabinet has been the appointment of advisors (Klein and Lewis, 1977). Advisors join ministries in a variety of ways, and the controversy surrounding their use again reveals the secluded atmosphere that Whitehall prefers, and that may be essential to cabinet government. There were thirty-four such appointments in the Wilson government; thirty-one under Heath; and twenty-four under Callaghan (*Economist*, Aug. 21, 1976). Wilson in particular felt the need for independent advice on economic policy and brought Thomas Balogh (now Lord Balogh) into his government as chief economic advisor (outside the Treasury). There have also been numerous "irregulars," or temporary departmental advisors, brought into government for special tasks. Heath appointed a team of businessmen to implement changes in the Civil Service Department, and in 1979 Thatcher again brought in business leaders to study departmental efficiency and to search for public spending cuts.

The intense controversies that have surrounded all these efforts to elaborate and expand the policymaking capacity of both cabinet and ministers suggests how difficult it is to change the political constraints on British policymaking. Ministers, junior ministers, and higher civil servants have found most innovations in policymaking at the highest levels of government unacceptable. Their opposition to change is echoed in the press, which sees most high-level policymaking experiments as diabolical designs of power-hungry prime ministers. Parliament views more sophisticated policymaking machinery as a threat to its representative functions. Certainly other welfare states also bicker over accommodating the difficulties and uncertainties of policymaking, but in Britain disputes over the organization and capacity of government to deal with the complexities of policymaking more often lead to stalemate. The concentration of power in the cabinet and Parliament presupposes that the initiatives of top policymakers be constrained by underlying rules that were, in fact, developed centuries ago when the power of the monarch was transferred to the cabinet. Without the conventions and customs that limit how ministers behave, British democracy would itself be jeopardized. The close interdependence of societal and elite consensus is in many ways the most serious obstacle to expanding the government's policymaking capacities. Hence, it is difficult to make political adjustments or to introduce new political actors into the system without upsetting the fundamental, if unwritten, principles on which the British political system is founded.

Ministers and Departments: Who Makes Policies?

The effective level of policymaking in the British political system is the department, which is supervised by a minister. In recent years an increasing number of ministers of important departments have been designated secretaries of state, an office reserved in the nineteenth century for a small number of ministers dealing with issues of paramount importance (defense, colonies, and foreign affairs), once linked to the Crown and used only for members of the royal court. Reinforced by the collective responsibility of the cabinet, ministers carefully guard their departmental domains, and their success as ministers depends more on how well they provide for the department in the annual budgetary battles than on policy innovation and experimentation. The ministers in charge of large departments and the more politically sensitive departments, such as the Foreign Office, have several assistant ministers, ministers of state. Even so, compared to the politically appointed component at the top of large departments in other welfare states, the layer of political leadership at the top of the departments is extremely thin. Combined with the long apprenticeship needed to acquire ministerial status, the small number of political appointments places limits on political intervention in policymaking and, some would argue, assures that ministers are so well socialized into the habits and preferences of top civil servants that policy innovation is discouraged.

The British see nothing strange in leaving the early stages of policy formation and the later stages of policy implementation almost entirely to a very few politicians, backed up by the civil service. Throughout the 1960s and until 1974, the number of departments was decreasing so that the scope of ministerial responsibilities was increasing. Both Wilson and Heath approved of large "super-ministries" that, it was hoped, would relieve the cabinet of detailed policy discussion and what often seemed to be interminable departmental axe-grinding. A reflection of the trend toward larger departments is the proliferation of upper-level civil servants. In 1976 there were 26 permanent secretaries, sometimes two or three in such key ministries as the Treasury; 20 "second" permanent secretaries (itself an indication of inflation of top civil service posts); 165 deputy secretaries, who run major divisions within departments; and 700 under secretaries, who are essentially the top-level managers of Whitehall. Like the prime minister, each minister has a small private office to conduct his political business and a parliamentary private secretary, usually a promising young MP, to help him keep in touch with the House of Commons.

One indication of the relatively fixed definition of policymaking responsibilities within British government is that so large an expansion of administrative advice and control could take place over the past two decades without anyone's questioning the relative decline of political actors in policymaking. There has been a fierce debate about the excessive influence of higher civil servants, but few serious proposals to increase the political component of departmental policymaking. Were this done, the keystone of British democratic institutions, ministerial responsibility, would be fundamentally altered. The policy effect has been that, even though British government went through substantial reorganization in the late 1960s, the political relationship between ministers and government was unchanged.

The urge to reorganize in the 1960s arose from the feeling that somehow British government was poorly prepared to cope with the complexities of the welfare state. But the principles of change were not political, but increased rationality and efficiency. DHSS, the Department of Health and Social Security (see Chapter 6), combined health, national insurance, and welfare assistance. The Department of the Environment (DOE) merged the problems of local government, housing, planning, and transportation. The effect was to make ministers even more dependent on their top administrators, and most commentators agree that the policy process within departments changed very little. In fact, the merged departments tended to remain compartmentalized from each other, and there were few benefits of more closely integrated, strategic planning. As Jordan writes (1977, p. 40), the departmental organization "appears as one of 'mad empiricism', governed solely by considerations of political expediency, where just knowing how to 'work' the system is an esoteric skill, a badge of belonging, and a political asset."

Nearly two centuries of reform and reorganization have not materially altered the relationship of ministers to their departments, to the cabinet, or to Parliament. After two decades of public expenditure planning, the departmental permanent secretary remains the responsible accounting official of his department. Departments have Management Units, but ministers and their top officials decide how these units are organized, define their objectives and projects, and ultimately rule on whether the results of management studies will be applied. External management studies, under the Treasury, are conducted only with ministerial permission and their results used only with ministerial discretion. In 1979, Thatcher discontinued the Programme Analysis and Review (PAR) projects, which Heath, another Conservative prime minister, had initiated in an attempt to get better policy coordination and overall planning within departments. Ministers and top civil servants resent intrusion into their departmental fiefs. Sir Douglas Allen, former head of the civil service, made it clear to the Expenditure Committee (1977, p. 53) that efforts to change the system of departmental control are easily appealed to the cabinet, where the mutual self-interest of ministers makes it unlikely that a department will be forced to change its habits.

Essentially, the politics of policymaking in British government runs in a small circle that quickly leads back to the cabinet. The concentration of power is difficult to penetrate from outside the highest levels of government. More diverse forms of political control would, of course, raise dilemmas for the British constitution, but more political involvement in policymaking might also help avoid the expensive, and on the whole ineffective, massive reorganizations, the constant shuffling of governmental agencies, and the resistance to interdepartmental planning that has plagued British government. The increased ministerial responsibilities combined with the ease with which ministers can repel reform has very likely made policymaking more confusing. For example, it is easy for ministers to "fiddle" more general policy guidelines. There is considerable evidence that hiving off can be manipulated to increase public employment while official policy is to reduce public employment. The Manpower Services Commission began as a small, detached agency at the Department of Employment and now has about 24,000 staff. Hood (1978) suggests that in some instances hiving-off activities in new agencies may have a "Pontius Pilate" effect, meaning more intractible problems are simply excluded from departmental business, and ministers evade responsibility.

Compared to most democratic political systems, the external controls on departmental policymaking are relatively crude and mechanical. The success of ministers and departments in rejecting civil service reform (see Chapter 2) also avoided more sophisticated budgetary control, reducing limits on departmental spending to a confrontation over numbers of staff. Ministers and their top aides are skilled in showing how cuts in departmental budgets would eliminate the most essential services of government. When the Thatcher government imposed more drastic spending limits, the DHSS announced (leaked to the press) that waiting lists for hospital care would lengthen, and the DOE showed how local services for the elderly would be discontinued. For years the rapidly expanding staff of the Inland Revenue Service has threatened that any cuts would be immediately reflected in lower tax collection, although Britain has one of the most highly computerized and expensive tax collection agencies in the world. The point is not that ministers may be right or wrong in these disputes, but that no one else can judge whether they are. Even more damaging to policymaking is the fact that there are few incentives to devise less drastic solutions or to adjust the policymaking machinery to new conditions.

The net effect is that policy guidance over ministers and departments is weak, and once disaster strikes there are few options other than the most drastic and arbitrary of controls. Since 1968 the Treasury and the Civil Service Department have been uneasy allies in a struggle to fashion more sophisticated planning and spending controls over departments, but, as we shall see in Chapter 2, the coordination and expenditure plans of departments barely gave way to these efforts. Because the Treasury was unable to devise effective controls, there was no alternative once financial disaster loomed in 1975 but the most arbitrary and indiscriminate of controls, "cash limits" or simply forcing departments to confine spending to arbitrary levels. Even so, ministerial prerogatives meant that relating cuts to policies within departments was left to ministers and top civil servants.

Perhaps the hallmark of policymaking in the welfare state is that there is an enormous amount of interdepartmental business. As the state does more, policies presuppose better cooperation among departments. Some of the interdepartmental clashes of this kind are notorious within British government, and seem almost impossible to resolve. For example, the care of children is divided between the Home Office and the DHSS, whose struggle for pre-eminence in this area can be traced back for at least a decade. The plight of inner cities is another example; here, even having most of the concerned departments within a single super-ministry has not assured close cooperation and coordination. The main device to resolve interdepartmental problems involves creating a committee of civil servants, though ministers are called in once departmental turf seems seriously threatened. There is, of course, the ultimate appeal of a minister to the cabinet, but this is a risky strategy, for it may reveal ministerial weakness or incompetence.

The cabinet has about 150 committees, some organized around broad strategic questions such as economic policy and chaired by the prime minister, and others on more specific, but intricate, problems such as relations with the European Economic Community. Probably fifteen or twenty are active (politically controversial) at any one time. Officially, cabinet committees do not even exist. They are appointed by the prime minister in consultation with ministers and the cabinet secretary. In at least a few instances, it appears that they have been selected to make sure that the most concerned ministers are *not* involved (Page, 1978). Their procedures and organizations are put forth in a confidential (but now leaked) volume, the *Organization of Cabinet Committees*, which ministers read as part of their initiation rites. One of the reasons Wilson was suspected of being a "presidential" prime minister was that he ruled in 1968 that no matters should come before the cabinet until the appropriate cabinet committee reached agreement. As further testimony to the power of ministers, the rule was soon rescinded.

The strong political consensus surrounding the top levels of British policymaking, and the exclusion of competing as well as most supporting MPs from the policy process, means that we know little about important decisions. In recent years, there have been more intentional and unintentional leaks to the press, and some revealing ministerial memoirs. Even these partial, and quite possibly misleading, accounts are strongly disclaimed, and a court battle went on to prevent Crossman from publishing his *Diaries*. The most curious part of the process is no one seems to like it very much, but no one wants to change it. A leading Labour Party minister, Barbara Castle, wrote that when "departments did the horse-trading" through committees, the purpose of policies would be diluted (*Sunday Times*, June 10, 1973). Another Labour minister, Roy Jenkins, wrote that interdepartmental consultation in the hands of civil servants "effectively removed the point of decision from the Home Secretary" (his former post) and that "co-ordinated views on paper tended to produce co-ordinated silence around the table" (*Sunday Times*, Jan. 17, 1971).

Many would argue that the true policymakers are the permanent secretaries and top civil servants and each new minister runs a gauntlet in his early weeks in office to see whether he or they will set priorities in the department. The discreet Monday lunch of the cabinet secretary, the head of the civil service, the head of the diplomatic service, and the chief permanent secretary of the Treasury probably has policy significance comparable to cabinet meetings. Top civil servants, or "mandarins," brief the minister on departmental legislation, advise him on how ministerial proposals will affect the department, and work out the detailed plans for implementation of new laws, and many of the more trusted become his antennae to listen in on rival departments and ministers. There is no question that the mandarins wield enormous influence over policymaking. In nearly every other democracy, much of this work would be done by elected officials, who would, in turn, learn the details of policymaking and view policy results at close quarters. The exclusiveness of British policymaking makes direct feedback of the results and frictions of implementation virtually impossible.

The standard justification of dependence on the higher civil service is that they are politically neutral. The more difficult question, which neither the mandarins nor the ministers address, is whether a suitable blend of political judgment and effective action can be accomplished in such a small circle of officials, when the top political officials are distracted by a multitude of other responsibilities to their party, Parliament, and constituents. How departmental political defenses operate can be seen in nearly all the policy analyses to follow, but it is nowhere more obvious than in the execution of administrative reform, discussed in Chapter 2. The elaborate precautions to assure the political neutrality of the civil service have no parallel in any other democracy. No modern government can work without impartial and objective advice, but few so abruptly and decisively demarcate at high levels where and how political judgment may be introduced in policymaking.

In return for their loyalty, civil servants extract anonymity and security. A minister cannot remove the permanent secretary he happens to find in his department. Top administrative appointments are made by the head of the civil service in consultation with the prime minister and other leading mandarins. The House Expenditure Committee (1977) created a furore by suggesting that a minister ought to be free to choose a limited number of top officials. There is a certain irony that it was a Labour prime minister, Callaghan, whose colleagues seemed less comfortable when confronted with civil service influence, who rejected this relatively modest compromise.

Ministers have a number of policymaking aids at their disposal, but boundaries between political judgment and policy proposals are carefully demarcated, and only rarely does a body outside the inner circle of policymakers raise questions about the existing framework for exercising political influence on policies. There are, first, Royal Commissions, which conduct exhaustive studies of major reforms. Their "mandate," or directions, usually excludes considering the top levels of policymaking, and they are appointed by the prime minister in consultation with the most concerned minister or ministers. In most cases where top civil servants are essential to an inquiry, a Committee is used so that civil servants will be spared entering a public debate on policy matters. A third instrument is the official inquiry. This can range from a relatively minor review of planning or housing decisions (there were 7,500 in the Department of the Environment in 1970) to such impassioned investigations as those into the third London airport or the reorganization of London transport. Ministers are under no obligation to take such advice nor even to respond publicly to these findings.

The remarkably thin layer of politicians overseeing the British policymaking process achieves its most dramatic form when considering "quasi-non-government organizations," or QUANGOs. No modern government can operate without this bewildering array of quasi-judicial boards, specialized regulatory agencies, elaborate organizations of implementation, and system of administrative appeals. But the limits on executive and legislative powers, and better-defined systems of administrative law provide most other countries with ways of relating organizational complexity to the policy process. For the historical reasons outlined above, Britain had no such alternative, so virtually all the organizational apparatus of modern government operates under the discretion of ministers and civil servants.

Enormous bodies of delegated legislation go formally unreviewed. Jurisdictional and organizational disputes have no clear channels for resolution. Each department is left to fashion its own procedures for the collection of evidence, the adjudication and appeal of administrative decisions, and the regulation of top-level administration. Administrative justice is a tangled web of appeal tribunals and administrative agencies that have indirect and often ambiguous relationships to the courts. One can only admire the ingenuity that British policymakers have displayed in dealing with the organizational complexity of modern government, but it has been achieved at very high cost and by increasing ministerial powers in ways that were never anticipated.

Until recently the huge areas of discretion were seldom discussed. Indeed, a careful debate is impossible because government itself has only a rough idea of the number, type, and powers of governmental organizations. The public debate began when a Labour MP (Edelman, 1975) asked carefully designed questions in the Commons to show that ministers now had powers of appointment involving a total remuneration of about £4 million. A more explosive study followed, by a Conservative MP, showing that ministers make some 18,000 appointments to 785 bodies, tribunals, agencies, and boards outside government, having a total budget of over £35 million. Suddenly the barely concealed patronage of American and French politics seemed less strange. For years the Civil Service Department has kept a secret list of suitable appointees (the List of the Great and the Good). What many modern governments do openly, and often with clearer recognition of the political calculations and with clearer provision for administrative justice, Britain had been doing all the time.

The diverse, and sometimes doubtful, legal basis for QUANGOs makes it difficult to define and therefore even to count them (Outer Circle Policy Unit, 1979). The largest category are "administrative tribunals" that are used for a wide range of policies and that often hear over 25,000 cases in a year (Wade, 1977, pp. 742–43). In recent years, industrial tribunals have acquired major importance (43,000 cases in 1976) in dealing with disputes over unfair dismissal, compensation for accidents, equal pay for women, and redundancy payments (compensation for lost jobs). There is no general right of appeal under British law, and each department works out its own system of hearing appeals.

No doubt, many civil servants follow the results of these hearings and many become known when individual grievances are submitted to MPs, but the divorce between the formulation of

British policies and the evaluation of their results is one of the weaker links in the politics of policymaking. Some appeals stop at high-level tribunals such as the Supplementary Benefits Appeals Tribunal or the Immigration Appeals Tribunal; industrial disputes go to a quasi-court, the Employment Appeals Tribunal; and others like national insurance disputes go to a commissioner (official inspector). Leaving aside how cumbersome these procedures are in handling individual claims, their diversity, complexity, and removal from policymaking itself makes it difficult for ministers to learn how past decisions have worked in practice and to some extent spares them from dealing with the consequences of their own policies.

The politically ambitious rarely want to be confronted with errors of judgment, but the ways in which British policymakers avoid the complexity of the modern welfare state are nonetheless striking. When some of these problems arose before a blue-ribbon Committee on Ministerial Powers in 1932, they were pushed aside. The proliferation of discretionary powers led to the Statutory Instruments Act of 1946, which requires that delegated rules of all kinds be placed before Parliament, but it appears that only 2 percent are even examined (Wade, 1977, p. 735). They can only be amended or annulled by Prayers, or special permission to reject an order of a Crown agent. There is little time in a crowded parliamentary agenda for these fine points and, of course, an MP of the ruling party does not gather favor by obstructing ministers. The political embarrassment created by the Crichel Down case (a dispute over an inquiry into restoring land requisitioned during the war) produced the Franks Committee in 1957, which again ruled that "general administration" was beyond its terms of reference and so did not pass judgment on discretionary power. Finally, a Council on Tribunals was established in 1958, but it has no power to see that its advice is heard by ministers nor can it require that a minister change procedures. Though centrally involved with the complexities of laws and decisions, it is an isolated and "an inconspicuous advisory committee" (Wade, p. 762) in the policy process.

Britain has not escaped the complexity of policymaking in the welfare state, but it has subordinated the proliferation of governmental agencies and the growth of discretionary powers to a virtually unchanged political framework for policymaking. Ministers have an enormous amount of patronage to bestow, but almost nothing is known of how this is done; with rare exceptions the posts are not advertised, and with what appears to be similar regularity the performance is not evaluated. When the question was asked in the House of Commons, MPs were told that how performance is assessed is confidential.

The multiplication of QUANGOs and appointments in an era of complex government is not surprising, but that their relation to policymaking should be so little debated is. The constitutional constraints on a dispersal of policymaking powers are great, but so are the rewards of compliance with the system. A study of the 321 Conservative MPs elected in 1951 showed that 123 became ministers or junior ministers, and were thereby launched on political careers, while the remaining 108 received appointments, titles, or honors (Sainsbury, 1965). Every political system must reward its loyal members, but one cannot escape the conclusion that in British politics helping maintain a narrowly conceived and highly concentrated power structure often takes precedence over dealing with the complexities of policymaking.

A frequently applied test of the viability of political institutions is their ability to withstand crises and to survive momentous social and economic changes. By this test the British political system has been an unqualified success because the complexities of policymaking revealed over a generation or more have not materially changed the role of ministers and cabinet in the policy process. The demands made on government in Britain, as in every other modern democracy, have grown, but the ways in which these demands are, in turn, converted into policy have changed very little. Compared to the policy process in most democracies, access to the highest levels of policymaking is restricted, and decisions are left to the political judgment of relatively few people. The nature of the British cabinet government requires that careful attention be given to maintaining elite consensus, and, in return, political leaders enjoy discretion and influence that is given to few leaders of democratic countries. Whether the exclusiveness and confidentiality of high-level policymaking has produced effective and sound policies is a difficult assessment, and will be considered in Chapter 8. One of the reasons policymaking has not been more severely judged is that Parliament, like the ministers and the cabinet, concentrates on formulating and expressing demands, rather than working out how government can respond to them. Just as the civil service spares leaders many of the complications of policymaking and policy implementation, so also does Parliament keep their sights fixed on elections and party competition.

Parliament and Policymaking: The Primacy of Electoral Politics

The fact that Parliament has no direct role in policymaking is of no surprise to most observers of British politics. One of the most strategically placed experts on Parliament, the deputy principal clerk of the Commons, wrote that Parliament "remains peripheral to the main political argument and national issues" (Ryle, 1975, p. 23). Parliament no longer has an active role in initiating and designing legislation, and in this sense Parliament is not a lawmaking body. On the whole, Mill's view that "a numerous assembly is as little fitted for the direct business of legislation as for that of administration" still prevails (quoted in Wiseman, 1966, pp. 23–24). Unless one takes into account the close relationship of cabinet government to parliamentary rule, it is difficult to reconcile the limitations of Parliament, now primarily those of the House of Commons, with policymaking in British government.

The responsibility of the cabinet was devised to curtail the unbridled powers of the monarch and, in particular, the tendency of George III to manipulate ministers through patronage and favors. The growing middle class and aristocracy were agreed that, if collective rule could overcome monarchial excesses, then Parliament would only need minor investigatory powers. Thus, Parliament emerged as a deliberative body designed, as Lord Campion, a leading constitutionalist, put it, "to ventilate" government business. The only specific power reserved to Parliament was to approve taxation and spending. The tradition that measures to spend money can only be introduced with the approval of the chancellor of the exchequer was initially intended to curb monarchial foreign adventures and the corruption of MPs. The task of Parliament was, and to a large extent remains, to question ministers, and in doing so to represent public opinion.

As Lowell put it (1908, p. 140), the point was to "know who to hang." His view is echoed by a leading political analyst of the left, Harrold Laski, who wrote (1938) that Parliament has the "immense advantage always to know who is to blame when something goes wrong." As we have seen, very few ministers are hanged, and when they are associated with major policy reversals they are most often given other ministerial posts. With the rise of mass parties and the emphasis on electoral politics, the aim is no longer to remove ministers in order to convey disapproval of policies. The intricacy of policymaking in the welfare state makes it virtually impossible to fix responsibility on an individual, in some ways even on a government. There is no way of knowing what decision, or even series of decisions, accounts for inflation, racial conflict, unemployment, or confusion in local government.

Parliament can do little more than cope with the consequences of policymaking as eventually perceived by the public. "In so far as there is a 'deliberative' stage in the legislative process, this is now found much earlier than the Parliamentary stages, in the interplay between political parties, pressure groups, Departments and Cabinet, which together form a complex decision-making structure, involving a variety of social and political forces" (Walkland, 1968, p. 71). In general, the Conservatives have been comfortable with the policymaking deficiencies of the House of Commons. In both the late 1960s and again in 1976, Labour tried to make procedural changes that would enhance the Commons' powers. The net result was a great deal of tinkering with parliamentary procedure, the handling of bills and the scheduling of debates, but when the distinguished clerk of the Commons wrote his summary of the legislative process in 1975 (Ryle, 1975, p. 11), he noted "how little it has changed in the last 25 years."

Part of the problem is, of course, the immense workload of Parliament, a problem it shares with every democratic legislature. But the British MPs are among the most oppressed, sitting about 1,500 hours a year. This is five times the hours spent on legislation by the French National Assembly or the German Bundestag. Measured in pages, the volume of legislation doubled between 1952 and 1972, and committee meetings quintupled. Under the best of circumstances, the Commons can act on roughly fifty government and about fifteen private (individually sponsored) bills each year. The Opposition is, of course, excluded from the drafting and design of government bills, and a great deal of this burden involves consolidating and updating earlier laws.

There are at least three ways to illustrate the declining powers of the Commons to scrutinize the workings of the cabinet. First, the Commons has no time to investigate the use of discretionary powers in any systematic way, although some of the more outrageous injustices still find their way to the floor. Since Parliament has neither the facilities nor the inclination to examine the whole body of British law, most existing executive powers are routinely renewed each year in a single act. Second, there are over a thousand "statutory instruments," or executive orders, placed before Parliament each year. The Select Committee on Statutory Instruments (since 1973 a Joint Committee with the Lords) does its best to churn through these measures. From this morass of ministerial orders, about a hundred are studied more carefully and about a dozen reach the floor of the Commons for debate (Select Committee on Procedure, 1978, pp. xxxi–xxxiv). Twenty MPs can, and often do, block such debates to save time for more politically rewarding issues. A third, and rapidly becoming the most severe, strain on parliamentary surveillance is European Community legislation. Since 1972 there has been a Select Committee on European Legislation (now also a Joint Committee with the Lords), which reviews nearly six hundred documents a year, about a hundred of which are recommended for debate and about thirty of which are actually considered (Select Committee on Procedure, 1978, p. xliii).

The parliamentary reform movement has attracted some support among distinguished MPs, but it has also run into formidable resistance in the Commons. The task of the Opposition is to prove that it can govern, not to underscore its agreement with the ruling party. Crick calls this the "continuous election campaign of the whole life of Parliament" (1964, p. 26). But the obstacle to giving the Commons real investigatory powers is in many ways even more profound. Unlike the legislatures of most democracies, Parliament, to use an old-fashioned term, is sovereign in British politics. Providing alternative leadership is fundamental not just to the political system but to the constitution. Mass parties and mass electorates have reinforced this crucial role. It is to the advantage of the Opposition *not* to reveal its preferences. As Butt points out, "Debates are seen as too crudely partisan in point-scoring and yet tending to fudge real issues" (1969, p. 312). MPs supporting the government have even less reason to erode its attractiveness to the electorate. Behavior that might blur party alignments in the Commons or create more cross-pressure within parties would submerge the principles of ministerial and cabinet responsibility on which the system rests.

There is, of course, a great deal of intraparty consultation before the governing party brings a bill to the Commons. On basic structural changes such as reform of the House of Lords there is also much bipartisan exchange. But policymaking agreements cannot be allowed to become too prominent or the system itself would be undermined. Some issues may create serious cross-pressures within a ruling party, as regional devolution did for the Labour Party. When governments have smaller majorities, they are, of course, more vulnerable to backbench criticism. Even strong majorities cannot ignore backbenchers. Labour plans to strengthen labor legislation in 1969 were abandoned because fifty-three Labour MPs voted against and forty abstained from the White Paper proposing reform. Another divisive issue, the European Community, found sixty pro-European Labour MPs voting with the Conservatives in 1972. When internal party pressures become overwhelming, ministers can evade their responsibility by having a "free vote," but, done too often, this can make the ruling party appear weak. Major embarrassments of this kind occur most often on issues that inflame public opinion and outrage party activists, not on the more complex problems that regularly occupy the government in the welfare state.

Possibly the most dramatic illustration of the Commons' disinterest in the details of policymaking is the treatment of its most precious claim to influence, the powers of appropriation and taxation. Though its significance has diminished with inflation (see Chapter 3), the report of the Public Expenditure Survey Committee of the Treasury (PESC) was originally intended as a long-term projection of the government's spending plans that would stimulate a serious debate on resource allocation. But the Commons has never found more than two days for the PESC debate. Similarly, the debate on supply or appropriation has twenty-nine days put aside for it in each session, but the topics are chosen by the Opposition, which naturally picks those items that will make the government most uncomfortable. If any general trend can be detected, it is most often simply that government should spend more. The Commons has neither the inclination nor the capacity to make appropriation debates into detailed policy investigations. When a snap vote does convey partisan outrage (often by reducing the chancellor's salary), the government can muster its forces a day or two later and reverse the vote. Taxation legislation or the Finance Act is seriously debated, but in relation to the particular provisions that relate to an MP's constituency or party preferences, rarely in terms of overall financial or tax policy. Since 1970, public spending has been reviewed by the House Select Committee on Public Expenditure, which has much broader terms of reference than the discontinued Committee on Estimates and which has produced careful analyses of major public spending issues. But even when the House finds time to debate its reports, few MPs bother to attend.

Political reputations are not made in committees. Over the 1960s parliamentary reformers hoped that a stronger and specialized committee system would increase the Commons' policymaking role. The standard form of parliamentary committee is the Standing Committee, simply a group of MPs chosen in proportion to party strengths and routinely assigned bills to help the House scrutinize and digest legislation. Select Committees have specific tasks, but until recently had no staff and only minor powers of inquiry. Unlike committees in most legislatures, they cannot require ministers to explain their policies. Until 1967, when the left-wing Labour minister, Benn, appeared before the Science and Technology Committee, a minister had never voluntarily explained his policies before a parliamentary committee. Committees can ask civil servants for information, but even these requests may be overruled by ministers.

In much the same way that blurring the role of the Opposition would jeopardize key elements of the British constitution, so also more autonomous and more active parliamentary committees would muddy party alignments and multiply cross-pressures within parties. "Legislative Committees which could challenge, obstruct or overthrow Government policy would plainly be inappropriate in this system" (Butt, 1969, p. 358). Most MPs agree that the appropriate place to expose the weaknesses of ministers is before the entire House, and few welcome the drudgery of detailed committee work. When the Committee on Procedure raised the possibilities of more highly specialized and more influential committees in 1964–65, a leading Labour Party spokesman, Michael Foot, and the former Conservative whip, Sir Martin Redmayne, agreed that stronger committees would only detract from the debates of the House and weaken Parliament's traditional role of deliberation and scrutiny.

The pressure for stronger committees has arisen in part because Parliament is overburdened. Though possibly he intended them as a diversionary tactic to occupy the growing number of left-wing critics in the Labour majority, Wilson agreed to two experiments with specialist committees, but with the important provision that they change topics every two or three years. The committees quickly confirmed the worst doubts of ministers who were skeptical about committees. The Agricultural Committee was soon in a battle with the Foreign Office to obtain permission to visit Brussels and to examine Common Market agricultural policy. The fledgling Science and Technology Committee chose a no less sensitive issue, the development of the nuclear power industry. The government refused permission to debate its findings in the House.

The political pressures on MPs make them no less comfortable than ministers with stronger committees. From 1970 to 1978 only one report of the Committee on Nationalized Industries was debated, and on this rare occasion, committee members from the ruling party reversed their committee votes in order to support their government in the House. Nor do ministers enjoy using their powers against their own supporters in the House. There have been bitter departmental clashes with committees, but it is not difficult to find reasons to withhold information. Aggressive committees also make prime ministers appear uncooperative. Wilson refused to permit Harold Lever (now Lord Lever) to testify on industrial loans he had made earlier because he was no longer the responsible minister. When the Committee on Procedure asked for stronger committees in 1978, Callaghan resisted debating the report. Committee investigations strike at two cardinal constitutional principles: ministerial responsibility and civil service anonymity. Although the Conservatives accepted the report's recommendations in 1979 and agreed to form twelve permanent Select Committees aligned with major departments, ministers still cannot be compelled to testify and it remains to be seen how thoroughly MPs will undertake the tedious and generally unrewarding task of monitoring departments.

The most intractable obstacle to giving Parliament a more active policy role is the secrecy of government itself. The Official Secrets Act of 1911 was passed in one day under the shadow of war and makes even trivial unauthorized disclosures criminal acts. Labour came to power in 1964 pledged to support more open government. Five years later and just before an election, the government produced a weak White Paper (1969, cmnd. 4089) that avoided the most difficult issues. The Heath government conducted another inquiry (Franks Committee, 1972, cmnd. 5104), but again no action was taken. In no country in the world are ministers so completely shielded from public and parliamentary scrutiny. Sweden has had liberal information laws since 1809, and even cabinet minutes are public after two years. British investigators have had to turn to the American Freedom of Information Act of 1975 to acquire information about their own country that was withheld by Whitehall.

The restrictions imposed by the Official Secrets Act have become more onerous because of the complexity of policymaking. Although much more routine information is now made available to the public, in particular by the vastly improved reports on many specialized problems by the Central Statistical Office, there is almost no critical social or economic problem that can be studied without government information. For example, for many years the Treasury regarded its model of the economy as confidential even though similar models were devised by consulting firms and academic departments. Both ministers and top civil servants view more liberal access with alarm. When Callaghan considered revising the Official Secrets Act in 1978 (again just before an election), the largest civil service union protested and the elite First Division Association of top civil servants made its reservations public. In 1979 the Thatcher government proposed legislation amending the Official Secrets Act by defining criminality in ways that many felt would be even more restrictive than the original Act, only to withdraw it after numerous protests.

A curious development in British politics that stems from secrecy as well as unchecked executive power is the increasing role of the courts in challenging ministerial decisions. There is, of course, no judicial review, but courts can interpret the use of statutory powers and the grounds for administrative secrecy. For many years, constitutional experts have been agreed that the use of Crown privilege (action in the name of the monarch) has been applied excessively and incorrectly (de Smith, 1973). Recent court decisions have rejected some basic policy decisions, such as the ruling in the Tameside case to rescind a Department of Education order forcing a local education authority to produce a plan for comprehensive schools. Another major decision ordered the Post Office to deliver mail to South Africa after a militant postal union had refused to handle mail for that country. Of course, ministers can and do then produce emergency legislation to establish a statutory basis for their power. But Parliament has neither the time nor the inclination to explore such conflicts and their policymaking implications. Although it is the supreme lawmaking body, it has relatively little incentive to specify the contradictions and confusions of policies.

When a parliamentary ombudsman was first seriously proposed in 1961 (Whyatt Report), many thought this new office would strengthen Parliament in its dealings with ministers and higher civil servants. As finally defined in 1967, however, the parliamentary commissioner has only feeble powers. He has no legal investigatory powers and can only act on complaints made to him by MPs. Crown privilege was broached to permit departments to provide information, but their responses cannot be published. His annual reports are sent to the departments concerned, but they are under no obligation to respond or to act. In effect, every precaution was taken to see that the commissioner could not threaten ministerial or administrative powers.

While it may appear paradoxical that a legislature with the enormous powers of the Parliament has so little influence over policymaking, most MPs do not want to infringe on ministerial powers. The wide-ranging policy intervention found in the American Congress or the French National Assembly presupposes a flexibility of partisan alignments and party loyalties on various choices and issues. Despite the many pressures and controversies that urge MPs to acquire effective policymaking roles, elite consensus includes reluctance to cast doubt on fundamental constitutional principles, which restrains them. The Commons could pass any law it wished to check ministerial powers or to assert its primacy in the policy process. That it does not is the most compelling evidence of the durability and depth of political consensus within Westminster.

Parties, Groups, and Voters: A Passive or Satisfied Society?

As they have operated for over a century, British political institutions rely on two-party politics to sustain the stability of one-party government. In other political systems, multiple parties and rivalries between legislative and executive offices make the transformation of social support into political power clearer. Obviously, no democracy could exist without societal consensus about the form of government, but other societies also have deeper social cleavages and entrenched regional differences that make the confusions of party politics and diverse forms of policy intervention important. To most British the logrolling legislation of the American Congress or the vociferous factions of the numerous French parties are a mystery. Although British society is by no means as homogeneous as the strength of societal and elite consensus might indicate, a number of fundamental social, regional, and economic conflicts were resolved well before mass parties and mass politics developed in the late nineteenth century. Modern democracy emerged after the basic framework of political consensus was built and many social issues that might have splintered parties, and therefore have vastly complicated aggregating opinions and preferences around two major parties, had been resolved.

There were, of course, possibilities that effective reconciliation of mass politics and parliamentary institutions would not occur. One of the more glamorous late Victorian political leaders, Joseph Chamberlain, built his power on an urban caucus of the Liberal Party and his highly successful mayoralty of Birmingham. Until he was persuaded that even more power could be found in Westminster, there was a glimmer of a chance that a more decentralized and localized structure would overtake parties. The rise of the Labour Party posed another threat to the reconciliation of the party system with parliamentary power. But the Labour Party eschewed the more ideological course of socialist parties on the continent and did not foment class politics, in part because it had an unchallenged claim to worker votes. Though about a third of the workers consistently vote Conservative, the Labour Party itself was spared the competition for worker votes from the left that on the continent has intensified rivalries among parties of the left and, in turn, intensified political conflict to win over the working class.

In any event, had mass parties and their leaders encountered the social conflict and differences that were more forcefully introduced in the democratic evolution of other states, the British elite consensus would have been threatened. The success of the transition depended in no small measure on the readiness of the Conservative Party to adopt reforms and over the years to accept most of the progressive measures of both the Liberal and the Labour Parties when they were in office. In fact, there is some justification to the flattering image of the Conservatives as the "natural" ruling party of Britain. For nearly two-thirds of the time since the Reform Act of 1884, which established near universal male suffrage, they have been the ruling party. From the First World War until 1945, they were almost continually in office. Their strength in the heavily populated south and southeast of England raises the specter of the Labour Party becoming a party of the hinterlands.

For policymaking purposes, it is appropriate to distinguish political forces operating within Parliament from those operating through the party organization. The party leader, both in opposition and in power, takes special pains to keep in contact with backbenchers. The prime minister and his opposite, the leader of the Opposition, as well as leading ministers, frequently meet with the backbenchers. In the Conservative Parliamentary Party there is, not surprisingly, a group representing the right wing, the "Monday Club" of about fifteen MPs, and a more radical association, the Bow Group. The key backbench organization is the 1922 Committee, which sometimes makes public its reservations about Conservative policy. In 1979, for example, the 1922 Committee had frequent consultations with the chancellor of the exchequer to make known their alarm over higher interest rates, increased local taxes, and the effects of spending cuts.

The Parliamentary Labour Party (PLP) is in some ways more unruly than the Conservative Parliamentary Party (CPP), but it is doubtful if Labour backbenchers have necessarily had more effect on government priorities. Labour has never been a militant socialist party on the continental model, but there is nonetheless a sizeable body of about eighty MPs linked to a militant Tribune Group that publishes a weekly journal. As internal party schisms deepened in the 1970s, the Manifesto Group of about ninety moderate and right-wing Labour MPs was formed to counteract the Tribune Group. The struggle intensified in 1973, when the militant left formed the Campaign for Labour Party Democracy, involving numerous MPs, to persuade the party to elect its leader in the Annual Conference and to bind him to a popularly written party manifesto. Their fight to democratize the party stimulated the formation of the Campaign for Labour Victory in 1977 to defend the moderate views of the PLP.

Although both major parties have undergone severe internal strains over many difficult decisions in the past decade, internal fights in the Labour Party are more public and the party leader is more frequently repudiated in the Annual Conference. After the electoral defeats of 1951, 1959, and 1979, there were serious splits at the top levels of the party. Both parliamentary parties select their own leader, who, in turn, selects his cabinet or shadow cabinet, although in opposition the Labour shadow cabinet is more democratically selected. The 1979 Labour Party crisis arose over preparing the election manifesto. The manifesto is in fact only a crude description of what a party would do in office, and is written to mobilize votes rather than to guide governments. Neither major party departs much from its manifesto, but this is hardly surprising given its generally broad and sweeping language. The party leader composes the manifesto in consultation with other party leaders and the party organization. At the core of the 1979 fight within the Labour Party was outrage that the party leader, Callaghan, had excluded from the manifesto several issues dear to the militant left wing, in particular abolition of the House of Lords.

If binding external controls are placed on the PLP, the principles of British democracy will undergo a severe strain, though it should be noted that in countries with more ideological and less disciplined parties, the proposals of the Labour left would not seem very radical. The constitutional dilemma is more acute where there is such a concentration of power in ministers and Parliament, which, in turn, means that national elections are a critical check on the direction of government. A more deep-seated problem is the gradual erosion of general support for the two major parties. Until 1979, the proportion of the total vote captured by the two major parties steadily declined. Using a more demanding definition of support, we can say that no party has been elected to office by a majority of eligible voters since 1935. Britain has had "minority" government since 1945, the last time a government was elected with a majority of votes cast.

The strength of the British concept of political consensus is revealed in the alarm that is sometimes voiced over the weakening of the major parties and more acute internal party conflicts. But as Beattie has pointed out (1975), political stability was similar under past coalition governments and under stronger parliamentary majorities. France has been governed by a coalition throughout the Fifth Republic, and the reshaping of party coalitions is central to American party politics. As Beattie states (p. 299), much of the concern over the demise of the two-party system stems from the presumption that only internal party cohesion, and the clear opposition of "ins" and "outs," can provide stable government. There is no reason why winning coalitions cannot be built from party factions and small parties. Indeed, Britain had government by a minority party over the last year of the Callaghan government, and there were few visible signs that the handling of legislation, the workings of the cabinet, or even the lawmaking process were radically changed.

The normal pressures of government plus unexpected crises and events mean that a government that takes power without a fairly clear idea of its policy goals is at a severe disadvantage. For this reason, the capacity of party organization and party leaders to assemble well-thought-out proposals before taking office is important. On the whole, the more unified and paternal Conservative Party has had more success in preparing for office. In the postwar reorganization of the party, a strong Research Department was created and, through the party leader, is closely linked to fashioning new policies, dredging for new ideas, and even briefing backbench MPs on party objectives. Heath launched an intensive series of meetings and mobilized numerous advisors in the years preceding his 1970 government, culminating in the now famous Selsdon Park meeting of his entire cabinet to discuss how they would implement their designs. Less confident of the party organization, Thatcher relied more on the Centre for Policy Studies, organized in 1975 by the unreconstructed liberal Sir Keith Joseph to advance his concept of a free, market society, and on taking office merged the Research Department with the party Central Office.

Controversies within the Labour Party and dependence on the TUC have made it more difficult for them to prepare for office. Wilson acknowledged that the party took office in 1964 with few defined ideas of its aims. The Labour Party has a small Research Department, but party workers are both underpaid and distracted by internal party strife. The complexity of Labour's organization itself makes the evaluation and use of policy advice awkward. Nine-tenths of the votes in party conferences and nine-tenths of party finances come from the Trades Union Congress (TUC), which has more extensive research facilities and its own objectives. When a Liaison Committee involving the TUC, the PLP, and the party was formed in 1971, policy leadership shifted to the committee, but the main concern was undoing antiunion Conservative legislation (see Chapter 4) and working out a new basis for union-government cooperation once Labour regained power.

The comparatively low capacity of parties to formulate and to influence policy may stem from their social setting. British parties seem more immune to conflicts and even the demands of society than do the multiple party systems and factionalized parties of most European political systems. Whether Britain has been spared social conflict or chosen not to recognize it is not easy to decide, nor is this question the primary purpose of our study. Despite the deterioration of British parties, detectable in the declining number of party agents and party members, societal consensus for the British system of government remains strong. Possibly the persistence of two-party politics encourages neglect of social change. In examining the "two-party legend," Beattie (1974, p. 229) suggests that parties should observe "the effective accommodation of interests rather than the pretence that they do not exist." Perhaps the relative ease with which social agreement *about* government has been elicited has, in turn, produced complacency about the significance of agreement *within* government.

Westminster has an enormous burden of responsibility, not just for policymaking but for aggregating interests and sensing public preferences. Undoubtedly, Parliament, parties, and constituents help keep government alert to new demands and discontents. But grassroots influence is not only resisted at the top levels of policymaking but is minimized, as we shall see, by the electoral system. "British democracy is highly elitist, more so than that of many other states with parliamentary systems. Britain has never known the referendum, the popular initiative, the nominating convention, the primary or the write-in vote, and the prospects of these being introduced seem remote" (Pulzer, 1975, p. 146).

Despite the protests of Labour Party militants in 1979, deference (Kavanagh, 1971) still seems to prevail. A less flattering version is that the *embourgeoisement* of British electoral and party politics spares leaders from the social protest and crippling party schisms that are common to most democracies. In most sociological studies of British politics, social class emerges as the most important determinant of voting behavior. But, as Pulzer notes, social class may be statistically important because modern Britain was spared the potentially paralyzing social cleavages of race, religion, and regional loyalties. A second possibility, more closely linked to government, is that it is relatively easy to translate social differences into concrete benefits and services. Social class is a highly subjective concept, and so long as the welfare state can remove the most onerous of the objective differences among classes, the political system is secure.

If one examines the electoral system more closely, it appears that, although elections may serve as the ultimate check on government, there has nonetheless been resistance to electoral reforms that might destabilize the political system. The single-member plurality voting system means that in two elections (1951 and

1974) a party acquired a majority of seats while having fewer votes than the losers. Though MPs pay close attention to individual complaints from their constituencies, about two-thirds sit in secure seats and are not required to examine party policy closely. There is also considerable variation within the electoral system in the size of constituencies. The average constituency has 64,000 voters, but in 1974 constituencies varied from 26,000 to over 96,000 persons. The inequities are greater than in the United States.

Rather than risk the uncertainties of a more equitable electoral system, the leaders of the two major parties are content with a system that gives Labour undue advantage in urban areas and the Conservatives advantage in rural areas. The net effect is that over 5 million votes in England are "wasted"; that is, they have no effect on electoral outcomes (Johnston, 1979, p. 180). Although Britain has automatic electoral redistricting under a statutory Boundary Commission, ministers are not unwilling to bend the law to their electoral advantage. Fearing a close outcome in the 1970 election, Labour postponed redistricting recommendations in 1969 that might have cost them about ten seats. The main losers of this system, of course, are the minority parties, especially the Liberal Party, whose supporters are scattered. In the October 1974 election, the Liberals' 6 million votes gave them only thirteen seats, but the spatially concentrated 630,000 votes of the Scottish Nationalists gave them eleven seats.

The "winner-take-all" system places great emphasis on national elections and the party leader, but it also makes it relatively easy for leaders to calculate exactly where and how many votes are needed to win. While it is true that electoral campaigns are shorter, less expensive, and in general less melodramatic than elections in most democracies, it is also true that the reluctance of major parties to reform the system presents the powerful with fewer uncertainties. There is very little risk of the three-cornered contests that are commonplace in the French multiparty system; almost none of the bargaining needed to bring diverse local party organizations into line as is found in the United States; and, until the Scottish Nationalists could maximize their influence because of the small majority of the Labour Party after 1976, very few of the regional trade-offs found in German elections and party politics. The Scottish Nationalists are an exception that proves the rule because with a very small number of seats they were able to force Labour to pursue devolutionary policies that not only tore the Labour Party apart but monopolized political debate for nearly two years. In party and electoral systems that require more bargaining over policies in order to function, political compromises are commonplace. They are also an important way that political actors outside the inner sanctum of policymaking can raise issues and influence policies.

To a much greater extent than in most modern democracies, it has been possible to organize both parties and elections so as to minimize penetration of the top levels of decisionmaking. The electoral system reinforces two-party politics and maximizes the chances of one-party government, thereby providing less incentive to rethink the nature of political consensus. A more complex party structure would almost certainly imply compromising cabinet control over policymaking in Westminster and Whitehall. Much the same relationship has been worked out to accommodate the complications that powerful interest groups might generate for the British political system. British pressure groups, professional associations, and clientelist organizations do not work through parties and elections to gain influence and to achieve their aims. There is nothing particularly conspiratorial or even corrupt in the way British pressure groups operate, but their needs can be readily met by working through Whitehall. British administration mastered the principles of cooptation and mutual self-interest long before the "corporate state" became a political science buzzword.

Pressure groups wield immense influence in every modern democracy, and as the development of the welfare state has complicated the tasks of government, they often become critically important links to the beneficiaries of government. In some ways, British pressure groups are more sheltered from public scrutiny, for they can operate beneath the cloak of confidentiality surrounding nearly all policymaking. In nineteenth-century Britain, their dependence on MPs was more pronounced. The great railway companies controlled nearly a third of the MPs; the local government associations operated through a network of several hundred MPs, who reciprocated each others' support in passing bills to help individual localities; and agriculture almost effortlessly worked through the landed aristocracy in Parliament to avoid taxation. It is difficult to weigh the costs and benefits of the more overt, political manipulations of Victorian pressure groups against the interlocking administrative structure that now shields them from the public political arena.

However much we may lament the huge bureaucracy on which the welfare state depends, this vast administrative apparatus could not operate without an even more intricate, specialized array of organizations of clients, experts, and beneficiaries. What differentiates Britain from most democracies is that, once the transition to the welfare state heavily redirected pressure groups toward the administration, Whitehall, in turn, could operate under peculiarly sheltered conditions created by the special relationship of ministers to civil servants. Many feel that administrative dependence on groups is greater than in most countries because the generalist tradition of the civil service provides even less technical and practical knowledge. In any event, the accommodation of mass democracy and party politics in the British political system makes politicians less important to pressure group activities and further concentrates power in the executive.

Because the particular groups affecting a variety of policies will be described in the policy analyses to follow, a rough description may serve as an introduction. There are, first, groups that represent widely scattered interests and mobilize opinion. For example, Shelter is a nationally organized group to defend public housing; the Child Poverty Action Group supports more benefits and care for children; and the Joint Council for Welfare of Immigrants works for racial minorities. In general, groups of this kind do not seek to influence party and voting behavior as much as to publicize inadequacies and injustices of policies. Because the policies they are interested in are not only controversial but technically complex, they must constantly struggle not to be coopted into government.

Second, there are the more common clientelist groups that are both beneficiaries of government and active participants in policymaking. The most important is the TUC, which represents half the British workforce and is consulted on conditions of work, unemployment benefits, incomes and pay policy, and the like by a host of administrative agencies. The National Union of Farmers has a virtually symbiotic relationship to the Ministry of Agriculture, and the Department of Education can make few moves without consulting the National Union of Teachers. For all the speculation about "pluralist stagnation," policymaking could barely proceed without groups of this kind. When they are not consulted in drafting legislation, issuing administrative orders, or fashioning policies, their outcry can bring Whitehall, if not political leaders, to a halt. Although they have their champions in the Commons, they are not dependent on MPs to mobilize alarm in government.

A third category are groups that have near total control of policies affecting their interests and that are almost indistinguishable from the administration. They not only have the ready access to government of the clientelist groups but provide indispensable advice and skills. The British Medical Association is perhaps typical of such groups. After thirty years of nationalized health and medicine, almost nothing can be done affecting the organization of care, hospitals, medical education, and medical fees without their consent. The nationalization of party and electoral politics has actually increased the influence of important groups of experts. National parties have little time for the vast area of policymaking involving local government, but Whitehall needs the active support of groups such as the Town and Country Planning Association or the Association of Metropolitan Authorities. "Producer groups," to use Beer's phrase (1965), have peculiar problems because confrontations with government threaten their privileges, while, in turn, the government would have difficulty performing its tasks without them. The diplomacy of mutual adjustment is essential to link them to government, and an important function of the bureaucracy is to carry on this complex game through the numerous decisions that daily involve them in policymaking. Politicians are virtually excluded from this exchange, nor does the political system provide incentives or opportunities for them to take an active role.

Dilemmas of Policymaking in a Consensual Society

In every democratic state the development of the welfare state poses a difficult choice between sustaining existing political institutions and adapting them to a more complex policy environment. If this choice seems less significant within the British political system, it is because British leaders and society accepted the welfare state without encountering severe political conflict and without being forced to reconsider key political relationships at the pinnacle of the policymaking process. In some respects, this is a notable accomplishment. Viewed in relation to the increasing complexity of decisionmaking, the problems of implementing and assessing policies, and the growing importance of the bureaucracy, the results may be less impressive. The game of politics may be going well when the policymaking process is going poorly.

How one answers this question depends very much on how the politics of policymaking is conceived and defined. The close relationship of societal and elite consensus and, in turn, the underlying principles of ministerial responsibility and cabinet government that connect policymaking to political institutions make these distinctions harder to draw in Britain than in most democracies. As we have seen, the relatively successful superimposition of mass party politics on parliamentary politics also placed less importance on these distinctions in the historical development of British democracy. Though there were periods of confusion, the two-party structure prevailed and the direct confrontation of the major parties fitted into old institutional frameworks. An effect, and possibly a necessary condition, of this metamorphosis was to increase the power of the executive. Even when the two-party underpinnings of government have appeared to weaken in recent years, concern is more that the simplifying structure of an Opposition battling a government will be eroded than that the political interplay at the top levels of policymaking will in some respects be inadequate to the tasks of a welfare state.

In the policy analyses to follow, the tendency to distill policy choices into confrontations of major contenders for power will be referred to as the primacy of adversarial politics in the British political system. The phrase is not being used in reference to the electoral competition and parliamentary accountability to the public that has prevailed in many recent studies of British politics. Even the complications of French and German parties, for example, produce crude, but differing, views of the future when elections are held. Our concern is not so much the dilemma of popular control of the welfare state as with the policymaking dilemma. In this context, the issue becomes how adversarial politics may relate to the performance of government, the forging of policy alternatives and compromises, and the unraveling of the interdependencies and conflicts that policymaking in a complex environment creates.

To reply, as many British politicians and even political scientists might, that this is simply not the job of British government as traditionally conceived comes close to being an admission that policymaking in a more complex world has nothing to do with higher-level decisions in British government. Without ignoring the stability provided by two-party politics and one-party government in Britain, reducing choice to a zero-sum game is not a particularly difficult feat. The more difficult question is whether the politics of policymaking reduced to the "ins" and "outs" is effective in a welfare state. If we look beyond political confrontation in the House of Commons, the answer is by no means self-evident.

When we look at the policy process in Britain, it appears that there are a large number of practices that prevent politics from entering into policymaking. Insofar as parties decide policies, choices are made by a small circle of politicians who are, compared to any other democracy, relatively immune to demands from their own party organization and party activists. Local government, as we shall see in Chapter 5, is a vitally important executor of national policies, but is rarely used nationally to mobilize public opinion or to criticize policies. Sectoral and functional divisions of policy correspond to the main departments of government, which are shielded by governmental secrecy and rely heavily on clientelist and producer groups, not on politicians. Put in simpler terms, adversarial politics is adept at creating, and then moderating, political confrontation, but it is doubtful if these clashes have policy consequences.

Compared to most democratic political systems, one cannot help being impressed with the ease with which leaders can exclude other political actors and political forces from policymaking. Party manifestos are written by the labor leader and, in turn, used selectively at his discretion; MPs labor in committees whose work is seldom debated and whose advice is easily ignored; once constituency associations have chosen a candidate, they are for the most part quiet spectators of the policy process; local politicians are swamped with tasks imposed by national government, and are either unable or unwilling to use their collective force to influence national policies. Cabinet and ministerial powers are exercised behind a cloak of confidentiality, which, of course, they may lift with impunity, but others may not draw aside. In addition, they have at their disposal an array of patronage, honors, and favors that, if less costly than patronage in the United States and France, is no less well orchestrated to tap the political values and motives that prevail in British society and politics.

Thus, the policy analyses to follow will concentrate on how the complexities of policymaking have changed, and on how the British response has been conditioned by the political constraints described in this chapter. As we shall argue in Chapter 8, consensus in British politics has often meant agreement not to change the politics of policymaking even though the state and its activities have become increasingly important, operationally interdependent, and hierarchically ambiguous. That top political and administrative actors should find the political setting attractive is hardly surprising. Whether British government can now cope with the problems of the welfare state is a difficult question that the policy analyses will pose.

2 Administrative Reform: Reorganizing for What?

The notion that the vast administrative machinery required to conduct the business of the welfare state is politically neutral, naturally accountable, and responsive to demands for efficiency is rapidly dying away. In fact, the entire concept of a politically detached administration is of relatively recent origin. As Weber and others argued at the turn of the century, the liberal state required impartial rulemakers and effective implementors of political decisions. The two kinds of decisions were thought to be and generally were distinct. Like most of the modern democracies, Britain has only had such an administration for about a century. The complexity of policymaking in the welfare state forecloses the possibility that administration and politics can be readily distinguished. The problem of administrative reform centers on how the liberal concept of administrative influence has been bankrupted by the welfare state. Since World War II, Britain and most of the other countries covered in this series of studies have been heavily engaged in trying to work out a new relationship between political and administrative decisions.

Comparing these experiences would be much easier if the interface between the elected and the appointed were similar in every welfare state. In Chapter 1 we saw that the British policymaking process has some distinct features that made the passage from nineteenth-century administration to the contemporary welfare state extremely difficult. Ministers are responsible for their departments, but collective responsibility within the cabinet means that intergovernmental and departmental decisions are shielded from the public and even from Parliament. Since roughly the turn of the century, the Treasury has relieved conflict by controlling the administration and budget decisions. By 1960 these controls were both too crude and too ineffective. The controversial decision to form a separate Civil Service Department in 1968 is only a more visible indication that the management and guidance of modern government have now exceeded the capacity of any single agency of government.

Context

In analyzing Britain's effort to come to grips with the organization and control of administration in the welfare state, it is important to see at the outset the peculiar difficulties of introducing new concepts of administration in the British political system. To a much greater degree than in other welfare states, the administration has few responsibilities to Parliament, and Parliament, in turn, has few ways of investigating what civil servants do. An indication of the concentration of authority in the cabinet is that these questions did not figure significantly in the early reform discussions. Crossman and other Labour leaders on the left wing of the party wanted more parliamentary accountability, and the restructuring of Westminster Committees (see Chapter 1) was part of the effort to achieve this. But the hope that an easily manipulated legislature could somehow deal with the complexities of administering the welfare state was ill founded. Once Crossman became a major leader in the Labour government, his enthusiasm for such reforms diminished. Even more ironically, his own consolidated department, Health and Social Security (see Chapter 6), was a creature of the reform effort of the sixties that made parliamentary penetration of administrative decisionmaking more difficult, and resisted reorganization at every step. Organizational complexity left the million public employees in the Health Service outside the scope of the Civil Service Department.

Parliamentary control of the administration is essentially limited to its powers to appropriate and to audit funds. As outlined in Chapter 1, parliamentary control over appropriation has become immensely complicated because of the intricacy of spending controls needed by the welfare state. Though a technical point, this is why the House of Commons Expenditure Committee has focused so heavily on the Exchequer and Audit. It is its most important power over the administration and one of the few areas where the responsible officials, the comptrollers auditor general, are required to provide Parliament with full details of administrative behavior. The Commons' Public Accounts Committee is supposed to be politically neutral and, under the Gladstonian notion of accountability, chaired by a member of the Opposition. Over the past decade these links proved inadequate, but neither ministers nor civil servants have incentives to change a system that so effectively isolates the executive from the legislature.

There are few reasons why either ministers or civil servants should welcome more parliamentary intervention. Ministers must work closely with their top civil servants, and civil servants, in turn, depend on strong ministers to defend the interests of their departments. Despite all the efforts to make ministers think more about long-term strategy, their eyes are naturally on the next election as well as on running their departments. From an administrative perspective, their success is judged very heavily by how readily they extract money from the Treasury (Boyle, 1965, p. 251). Moreover, there are reasons to think that a minister who is too burdened with departmental detail cannot develop his own plans and programs (Playfair 1965, p. 267). The proliferation of government under the welfare state has added to these dilemmas. As public spending grows, ministers are tempted to form coalitions to beat back Treasury cuts, and, as we shall see, it has been difficult to force ministers to control public spending or to make clear choices among programs and policies.

As we saw in Chapter 1, for over twenty years there has been a debate on secrecy within British government. While there is little doubt but that the British cabinet and departments are more effectively sheltered from public view than those of any other modern democracy, it does not necessarily follow that, were the flood of information and policy papers generated in Whitehall made more readily available, "control" would be established. Control presupposes that objectives are defined. The alliance between top civil servants and ministers has resisted more open government, but this does not mean that less resistance would make the ordinary citizen an enthusiastic follower of the battle between the Civil Service Department and the Treasury, much less a keen analyst of the relative advantages and disadvantages of hiving off such things as the Department of Employment's training and placement functions in a semi-autonomous Manpower Services Commission. One of the most troubling aspects of the welfare state is that the machinery that was thought essential to individual well-being and opportunity appears so irretrievably remote from citizens. Though this analysis will not dwell on how democracy copes with big government, it is important to recognize that neither citizens nor ministers have much reason to alter their behavior.

The machinery of government has become too intricate and too large to be easily changed, possibly even to be easily monitored. What differentiates Britain from other modern welfare states is that the formal concentration of power in cabinet government has made dispersal and delegation of authority more difficult. Parliamentary powers have not been (and possibly cannot be) adjusted to the welfare state. The small number of political appointees in departments makes ministers more dependent on their civil servants than in most countries. The spending and financial powers concentrated in the Treasury make reorganization difficult. As we shall see, the curious pattern of reform efforts over the past twenty years has been to minimize damage to this concentration of policy-making power, and to create numerous side issues. The interface between politics and administration has remained basically unchanged although it serves partisan interests to claim otherwise, and partisan interests often confused reform without clarifying objectives.

At the core of this acute dilemma is Wright's observation (1977, p. 299) that British civil servants have no general obligation to the state or to the public interest. It is not that they are not public-spirited or that there is no public recourse to their actions, but that British civil servants are not governed by public law or subsumed under administrative statutes that define their general responsibilities and status. For all the simplicity of the British political system, the relationship between administration and politics is remarkably complex. The most common definition of a "civil servant" is essentially a residual one taken from the 1965 Superannuation Act: "a person serving in an established capacity in the permanent civil service." The Act compounds the confusion by adding that civil service also means the "civil service of the State," one of the few occasions where this embracing term is used in British law. An additional definition is taken directly from parliamentary practice by defining civil servants as those persons paid directly from money voted by Parliament and therefore servants of the Crown. Since the Crown is a symbolic entity and its powers rest with the prime minister, one is led back to the near total dependence of national administration on a person whose powers are limited only by his ability to extract legislation from the House of Commons.

Deciding what the civil service is becomes more difficult as the public sector grows. This problem has plagued every welfare state, but the definition is even more ambiguous in Britain. There is, for example, a separate civil service for Northern Ireland, and nearly 160,000 "industrial civil servants" who work in Royal Docks, the Royal Mint, the Stationery Office, and other industrially organized activities of government. Outside Whitehall are roughly 2 million persons employed by nationalized industries, nearly 3 million working for local government, and a million organized within the Health Service. Total public employment in Britain is 7.8 million persons, about 31 percent of the entire workforce (Parry, 1979). As in most policymaking situations, crude figures tell us little except the relative importance of the issue. Clearly the organization and planning of British administration is, as in most welfare states, critically important.

One of the more curious features of modern government is just how hard it has become to tell how large the administration is. The national government makes only vague manpower estimates, and it seems unlikely that British administration, even if presented with a policy on public sector employment generally, could enforce it. Contrary to the popular image of bureaucracy, this is not because expansion has been so great, but because government is constantly changing the status and organization of major components of the administration. In fact, British national administration has not grown a great deal in the past twenty-five years. The huge increase was during World War II, when the nonindustrial staff (less the Post Office) tripled in size from 163,000 to 499,000. The number of nonindustrial civil servants (with whom this analysis is mainly concerned) actually diminished from 1945 until 1962, when it was about 394,000. In the last years of the Conservative government in the early sixties 20,000 persons were added; under Labour from 1964 to 1970 slightly over 70,000; and again under the Conservatives from 1970 to 1974 an increase of nearly 20,000. Labour again made large increases from 1974 to 1978, when non-industrial civil servants increased by nearly 50,000 persons to 566,000. These large-scale terms treat government as a manpower problem that can only be evaluated in broad economic terms. Bacon and Eltis (1978, 2nd ed., p. 120) estimate that between 1966 and 1975 non–market sector employment increased by roughly 1.2 million persons.

The more relevant question is not how many persons government employs but how it organizes itself, and this, too, confuses figures on the size of the national administration. In 1970, for example, 15,000 postal savings employees were added when the bulk of postal employees became part of a public corporation for the Postal Service. The flurry of reorganization activity created by quasi-governmental agencies (see Chapter 1) reshuffled civil servants throughout the late sixties and early seventies. More often than not, the resulting confusion was attributed to political motives to hide the true size of the administration and fueled an unproductive debate. The critical political interface with administration occurs, as one might expect, much higher in the political hierarchy and is seldom debated in public. While we shall examine many aspects of politics within the administration, our main concern will be how politicians are motivated to adjust the British administrative structure to the complexities and ambiguities of policymaking in the welfare state.

The liberal myth that administrative reform and decisions are not political dies slowly. Historically Britain differs from much of Europe in that national administration was intensely political until mid-Victorian England (Parris, 1969). As cabinet government developed over the eighteenth century, appointments as ministerial secretaries were a major form of patronage in a system that depended heavily on a spoils system to sustain ministerial power. In 1851, Whitehall had 40,000 employees, two-thirds of whom were in the Post Office. The Poor Law Board, one of the most ambitious reforms of early Victorian England, employed eighty-four persons (Brown and Steel, 1979, p. 24). Change began because the Reform Act of 1832 diminished the power of the monarch over ministers and, in turn, made ministers dependent on Parliament. This meant that ministers needed elaborate plans, and party competition, though still vaguely structured, began to produce major new proposals.

For our purposes two things stand out in the Victorian development of the national administration. First, unlike most of Europe, the growing complexities of policymaking in Victorian England were not directly linked to creating a civil service. The civil service was created to combat administrative corruption and to demarcate ministerial powers. In this respect, mid-nineteenth-century and more recent reforms are remarkably similar. Then as now constitutional and political reasons made it inappropriate to ask how the state was changing. Second, the early reform placed great emphasis on personnel and accountability in a narrow sense. To Gladstone, the chancellor of the exchequer largely responsible for the early progress of reform, accountability meant saving "candle-ends and cheese-parings." In 1968 the Fulton Committee made many of these same assumptions.

As Smith outlines (1971), there has been no shortage of reform efforts. Including Fulton, there were fourteen major studies of the civil service between 1850 and 1968. These have been well summarized by Bourn (1968) and cannot be fully analyzed here. Nearly all were concerned with the internal problems of the new civil service: promotion, pay, pensions, and the like, and, when reform was considered, the civil service generally got its own way. Had the Fulton Committee departed from this tradition and dealt more directly with the realities of administrative behavior, much time and money would have been saved over the past decade. Reform must begin with what governments do, not with what civil servants do.

Around the turn of the century, Whitehall began to spawn departments from the various boards and commissions that had proliferated in Victorian England (Parris, 1969). In 1914 non-industrial civil servants numbered 229,000, almost half their present numbers. By then it was apparent that what Wallas (1948, p. 254) called "the greatest invention of the nineteenth century" had substantially changed because the role of government had enlarged. By the end of the First World War powerful new ministries developed in areas that had gradually come under the influence of government: a Ministry of Labour for employment policy (see Chapter 4); a Ministry of Health to redress the shocking conditions exposed during the war; a Department of Scientific and Industrial Research to encourage research and development; and a strong Ministry of Education that had established its domain since the 1902 Education Act extended public education. For the first time British government began to wonder about how it should be organized and the Haldane Committee (1918, cd. 9230) was appointed to review this question.

Between 1939 and 1945, mobilizing for war again expanded the scale and scope of government. The most important change was the immense growth of departments concerned with social services, trade, industry, and transport, all areas that had been largely left to private sector decisions in the past. Between 1939 and 1950 these departments tripled in size (Abramovitz and Eliasberg, 1957, pp. 40–45). Although we now know that the cabinet gave serious attention to a major reorganization immediately after the war (Lee, 1978), demobilization and reconstruction left little time to restructure government. Although Atlee's new Labour government in 1945 worried about the cooperation they might receive from the elitist civil service, Labour had no designs to restructure government. In any event, the statutory expansion of services and benefits left little choice to the administration. Most of the Labour leaders had worked closely with top civil servants throughout the war. Though the welfare state began to take shape, Labour's aims could be added on to the existing functions of departments, and the new social benefits were relatively routine operations to redistribute funds directly to individuals or to expand existing services. The complexity of the welfare state did not become apparent until roughly 1960, and by then a new generation of leaders had arrived.

Agenda

Many events created a sense of *malaise* in the early 1960s. Britain's economic performance did not seem to be keeping up with that of other major European countries (see Chapter 3). The social security system was in deep trouble (see Chapter 4). Relations with the nationalized industries were confused, and continued efforts to reform local government had failed (see Chapter 4). The stage was set for a major inquiry into the problems of making and implementing policy in a more complex world.

This effort began with the 1961 Plowden Report on planning public expenditure, which is discussed in Chapter 3. Although Plowden did not anticipate major organizational changes, it was clear that structural change was imminent. When Plowden appeared, Norman Chester (later Sir Norman) noted that it paved the way for the separation of the civil service from the Treasury (1963, p. 10), although a Treasury expert on public expenditure, Richard Clarke (later Sir Richard) noted it did not "portend the ultimate division of the Treasury" (1963, p. 23). The battle lines within government were being formed well before Fulton appeared, and, as we shall see, Chester was right.

The intimate connection between spending and administration peculiar to British cabinet government is revealed in how Plowden led almost naturally to the Fulton Committee. In many ways the Fulton Report was, in Robson's words (1968), a "scapegoat for real and imaginary ills." The problem of managing a huge administrative system had become increasingly apparent, and important changes had taken place before 1968. In 1963 the Treasury established a Centre for Administrative Studies, and in 1962 the head of the civil service was made an equal with the other major secretaries of the Treasury. The Treasury had a committee at work on administrative training and had made considerable progress in devising better management methods (Clarke, 1978). This is why Chester called Fulton an "ungenerous document" (1968). A third administrative expert, Richard Chapman (1973, p. 39), agreed that the Report could be seen as "a political expedient for a government seeking to create a reformist image." Helsby (later Lord Helsby), who was the first head of the civil service after the Treasury reorganization of 1962, called it "a ferocious way to make headlines."

Such a study could not be conducted in any country without being intensely political. In Britain, however, the Report purported not to be political, though it was patently a Labour document. As Smith (1971, p. 272) notes, the conclusions were known before the Report appeared. A Fabian pamphlet of 1964 is virtually identical to the Report. Labour included administrative reform in its 1964 election manifesto, and one of Wilson's close advisors, Thomas Balogh (later Lord Balogh), made a bitter attack on the civil service (1959). Wilson approved one of the major recommendations, an independent Civil Service Department, the day after the Report was published.

Things would not change much, however. Both the Plowden and Fulton Committees aroused little public interest and had large quotas of civil service members, and their conclusions were implemented at the discretion of the prime minister. By 1960, government had already exceeded the ability of Parliament and the public to follow its decisions. In both cases the inquiries were forbidden to examine the relation of civil servants to ministers and the overall organization of government, though significantly neither could write a report without making some comments on this carefully protected territory.

All this is not to say that the Fulton Committee did not do a thorough job. In many ways its five volumes of evidence, studies, and testimony remain our richest source of information about British national administration. Though private consultants had previously been employed within government, it was the first time that a major consultancy study was done and made public (1968, vol. 2). The Fulton Report is too elaborate and too complex to be satisfactorily summarized here. Only the sections dealing with reorganization are reproduced (see Reading 2-1). The Report covers nearly every aspect of the formal administrative machinery of Whitehall: recruitment, training, career management, pay, pensions, efficiency, organization, and expenditure as well as ministerial and parliamentary relations to the civil service.

Possibly the most naive part of the Report was the conviction that if different kinds of people, presumably more socially representative and more professional, were put in the upper ranks of the civil service, then the policymaking process would be simultaneously more "democratic" and more efficient. Leaving aside the inherent contradictions of these objectives, which Fulton never tried to reconcile, there was the very unrealistic view that personnel reforms could somehow make government more responsive and more effective. There was a great deal of material, for example, on the devastating effects of 64 percent of the administrative class coming from Oxbridge. The Report itself (vol. 3, pt. 1, p. 83), however, showed that 55 percent of top managers and 44 percent of university teachers also come from Oxbridge. In 1974, 38 percent of the MPs came from Oxbridge. When the civil service was again scrutinized by the Expenditure Committee (1977, vol. 2, pt. 1, p. 83), Sir Douglas Allen, then permanent secretary of the Civil Service Department, neatly spiked the argument by noting that six members of Expenditure Committee itself were Oxbridge.

Such ideological arguments have little effect on policymaking, especially when they point to irreconcilable goals and are combined with doubtful means. In terms of more basic reform, there were two fundamental arguments. Rather curiously, the Labour government suggested ways of bringing into government the private sector notion of efficiency. There was to be more exchange with industry, more managerial training in the new Civil Service College, more systematic personnel planning, and more managerial methods applied to departmental planning and to the civil service as a whole. There was a great deal of admiration for the French Ecole Nationale d'Administration and the American Office of Management and Budget. The Report ignored that the former is even more exclusive than the upper ranks of the British civil service, and that the highly politicized American budget office could not operate under a cabinet system. As often happens when one tries to implement policies in the real world, the major stumbling block in achieving efficiency was much more prosaic. The departments of British government are ministerial fiefs. The new Management Services Unit of the CSD could only enter this political territory by consent, and, as we shall see, consent did not mean acceptance.

The second major emphasis of the Report was on personnel. As Chester pointed out (1968, p. 304), the administrative class had already become an anachronism in a world concerned with industrial efficiency, scientific and technical expertise, and rapidly expanding university education. To describe Britain's administrative system as divided between bumbling amateurs and frustrated specialists was a useless and inaccurate characterization. Lord Simey, himself a Labour peer, wrote a sharp dissent (vol. 1, pp. 101–4) to the Report's opening statement that the civil service "is still fundamentally the product of the nineteenth-century philosophy of the Northcote-Trevelyan Report." But the political naiveté goes deeper. The idea that government should be organized around problems (see Reading 2-1) was not new; what was new and treated lightly by Fulton was that government's problems now seem to change rapidly and interconnect in unforeseen ways. The plea for fewer levels of government and for better coordination through "joint hierarchies" not only flew in the face of cabinet government and ministerial prerogatives, but raised unanswered questions about the allocation of authority within the entire British political system.

In short, the Fulton inquiry, like many other inquiries noted in this book, was never expected to talk about the critical interface between political and administrative actors. The stress on efficiency and on personnel were magnificent evasions. As Sisson argued, "to be right by different criteria" says little about political incentives and political choice" (see Reading 2-2). What he called the "management hoax" confuses economics with government. It is interesting that Lord Armstrong, the first permanent secretary of the CSD and later a director of Midland Bank, in testifying to the Expenditure Committee in 1977 (vol. 2, pt. 2, pp. 648–58), pointed out that running a bank is not the same as running a government, where the uncertainties of policymaking and the ambiguities of political goals can never be removed. These factors fairly easily frustrated managerial enthusiasm of the period in Britain,

France, and the United States, since the welfare state changed policymaking requirements but left politics pretty much unchanged.
The state was not going to wither away as in the Marxian vision
nor was it any longer susceptible to governance by the marketplace as in the nineteenth-century liberal state. The role of government had grown, not diminished, and no amount of managerial
tinkering would make this reality disappear.

Process

   Whatever the political shortcomings of the Fulton Committee,
it cannot be said that Whitehall failed to respond. Whether these
efforts have changed national administration in ways that would
have happened in any event is, of course, another question. The
flurry of activity generated by Fulton is best recorded in the four
reports by the new CSD (1969, 1970, 1971, and 1972) and cannot be fully outlined here. As is often the case with policy decisions, the things that were not done are most interesting. Although
Wilson seized on the main recommendation with alacrity and the
CSD was formed, this was hardly major governmental surgery.
Treasury reorganization had already made the old Establishment
Division a virtually self-contained unit. In his speech on Fulton
to Parliament, Wilson made it clear that Fulton's suggestion that
the new head of the civil service should be given financial status
above the permanent secretaries (vol. 1, p. 83) was unacceptable.
The Committee had also recommended that permanent secretary
appointments be reviewed by a selection committee of top officials
(vol. 1, p. 84). This, too, was ignored, not so much because the
review happens anyway through the regular Whitehall network,
but because the recommendation raised delicate questions about
the office that no one wanted to discuss. As the minister responsible for the civil service, the prime minister is consulted in any
event, but formalizing this task would raise suspicions of an executive department under the prime minister, which has always
been resisted in the name of collective responsibility. There is little
doubt as well that Wilson had no interest in compromising his
informal powers and that the civil service mandarins had no interest in seeing their roles better defined. In general, only officials
lacking power see advantages in such formalities.
   Nonetheless, there were important changes in the administration. Wilson declined to give special preference in recruitment and
promotion to experts, but an inquiry (Davies Committee, 1969,

cmnd. 4156) was launched on selection procedures. The old
"Method I" procedure of a single general written exam was abolished, but the more widely used written and oral system under
"Method II" was applauded. The top civil servants who spoke out
on Fulton did not seem particularly disturbed and, as it turned
out, had no reason to be. Everyone knew the elite administrative
class was doomed, but they also knew that top civil servants would
oversee the reform. From the beginning of 1971 a new Administration Group replaced the old class system, and from the beginning of 1972 a new Professional and Technical Category merged
experts in one pool that would, it was hoped, overflow to provide
the technical and scientific talent Fulton thought missing in Whitehall. These changes were more apparent than real. In fact, merger
in the full sense of complete mobility among departments and
jobs was never extended below the under secretary level, the eight
hundred second-echelon officials.

The critical intervening event in the process of implementation
was no less political when the 1970 election brought Heath to
power. The Conservatives, of course, shared few of Labour's suspicions about an elitist civil service system. Were it not that Heath
had his own ideas about injecting managerial procedures into government, Fulton might have gradually sunk into oblivion. Much to
the alarm of his more conventional Conservative followers, this
was not to be the case. In an even more dogged way than Wilson,
Heath believed that Whitehall, the civil service, and even the
cabinet needed a thorough overhaul. Unlike Labour in 1964,
Heath's government came to power with some clearly formed
ideas about government organization. For the past two years he
had been consulting business and management experts, and the
Conservative Policy Centre under David Howell was energetically
producing policy papers for the new government. Howell's 1970
pamphlet, *A New Style of Government*, contained the germ of
Heath's new strategy.

In a more comprehensive way than ever imagined by Labour,
government was to be converted into a giant strategic planning
operation. The cabinet itself was to be smaller (and was for two
years), ministers were to fix their eyes on long-term horizons, and
governmental agencies were to become computerized digits in a
vast efficiency operation. In a curious way, Heath's ambition was
more threatening to the civil service than Wilson's opportunistic
approach. When Heath talked of efficiency, he meant cost-benefit

analysis and strict managerial controls. His attitude was clearly in evidence seven years later when he testified before the Expenditure Committee: "We must have a system whereby the chairman takes decisions and forces people to take decisions if we are going to produce results within a time which is acceptable to the Government, Parliament and the people in the country" (1977, vol. 2, pt. 2, p. 777). But Heath provided a radical departure from past treatment of administration not so much because of the managerial emphasis, which had been present since the early 1960s, but because he dared challenge some basic political assumptions of how British government is organized. The irony was that managerial ruthlessness was to do what British political leaders were somehow unable to do.

Using the Ministry of Defence as a model (Nairne, 1964), Heath's White Paper on reorganization (1970, cmnd. 4506) encompassed the whole policy process. There were to be "unified departments to propose and implement a single strategy for clearly defined and accepted objectives." Conflicts were to be resolved "within the line of management" rather than by interdepartmental compromise and improved resource allocation would in turn make possible "more effective delegation of executive tasks." To build this managerial edifice three things were needed: super-ministries would free ministers from daily chores and facilitate strategic planning; functionally distinct and operationally self-contained agencies would be hived off as autonomous activities run under strict management controls; and government would energetically pursue Programme Analysis and Review (PAR) studies to clarify resource allocation decisions and evaluate departmental efficiency. It would be a mistake to equate Heath's reforms with the simple marketplace strategems of orthodox Conservatives. As in modern corporations and modern unions, bigness in government was not to be a handicap. The problem was to organize decisions so size and scale no longer mattered. In this less overt way, Heath accepted the welfare state just as Wilson did, but without socialist political rhetoric.

Using the relentless analysis that makes permanent secretaries fearsome, Sir Richard Clarke (1972) put his thumb on the central dilemma of large ministries. Some very small ministries may have immense political importance, and some very large ministries may perform routine tasks and therefore be of little political interest. With the tact that makes the mandarins bearable, he then does not say that, this being so, political bargaining and leverage at the center may easily ignore the strategic objectives that this huge operation was initially designed to clarify. Put more crudely, why be a manager when one can have more influence being a politician? Johnson (1971) also observed that there is little reason to think that ministers will stop competing just because their goals are clearer. In addition, he points out, parliamentary accountability will be even more difficult.

The slimming operation at the departmental level had begun under Labour with the formation of super-ministries for Health and Social Security (see Chapter 6) and the Environment (housing, transportation, and local government). These transformations were completed by the Conservatives followed by the merger of the Board of Trade within a giant "private sector" ministry, Trade and Industry. "Hiving off" also advanced quite successfully, and was consistent with Fulton if aimed at an entirely new objective. But the more autonomous agencies such as the Manpower Services Commission and the Property Services Agency kept strong departmental ties. The Ministry of Defence Procurement Agency, which had existed for some years, was the model for these operations. These operations were crucial for the success of Heath's strategy, for the first task was to demonstrate that management techniques could be applied. A much more difficult second stage was to convince the departments that they should also apply this kind of analysis. This task fell to the new CSD's Management Services Unit. Most departments expanded their management analysis units, and six went the full way and created the operational research units essential to full-blown corporate planning (Expenditure Committee, 1977, vol. 2, pt. 1, p. 105). The under secretary in charge of CSD Manpower Services testified that forty management objective, or PAR, studies had been done by 1977 (vol. 2, pt. 1, p. 91). This was the essential first step, because costs and benefits cannot be evaluated and compared unless top officials agree to specify their goals (Klein, 1972).

As the testimony also made clear, the Treasury has only persuasion to get a department to make such a study, can only advise in its execution, and has no authority to see that its results are ever used. Because the PAR studies are confidential, ministers and top civil servants are spared embarrassment as well as responsibility. All this is not to say that efficiency studies have not had some beneficial effects, but Lord Armstrong himself confessed to the Expenditure Committee (Expenditure Committee, 1977, vol. 2, pt. 2, p. 653) that the PAR analyses have not gone well. Without them there are no building blocks for strategic planning. Ministers do not want to be exposed to criticism within the government, nor do they wish to be occupied with showers of questions in Parliament and the press. Much less do they wish to provide the Treasury with the ammunition to shoot holes in their departmental budgets. Perhaps most difficult of all, political animals do not enjoy the philosophical discussion needed to clarify objectives nor do they see any reason to think about a future when they may not be in office.

To understand the most difficult obstacle to Heath's plans, one must return to the role of the Treasury. Were management by objectives to be fully implemented, resource allocation, and through it public spending, would be discussed around the shrunken cabinet table that Heath envisaged. The Treasury would be reduced to its nineteenth-century role of being the financial and monetary agent of government. A strong Management Services Unit within the CSD would be much more devastating to the Treasury than the 1968 hiving off of personnel functions. In this respect Heath's proposals were both administratively and politically radical. To see how this possibility developed, one must consider the Public Expenditure Survey Committee (PESC), whose economic planning role will be discussed in Chapter 3. Changes in public expenditure planning in 1961 gave the Treasury a new weapon to control public spending. Although there is little evidence that the public expenditure forecasts ever reduced spending until the severe inflation and economic decline of the mid-seventies, the Treasury was able to extract more accurate information from departments and to formulate independently the relation of resources to future spending. Ironically, the Treasury had first thought of Fulton as a respite from increasingly insistent demands from ministers to get public spending accounts and controls in workable form. What transpired was that once the CSD was created in 1968, the possibility arose that the CSD, not the Treasury, would control manpower estimates and thereby determine half or more of public spending.

Top civil servants were (and are) bright enough to know that personnel was not the key issue. The crippling constraint on the Treasury after 1968, as Sir Douglas Allen made clear before the Expenditure Committee (1977, vol. 2, pt. 1, p. 56), was that "the old mystery of the Treasury, where it was hitting you, has gone." From 1968 there was dual control of public spending because spending limitations on personnel rested with the CSD, which had little incentive to reduce staff. PAR had the oddly counterproductive effect of making it even less advantageous for the CSD to try to discipline departments. Their most important job under Heath was to get management studies done, and to do this while also cutting back departmental staff in more arbitrary ways was obviously impossible. The beauty of Heath's strategy was that, given close cooperation between the CSD and departments, public spending control and resource allocation would be provided simultaneously. The relationship between the CSD and the Treasury was further aggravated because the CSD determines pay policy.

As he did with economic policy more generally (see Chapter 3), Heath made a daring gamble that he might be able to control public employment and governmental organization through new techniques. What has been less often realized is that this meant downgrading the public expenditure forecast (PESC) in hopes of getting a more direct and a firmer grip on public spending. Later events were to demonstrate that he was right, because inflation in the absence of an incomes policy for the public sector sent public spending soaring. When this happened, roughly from 1974 to the present, public sector incomes policy became critically important. PESC emerged from the Plowden Report and has incorrectly been most often viewed in terms of economic policymaking. In fact, its political ramifications were much wider and touched on critical relationships within the policymaking process, most importantly the powers of the prime minister, the Treasury, and the departments.

As a tool of economic policymaking, PESC possibly did more harm than good. (The ramifications in relation to the private sector and macroeconomic objectives will be discussed in Chapter 3.) The weaknesses of PESC are well known: there is no connection between the spending forecast and future tax policy so the government in office is promising funds without showing how it intends to raise them; for political as well as economic reasons the chancellor of the exchequer does not want to publicize employment or inflation forecasts so two of the most critical causes of increased spending are simply omitted; and as is apparent in the published forecasts (since 1969) the temptation is overwhelming to overestimate growth in order to justify expanded services and benefits. While it may be true, as Heclo and Wildavsky argue (1974, p. 202), that "no nation in the world can match the sophistication or thoroughness found in the British process of expenditure projection," it is also probably true that this process is subject to more political influence and opportunism than in any other country in the world.

The most persuasive evidence comes from Sir Richard Clarke, who was instrumental in assembling the public expenditure control machinery in the Treasury. As he notes (1978, p. 133), the four-year time cycle is too short to get control of long-term commitments and too long to persuade ministers that they should observe its guidelines. There are a host of technical problems: constant prices invite underestimating spending; the inability to translate it into budgetary (department by department) terms means that ministerial responsibilities, even if they were spelled out within PESC, are difficult to state in current spending terms; and the inability to translate it into economic terms (income and taxation implications) means that it is of doubtful value in economic policymaking. PESC invites the political reversals and partisan tinkering that plagues much policymaking in Britain (Clarke, 1978, p. 137n). The public sector generates its own complexities that easily exceed capacity for political control. For example, the "relative price effect" (an allowance for higher price increases for government than those expected in the economy) was devised because of the large wage component of the budget and, in turn, means that "the public sector's labour force may increase without control over time" (Maynard and Walker, 1975). Administrative reform is virtually impossible, which explains why in 1977 Britain relived the entire issue.

Heath saw a new way of controlling expenditure and administrative decisionmaking by making departments more responsible through corporate planning. Even if the economic crisis of 1973 had not wrecked these plans, he faced formidable opposition from a Treasury that had already been downgraded by the formation of the CSD, and from ministers of spending departments who did not want to be haltered. Heath was often criticized for his "presidential" tendencies in government reorganization, but his proposals were in many ways the most original and far-reaching administrative reforms yet produced. Heath did not ignore the unfortunate split between personnel policies, vested in the CSD, and spending control, but he did not have confidence that the civil service left to themselves would, in effect, place their heads on the block of corporate planning. The implementation of Fulton, however poorly conceived the Report, seems to confirm his doubts.

Consequences

In creating a vision of a harmonious, enlightened, and industrious civil service, Fulton is in many respects the last chapter of Victorian views on administration rather than the prelude to administrative complexity in the welfare state. In fact, in 1977 the Expenditure Committee notes in opening their report that a House of Commons committee had not had the audacity to survey the civil service as a whole since 1873. There is more than a little irony that Parliament was mobilized at that time because of the tremors sent through nineteenth-century Whitehall by the initial administrative reforms. Now, as then, reports and recommendations have no chance of being accepted unless they please the cabinet.

One item in the Committee's inventory of failures and successes from 1968 to 1976, based on a memorandum from the CSD (Expenditure Committee, 1977, vol. 2, pt. 1, pp. 1–49), was recruitment. Oxbridge was still providing over half the successful candidates for the higher levels of a now "unified" civil service. As the Committee on Expenditure noted (p. xix), "Presumably people who pay for their children's education expect them to receive a good one," one that will give them an advantage at the anonymous stage of selection, the written examination. The Civil Service Commission was not even keeping statistics that would permit analysis of why "generalists" were still more successful than scientists and engineers. Despite unification, the CSD had also introduced a "faststream" for distinguished graduates so that they could jump several grades on entry. Unification within the classification system seemed pretty well bogged down. In 1968 there were 47 general grades (classifications used by more than one department) and 1,400 departmental grades; in 1977 there were 38 general grades with 500 departmental grades. For reasons never explained to the Committee, efforts to advance uniform grading stopped in October 1975 (Expenditure Committee, 1977, p. xxvi).

As we shall see in Chapter 3, one of the major problems of economic policymaking in the welfare state is that continued tinkering, much of it for political reasons, not only has little effect, but creates confusion throughout the economy. By 1975, Fulton and its consequences were having similar effects within the higher levels of the administration (Painter, 1975). The Civil Service Department (1975) published a report suggesting that the time had come to revive administrative morale. That the huge administrative machine could organize a counterattack is not so surprising. More revealing of the politics of administration was the disclosure that a small unit had been confidentially organized in the CSD to improve the image of the bureaucracy (*Times*, Aug. 31, 1978). The growth of services and benefits made administration into a scapegoat to explain poor political judgment and economic failure. As Lord Armstrong once said, civil servants become "grouped with mothers-in-law and Wigan Pier as one of the recognized objects of ridicule." What differs from other welfare states is that the top British civil servants are trapped between the anonymity required by cabinet government and the attractions of having immense political influence.

From 1973 another dilemma arose when inflation made public sector pay a sensitive issue. A Top Salaries Review Body had been organized to assess salaries of under secretaries and above, while other salaries were judged on comparability with the private sector by the Pay Research Unit, formed in 1956. With inflation, the large and often unpredictable public sector wage bill means that, contrary to the Committee's feelings, it has been virtually impossible to devise a national pay policy independent of the government. Indicative of the secrecy that abounds in Whitehall, the director of the Pay Research Unit needs ministerial approval to publish his findings. Neither are the productivity studies of the Manpower Services Unit in the CSD published. PAR had, of course, envisaged bringing these two kinds of analysis together so that costs and benefits of departmental work could be specified. There was little evidence that this was being done, and there is a great deal of evidence that ministers would not approve. The split between the management of the civil service and the Treasury also makes it virtually impossible to implement such decisions even if they were made.

In another area of fiscal responsibility, the Expenditure Committee closely questioned the Inland Revenue (the tax collection agency under the Treasury) on whether they ever studied the relative economic advantages and costs of various kinds of taxation. The Inland Revenue is sensitive to criticism because of it huge rate of increase in staff (56,000 in 1965 to 73,000 in 1975), but the testy responses of its under secretary, if made before an American congressional committee, would be fatal (1977, vol. 2, pt. 1, pp. 114–34). A more important illustration of organizational problems is the fact that the Exchequer Audit extends only to expenditures, not to revenues, unless instructed otherwise by its own superior, the Treasury. Thus, neither the fiscal nor the financial side of the Treasury was assessing the cost effects of the most crucial policies within government, taxation itself. The evidence goes far toward vindicating Heath's insistence that PAR be implemented, even though Clarke (1978, p. 99) says that Heath was "inventing the wheel." The Treasury has had the capacity to conduct such studies since program budgeting was applied to the Ministry of Defence twenty years ago, but it has never done so.

Some of the Expenditure Committee's most important recommendations are reproduced in Reading 2-3. As we saw in Chapter 1, ministers have few direct controls over civil servants even though the normal pressures of business and mutual interest usually prevent serious breakdown. The Fulton Report skirted the delicate issue of ministers and civil servants, only making the curious comment that "Ministers should not be stuck with Permanent Secretaries who are too rigid or tired" (1968, p. 95), but the Committee recommended that ministers "should be able to have any civil servant with whom they find it difficult to work moved for reasons of personal or political incompatibility." This is more than a question of ministerial authority. Would the prime minister want to lose the leverage that his approval of high civil service appointments provides in restraining zealous ministers? Would the ministers themselves, apart from a few known serious conflicts with permanent secretaries, want to have their responsibilities specified more clearly? Would the upper reaches of the civil service wish to shed this crucial informality, which in effect gives them more autonomy and anonymity than is found in any other political system?

Within the public sector the paradoxical effect of inflation has been both to expose the weaknesses of PESC and to help to restore Treasury power. This meant, in turn, that public employment generally and the effectiveness of spending controls specifically again came under scrutiny, with the chancellor of the exchequer taking the leading role. Although the implications for the administration and governmental organization did not appear immediately, after 1974 Treasury quickly acquired stricter controls over departmental decisions. In September 1975, departments were required to have monthly (formerly quarterly) spending accounts in the hands of the Treasury within ten days of the next month. The 1976 PESC forecast (1976, cmnd. 6393, p. 4) anticipated no increases in public spending for the next three years. The most severe control of all, cash limits, was set forth in a White Paper (1976, cmnd. 6440). This meant that roughly two-thirds of government spending was strictly limited to the previous year's level after allowing for inflation (Wright, 1977).

Austerity impinges directly on the public sector and, in turn, on governmental organization and employment. Faced with these difficult decisions, the prime minister found it hard to avoid having a public sector incomes policy, and even using it to set private sector standards. One of the paradoxes of the welfare state is that public employees are both a more visible and a more vulnerable focus for economies. In Britain this problem is accentuated because of the problems in constructing a private sector incomes policy (see Chapters 3 and 5). Complexity is compounded because the CSD and the Treasury work out public sector pay policy, while incomes policy is determined by the Treasury and the Department of the Employment.

The most important recommendation of the Expenditure Committee was that the management functions of the CSD should be returned to the Treasury. They realized what most within Whitehall already knew: that the "division of responsibility for control between the Treasury and the CSD [is] obsolete"; that "responsibility for monitoring the control of efficiency should be vested in the Treasury"; and that the management carrot disassociated from the spending stick had little effect on departments (1977, pp. li–lix). There was wide agreement among the mandarins of Whitehall: Lord Armstrong admitted that the division had produced a stand-off on management reviews (vol. 2, pt. 2, p. 650); Sir Douglas Allen confessed that the CSD had diminished the Treasury's power (vol. 2, pt. 1, p. 58); and Sir John Hunt, a widely respected secretary to the Cabinet Office, called separation "illogical" (vol. 2, pt. 2, p. 747). He outlined three possibilities: put public spending controls with the CSD, which would leave the Treasury a ministry of finance; restore CSD management responsibilities to the Treasury, leaving the CSD essentially a personnel agency; or keep the status quo with improved coordination (see Reading 2-4).

Callaghan's belated reply to the Committee on Expenditure (1978, cmnd. 7117) is a bland and indecisive document, essentially endorsing the status quo. He was reluctant to act because of the approaching election and, not unrelated to this, the severe conflicts he was experiencing with public sector unions. National incomes policy was completely shattered by 1978, and the 5 percent wage restraint could only be imposed on public employees. Their animosity, combined with near paralysis of many public services over the winter of 1978–79, were crucial in Callaghan's defeat in the 1979 election. Under a negotiation procedure established in 1919 (National Whitley Council), labor relations with nonindustrial civil servants had been relatively harmonious until 1973. But over the next decade public sector unions consolidated more successfully than private sector unions (see Chapter 5), and by 1979 80 percent of the public sector employees (compared with 35 percent of the private sector) were organized.

The overall effect has been that the civil service unions have become a critical group in forming a public sector pay policy, while their security within government structure makes them the most difficult to negotiate with. Agreement is essential for any harmonious reorganization of government, but government, in turn, does not have the leverage of the marketplace to decide how many civil servants are needed, much less reliable measures of productivity and costs that permit it to judge their most effective deployment. Heath's reforms were aimed at developing such measures, but it seems unlikely that strong public sector unions would permit their application. The 1974 Labour government was so heavily dependent on the unions that these avenues toward reorganization were effectively cut off. By 1979 pay awards in the public sector were often more controversial than in the private sector. Like Callaghan, Mrs. Thatcher also singled out public sector employees to achieve pay restraint.

In effect, a decade's effort to make government more effective and more accountable is vulnerable to demands by public sector unions. There are no clear solutions to this dilemma. Though the unions would hotly deny that they hold a privileged position in the British power structure, they are critically important in devising incomes policies and in government reorganization. Nonetheless, stringent public spending controls (see Chapter 3) have more direct impact on civil service pay, and on public sector incomes policy generally, than ever before. When government announces expected increases in local government or nationalized industry subsidies, for example, its forecasts are immediately translated into an incomes policy. When Sir Keith Joseph, secretary of state for industry, announced his future plans in 1979 (17.5 percent subsidy increases), these were seized upon as future public sector pay policy guidelines. The embarrassment was compounded because the Thatcher government was on record as opposing an incomes policy.

In 1976 the Labour paymaster general, Edmund Dell, and the Treasury asked a distinguished group of operations research experts to analyze how advanced techniques might be integrated into British public spending procedures. The report of the Committee on Policy Optimisation (Ball Report, 1978) is a fitting conclusion to the long and unproductive struggle to provide a coherent and manageable structure for the British welfare state. Its more general significance in this struggle is that it marks the resurgence of Treasury influence, which was of course inherent in the economic crisis and the determination of both Labour and Conservative politicians to reduce public spending. In brief, the application of optimal control theory by the Treasury would be to impose through a single department what many spending departments refused to do for themselves under the impact of Fulton, PESC, and later Heath's PAR.

The Ball Report is an extremely frank account of the obstacles to reform. Among the practical difficulties, they note (pp. 101–2) that ministers would fear "a loss of control over the policy-making process and a failure to keep their options open, a feeling that would make them hostile to the whole process"; that ministers would not want "to commit themselves to decisions in advance of events, or to answer hypothetical questions"; and that ministers and governments change their minds. The realities of policymaking should be compared with these political objections. To what extent can it be said that a British minister, or those of any other advanced welfare state, indeed have a clear notion of their options, are ever free from the accumulated decisions of the past, or have in fact been able to translate the vague prescriptions of parties into meaningful policy language? There is very little evidence that the computerization and sophistication of decisionmaking over the past two decades of governmental reform and reorganization has replaced judgment or eliminated choice.

In the final analysis the resistance to modernizing British government does not come from the administration, as more conspiratorial thinkers of both the extreme left and right are likely to suggest, or from the highly technical and often obscure techniques needed to run modern government. As will be argued in more detail in Chapter 8, resistance is deeply rooted in the constitutional and political principles of cabinet and parliamentary government as they have evolved in Britain. Refusal to confront structural constraints is a political problem. As we shall see in the cases to follow, when faced with issues that raise such fundamental choice and, in turn, cast doubt on British political traditions, policymakers have retreated with an alarming regularity.

Readings

2-1. THE STRUCTURE OF DEPARTMENTS AND PROMOTING EFFICIENCY*

The Fulton Committee on the civil service studied every aspect of British national administration. Among their most important recommendations was that modern managerial methods and efficiency should be improved, but they were unclear on how these reforms should be implemented.

157. Further changes in the way in which many departments organise their work are also needed if the principles of accountable management are to be applied as fully and as widely as they ought to be. Three main obstacles at present stand in the way of the effective allocation of responsibility and authority.

158. The first of these arises when several departments, or several branches within a department, have a substantial interest in the same problem. With responsibility diffused, the need for wide consultation may mean that all can move forward only at the pace of the slowest. This limitation is inherent in much government work. Despite this, it should be possible, especially where

The Civil Service (Report of the Fulton Committee), vol. 1 (cmnd. 3638; London: HMSO, 1968), pp. 52–54. Footnotes have been deleted.

the problem is reasonably self-contained, to devise methods of concentrating in one man or group the responsibility for organising the relevant material and putting forward a solution. Where problems involve several departments, it may often be the right course to set up a team. This is, in fact, often done now. There is, however, too much of a tendency at present for members of groups of this kind to try to carry their departments with them at each step of the way. We feel that more specific allocation of responsibility to individuals, both departmentally and interdepartmentally, is needed. The interests of many different Ministers are often, if not usually, involved. Nevertheless, the problem-solving approach, has great value, since it reduces the temptation to "pass the buck", and it can do much to develop the competence and confidence of the individuals concerned. We recommend that departments should make opportunities for adopting it whenever they can.

159. Another general obstacle to the clear allocation of personal responsibility and authority frequently arises from the number of levels in the hierarchy of most Whitehall departments. Usually there are at least seven organisational levels in administrative work (from Executive Officer to Permanent Secretary), rather more than there would be in a typical industrial situation, and spans of control (i.e. the number of subordinates reporting directly to a superior) are very narrow, usually only two or three. Similar narrow spans of control are found in other hierarchies, e.g. in the organisation of much engineering work. Often, from Executive Officer upwards, each level "has a go" at a paper or a problem, adding comments or suggestions as it goes up the hierarchy until it reaches the point at which somebody takes a decision. This point is often higher than it would otherwise be because decisions may involve the Minister in having to answer for them in Parliament. In consequence, personal responsibility and authority are obscured; delay follows. We think that the number of working levels in the traditional organisation of the flow of business should be reduced. The level or levels omitted will obviously vary in different situations. Much more often than now, for example, an Executive Officer should work direct to a Senior Executive Officer, or a Principal direct to an Under Secretary. With "flatter" structures there can be a more precise allocation of responsibility and authority. We think the Service ought to make bold experiments in this direction.

160. The third obstacle arises in those areas of the Service where administrators and specialists (e.g. engineers, architects, quantity surveyors and planning officers) are jointly engaged on a common task like the design and preparation of military installations and the supervision of their construction by outside contractors. Where this happens, the two main systems of organisation at present are known as "parallel hierarchies" and "joint hierarchies". In parallel hierarchies, the responsibility is bisected: financial and overall policy control is entrusted to administrators organised in one hierarchy, while advice on the technical merits of a case and the execution and development of technical policy is laid to specialists organised in a separate but parallel hierarchy. In joint hierarchies, an administrator and a specialist are designated joint heads of a block of work but at lower levels the separation of functions still occurs, with financial control in the hands of the administrators. The way these arrangements work is described in more detail in the report of the Management Consultancy Group.

161. We are aware of the advantages claimed for these forms of organisation, but we are satisfied that they are outweighed by their very considerable disadvantages. They produce delay and inefficiency because of the need for constant reference to and fro between the hierarchies. They prevent the specialists from exercising the full range of responsibilities normally associated with their professions and exercised by their counterparts outside the Service. In particular, they obscure individual responsibility and accountability; no single person at any level has clear-cut managerial responsibility for the whole task.

2-2. RESISTANCE TO CIVIL SERVICE REFORM*

The Fulton Report soon evoked criticism for its political unreality and the difficulties of reconciling its recommendations with cabinet government.

One must not expect too much of an organisation which has to take cognisance of all the muddled business which pushes itself before the attention of a modern government. It might be better if its existence was not admitted at all, as an entity, and there were

*C. H. Sisson, "The Civil Service—Can Anything Be Done about It?" *Spectator*, March 6, 1971 (selections).

just several hundred thousands of people, split up into groups more or less usefully and certainly very variously employed. The conception of the existence of the Civil Service as a corporate entity produces a dull intoxication, merely on account of numbers, and it even gives rise to the illusion that there are people who control it. At the same time, curiously enough, it produces a conviction that 'the old doctrine of ministerial responsibility' is 'a myth', though that doctrine has at least the merit of being part of an intelligible political system, and meaningful in a way that the conception of the responsibility of the bland officials who smile their way through successive changes of policy is not.

The recommendations put forward by the Fulton Committee were mostly pointed in the wrong direction—towards the melting of all classes into one, instead of the articulation of departmental and sub-departmental groups, and towards a conception of management detached from any intimate knowledge of the substance and purpose of particular pieces of work to be done. If there had to be a 'Civil Service Department'—and clearly it would not be practicable to pay so many people out of one purse without having some measure of co-ordination—it ought to have been established as a subordinate service department, leaving the major initiative and authority at various departmental points stretching out to the periphery. It is not self-evident that such a functionary as a Head of the Civil Service is wanted at all; he is the embodiment of a bogus unity. Of course there would be central questions to be settled, on which ministers would need some advice on a service-wide rather than on a departmental basis, but there is no reason why such questions should not be dealt with by a committee of Permanent Secretaries, with changing membership and, of course, changing chairmanship.

Of course any radical change in the Civil Service must come from new ideas of government, not from Civil Service tinkering and techniques. The Civil Service is a subordinate institution and should always be treated as such. A much more rigorous analysis of function than has been customary for some years must take place, and Departments must be organised strictly to carry out those functions and not to 'think', an activity which, detached from performance, never got anyone anywhere, least of all a government. It is unfortunate that so many people in senior positions in the Service have never, before they reached their final eminence, had any experience of management to speak of. The typical career of the bright administrator is in essay-writing—which is usually called policy-making—and secretarial work of one kind and another. The direction of the eyes has always been upwards, to see what will please, not downwards, to see what is going on in the expensive organisations which are supposed to be under their control. This can result in an appalling incapacity in people who are rather intelligent than otherwise. Desirable though some technical improvement in management certainly is, in certain areas, it is the development of sensitivity down as well as up the line which is the greatest managerial need in Whitehall.

It does not do to expect too much of reform, or perhaps to think too much of general reforms at all. There are a number of particular problems rather than a general one. Nothing is easy, and all one can hope for is the removal of some of the prejudices which make things more difficult than they need be. Perhaps the era of freer discussion forseen by Sir William Armstrong will help to alleviate the prejudices. That depends on how free the discussion is and there are, as Sir William has pointed out, strict limits to that, though in the realm of Civil Service organisation they do not seem to be very serious ones. It is only the servants talking among themselves, about their own affairs not about those of their masters, though to be sure radical action depends in the end on politicians. But the fact that Whitehall is parasitic—though many of the executive organisations embedded in the Service, and serving the public directly, have their own raison d'être—should not make discussion impossible, though too many talking parasites would be a nuisance, one can see that. From that danger the desire to please, deeply institutionalised in the hierarchy of the Service, should protect us. A greater danger is the promotion of pseudo-discussion, with the pattern of right-minded determined from the top. From that, according to what we are usually taught, the robust traditions of our country should save us. I am not so sure, for vast modern organisations of their very nature induce pressures with a strong resemblance to those experienced, we understand, under the sway of the Czar of Muscovy.

It takes a long time for ideas to make their way in the world, and we must not complain too much if those which are being promulgated in Whitehall have a rather tatty look. It is the business of a democratic administration to pick up and diffuse ideas rather than to invent them, and too much novelty would hurt. But we should complain a little, because it is only in this way that cracks are opened through which hitherto unacceptable ideas filter in. Complaint comes better from influential quarters outside, and the source of much of what now passes for new in Whitehall is the academic thought of some years ago. But one of the dangers of leaving complaint entirely to outsiders is that they very rarely know enough to hit the mark exactly. Businessmen are aware of the pervasion of unfamiliar criteria, so that even where they see accountability they do not necessarily see what people are having to account for. Academics are apt to inflame themselves about obsessive questions of economics or sociology, or to pursue the dogmatism of a technique beyond what is reasonable. These points of view are valuable because of their lack of sympathy, but they supplement, and do not replace criticism from within the Service itself. Admittedly the combination of one or two ideas with first-class practical experience must amount to something which is only just on the right side of insubordination.

2-3. RELATIONS BETWEEN MINISTERS AND CIVIL SERVANTS*

The Expenditure Committee Report on the civil service of 1977 surfaced a number of conflicts between parliamentary accountability, ministerial powers, and civil service reforms. Among the most important was the ambiguity of the relationship between ministers and their top civil servants.

137. All civil servants naturally say that they exist solely to serve the Government and that they take their policy instructions automatically from Ministers. They could scarcely be expected to give your sub-committee evidence other than to this effect. However, many who have been, or who are, Ministers believe that Ministers do not always get the service which it is claimed that they get. They say that they find on their coming into office that some Departments have firmly held policy views and that it is very difficult to change these views. When they are changed, the Department will often try and reinstate its own policies through the passage of time and the erosion of Ministers' political will. Many Departments are large and it is not difficult to push forward

*The Civil Service, vol. 1 (Eleventh Report from the Expenditure Committee, Session 1976–77, House of Commons Papers, 535-I; London: HMSO, 1977), pp. lxiii–lxiv. Footnotes have been deleted.

policies without a Minister's knowledge, particularly if there is any lack of clarity in defining demarcation lines between different Ministers' responsibilities, as has been known to happen.

138. Further it is often said to be extremely difficult to launch a new policy initiative which is not to the liking of a Department. Delay and obstruction are said to be among the tactics used, together with briefing Ministers in other Departments to oppose the initiative in Cabinet or Cabinet Committee. The workload on Ministers is immense and procrastination or repetition of the difficulties of a policy would be tactics that Ministers would find difficulty in overcoming.

139. In considering these allegations it is necessary to make two points which to some extent would justify these practices to the extent that they may exist. First, the workload of most Departments is so great that all decisions cannot be taken by Ministers. It is natural in these circumstances that Ministers would want to delegate some matters for decision to the civil service. We merely observe that any such delegation should be decided by Ministers, not by civil servants, and the succeeding incumbents in the relevant ministerial offices should be informed of it.

140. Secondly, the civil service has a duty to preserve the overall consistency of Government policy when a Minister embarks on a course conflicting with that of a Minister in another Department. It may be right for the one Minister to be frustrated, and the other (or the Prime Minister) alerted, until such time as the two have met and argued the matter out to a decision, either in or out of Cabinet. In addition, when a Permanent Secretary considers that his Minister is acting improperly he has a right to appeal to the Prime Minister and should do so.

141. Beyond these instances, however, there seems to us to be no justification for any of the practices mentioned in paragraphs 137 and 138. It is often argued that the civil service is entitled to prevent what is called "the worst excesses of left or right" in the interests of stable Government policy. This point of view used to be argued, particularly in relation to Britain in the years following the last war. It is still thought by some to be a justification for the civil service resisting measures which Ministers might wish to take, which in the opinion of the civil service are "going too far". In the opinion of Your Committee the duties of the civil service should be limited to pointing out the possible consequences, including the political consequences, of any policy but should not

include opposing or delaying the policy. If the policy indeed turns out to be unwise or destabilising, the political party in office pays the price. They carry the responsibility, they should have the power to implement their policies.

142. The danger with the argument of preventing "the worst excesses" is that it becomes open to civil servants to decide what are and what are not "worst excesses". If they assume the right to do that, then the step to assuming views on all party matters is but a small one. Whatever the truth of the allegations discussed above may or may not be, it is relevant to consider the powers of Ministers in relation to their advisers so that they may best discharge their responsibilities.

2-4. MAKING ADMINISTRATION ACCOUNTABLE*

By 1977, British government was again confronted with complex problems of aligning the civil service with modern management. The contradictions this created for cabinet government were spelled out by a London Times editorial.

It has been the custom of constitutional theorists to depict the United Kingdom as one of the most over-centralized nations in the developed world. Yet it is a paradox of Whitehall itself that its own centre does not hold. There is no single central department of state to dominate all others. Power is dispersed between the Treasury, the Cabinet Office, the Civil Service Department and, to an extent that is not generally realized, the Prime Minister's private office and Policy Unit in No. 10 Downing Street. When reform is in the air, as it is at present with a Prime Minister dissatisfied with the service he receives from his bureaucracy, an Expenditure Committee report urging specific changes and a new Head of the Home Civil Service to be appointed, the blurred and overlapping responsibilities of the central departments look especially messy. The possible reconstructions seem rather untidy also, unless Mr. Callaghan, against all indications, rejigs the Cabinet Office as a fully fledged Prime Minister's Department, establishing its primacy once and for all.

*"At the Centre of Government" (editorial), *The Times* (London), Oct. 6, 1977.

Over the past seven years the drift towards such a body has proceded piecemeal. The foundation of the Central Policy Review Staff in 1970, the growth in the influence of the Prime Minister's private office under Mr. Robert Armstrong between 1970 and 1975, the creation of a Policy Unit in No. 10 under Dr. Bernard Donoughue in 1974 have marked the stages of development. Above all, the increased might of the Cabinet Office, especially in economic affairs, under the stewardship of Sir John Hunt has tilted the balance of power in Whitehall. Should Mrs. Thatcher after a Conservative victory at the polls install a minister alongside her as a chief-of-staff, another significant landmark will have been passed on the road to a Prime Minister's Department.

In the meantime the abolition of the Civil Service Department is due and a reconstitution of its powers in other ways and other places. Firstly, responsibility for manpower and Civil Service pay should be joined with its natural twin, the control of public expenditure, in the Treasury. This would not be the regressive step that is often alleged. In pre-Fulton days, the pay and management side of the Treasury was virtually separate from all else in Treasury Chambers. Their proper union would be a sensible step in the welcome climate of efficiency and economy reflected in the recent report of the Expenditure Committee.

Shorn of responsibility for manpower the Civil Service Department would lose its title to separate existence. Its remaining responsibilities for recruitment, promotions, honours, patronage and dealings with the unions on conditions of service and professional ethics could pass to a new foundation—a Public Service Commission. The Head of the Home Civil Service would preside over the new body. He would be answerable to the Prime Minister but, as professional head, he should speak publicly and widely about the Civil Service before select committees and through an annual report. His commission could be made accountable to the wider public, as well as to Parliament through the person of the Prime Minister, by the appointment of outsiders to its membership.

A Public Service Commission would provide a base from which to launch the reform of Whitehall. A determined insider using the external stimulus of the Expenditure Committee report could succeed where other attempts, notably in the wake of Fulton, have failed to achieve necessary and lasting change. He would, however, lack two of the chief sources of authority in Whitehall, a department of state at his back and responsibility for a large block of public expenditure. The lack could be made good only by the conspicuous and sustained backing of the Prime Minister.

Once its reforming brief was exhausted, much of the commission's *raison d'être* would be lost. It would be a child of its time, as the Civil Service Department was the progeny of Fulton. A Prime Minister's Department would seem a more permanent settlement of the problem of the central departments, but the innovation would provoke resistances and objections of its own. If he does nothing else at this stage, Mr. Callaghan must make the headship of the Civil Service, whatever the body to which it is attached, a job worthy of a Whitehall heavyweight.

3 Economic Policymaking: Public Expenditure for What?

The image of Britain as a profligate and irresponsible dispenser of public money does not bear careful examination. There were nine European countries in 1974–76 whose governments spent a larger share of gross domestic product (GDP) than Britain (36 percent) (OECD, 1978, p. 43). Nor, as we shall see in Chapter 6, does Britain appear to have lavished spending on social services and benefits. Several more politically conservative countries, France and Germany, for example, spent more on welfare and collected more taxes (OECD, 1976). What distinguishes British public spending from that of most of Europe and Japan is how government spending in the aggregate seems to have dominated the economic debate. One feels that British parties and institutions created the illusion that government was spending a great deal. Britain did not become a "big spender" among the welfare states until the 1970s, and by then it was increasingly difficult to tell whether high spending was a function of inflation or of deliberate choices.

Separating political and economic forces as they affect the economy is not easy, but it is perhaps easier to do in Britain than in most countries. Adversarial politics tends to simplify economic choices. Labour and the Conservatives invariably run on platforms that promise to "put things right" and public expenditure helps crystallize these choices in readable, if not workable, form. The annual cycle of fiscal and financial legislation occupies half or more of Parliament's time and fuels lively debates that everyone knows will change nothing. Parliament's ability to alter spending proposals of the cabinet and ministers has been described as "ludicrous" and "complete nonsense" (Expenditure Committee, 1978, pp. 81 and 117). Since 1970, there have been some small incursions into ministerial territory and important steps toward clarifying the meaning of public expenditure, itself an ambiguous phrase, but what spending is supposed to do to the economy has never been very clear. Of all the policy problems considered in this volume, the aims of economic policy are the most elusive and as economic conditions have worsened, seem to incorporate impossible contradictions. The common phrases, full employment, balanced trade, and price stability, really say almost nothing about what decisions should be made. It is also important to remember that in the 1960s and early 1970s, when many of the policy choices described in this study were being made, errors could still be absorbed by modest growth rates and by manipulating slack in ministerial budgets. Countries were not undergoing double-digit inflation nor were they seeing whole percentage points stripped from their rate of growth and often added to inflation by rising oil prices.

What has "control" of public expenditure meant in Britain? If it means simply limiting the proportion of GDP spent by government, then Britain has been an abject failure. Until 1975 the proportion of national income given to public spending constantly rose. There were cries of alarm when public spending reached 50 percent of GDP in 1970–71, but this figure was inflated by including transfer payments (money given to individuals and to other agencies of government to spend) and by several forms of double counting of public expenditure (see Wright, 1977). To understand the politics of public expenditure there must be more precise measures of what is happening. There has been no "control" at all in the sense of MPs being able to influence future economic choices of government. One device to circumvent Parliament's power of appropriation has been the Contingency Fund, which steadily grew in the early seventies to over £800 million (Expenditure Committee, 1978, p. xxi). In fact, parliamentary budgetary procedures, which many consider the bedrock of British democracy (see Chapter 1), involve less than half of total public spending, and Parliament is left to make what sense it can of the various other appropriations that pass before its eyes. Under inflationary pressures there are now at least two, sometimes three or four, budgetary bills a year, often embodying contradictory economic policies.

Another definition of "control" might be the ability of Parliament to find out whether the money they appropriate is used in the way they decide. In fact, much spending legislation is discretionary, not unlike that in France. One economist has calculated (Godley, 1975) that unknown to Parliament nearly £6 billion were added to the official 1970–71 forecast for the year 1974–75, roughly double the planned rate of increase of public spending. Even more damaging to parliamentary control has been the draconian device of "cash limits," which places immense discretionary power in Whitehall. The Expenditure Committee (1978, p. 89) was told that the amount affected by cash limits actually *exceeds* the amount approved under the normal Supply procedure. MPs do not see the official audit, which is itself a rather barren account and tells little about effectiveness of spending, for nearly two years after decisions are made. In an age of rapid inflation, this can be little more than poring over the ashes of the past. For all the innovations described in Chapter 2, the control of public spending has changed remarkably little from the Gladstonian notion of accountability introduced in the 1860s.

Context

One should not ignore the possibility that leaders do not change the present system, however much lamented when economic results are poor, because it serves their immediate political interest very well. The evidence for this is very strong no matter which major party is in power. When the economy was clearly booming in early 1964, the year of a crucial election, a Conservative government increased benefits and created an £800 million deficit. When Wilson came to power with a slim majority, he refused to discuss much-needed devaluation until the 1966 election made him secure. On the other side of the ledger, there is little doubt that the stringent budgets of Jenkins in the late 1960s contributed to Labour's loss in 1970, even though they were doing the "right" thing in economic terms. Again, in 1974, Heath was clearly undone by economic disasters. Competitive parties face these choices in every modern democracy, but the British political system makes such manipulation easier, possibly necessary, in order to win elections. Cabinet government means that chancellors of the exchequer who resist public spending increases take grave risks.

The opportunity for such manipulation is provided by the power concentrated in the Treasury. While there is no doubt about the central importance of financial and fiscal power in the British political system, there are also numerous examples of the Treasury not getting its way in recent years. Until economic stagnation, the Treasury had little influence over public spending in either the absolute sense of limiting the total amount or in the more complex sense of guiding ministerial decisions to support larger economic objectives. So long as the economic policymaking debate focused on public expenditure, as it did until the Heath government proposed an industrial policy, the Treasury was never expected to have wide-ranging interests in spending decisions, nor is there much evidence that they wanted such a role (Heclo and Wildavsky, 1974). Neither the politics of public spending nor the more recent industrial strategies encouraged the Treasury to depart from its formal role, which is, in turn, reinforced by cabinet government.

What the Treasury does *not* do is more important that what it does. There has been important progress in forecasting and other techniques of economic planning in the Treasury, but Britain's central economic ministry contrasts sharply with the workings of other finance ministries. What modern governments need is an organization that can reach into the productive sector of the economy and that can effectively communicate with the proliferating levels and activities of government itself. In Germany this has been accomplished by coupling an effective labor movement with a strong banking system. In France there has been much less effort to preserve the formalities of public and private sector interests. Japan has used an even more expedient system by placing enormous economic power in monopolies. In a curious way the growth of the welfare state has made it *more* important that economic decisions be promptly and effectively communicated to actors outside government. The most interesting thing about the Treasury is not its strategic role *within* the spending process of government, but its remoteness from economic decisions *outside* government.

Public expenditure and larger economic objectives are often in conflict. Viewed from this perspective, the concentration on planning public spending diverted the Treasury from the broader examination of the economy that went on in most European countries in the 1960s and earlier. The Treasury can, of course, simply say that they are doing "their masters' bidding" while the economy steadily deteriorates, and cabinet government provides this defense. To be fair, it must also be acknowledged that until relatively recently Keynesian doctrine prevailed. The Treasury's job was mainly to expand and contract consumption (aggregate demand). Government was supposed to "fill the hole" left by unemployment. What was shoveled into this economic void did not seem to matter much. All this, of course, fits well with adversarial politics, for Labour could always claim that spending more was creating jobs and increasing consumption, and Conservatives could always claim they were strengthening the so-called private economy and protecting the pound. The political requirements of more recent monetarist theories of economic behavior are not essentially different. Instead of debating about a vague figure representing additional spending, one can now have an equally adversarial debate about an unforeseeable amount of public borrowing.

Space prohibits looking at all the subthemes to the simplified concept of public expenditure that suits British politics. Perhaps the most dramatic has been the changing policy toward nationalized industry. Labour came to power in 1945 committed to making massive transfers in ownership from the private to the public sector by bringing roughly a tenth of British productive capacity and about two million industrial jobs under government. In effect, government was burdened with many failing industries. Even worse, nationalization made a political football out of some deeply rooted economic problems. Labour was handicapped in making changes that would cost jobs, nor could they influence these industries through prices for fear of increasing the cost to the consumer of some vital services. Although the Conservatives protested loudly and made the nationalization of steel a political issue, they most often chose not to reverse these policies in order to observe the formalities of parliamentary consensus and from fear that they would alienate the worker votes that they needed to be elected to office. By about 1960, both parties saw that this vicious circle had to be broken because it was economically disastrous. But the major cost of this gargantuan experiment was distraction from other economic and industrial problems. Nationalized industries fueled a partisan debate, and, as we shall see, new solutions to problems of nationalized industry presupposed longer-term, bipartisan policies.

One cannot escape the impression that the formulation of economic choices riveted the attention of Westminster and the public on what divided the parties and what presumably divided the society. Some choices were ignored while other economic decisions were shaped to suit the requirements of politics, thereby disregarding the intricacy of how public and private interests overlap, the sensitivities of both managers and workers to changes in their circumstances, and even the growing inability of the British machinery of government to effectively design and implement economic policy. Political rhetoric was well served by viewing the economy as

an ideological battleground, though neither major party had very
clear ideas about how the machinery of Westminster and Whitehall
might actually influence lower-level decisions and deal with problems cutting across economic sectors. Complexity was ruled out.
On the one hand, Conservatives tended to treat the "City" (the
finanical and commercial center of London) as a sacrosanct preserve not to be ruffled by government. On the other hand, the
battle over economic doctrine within the Labour party meant that
it had to glance constantly to the rear to see whether trade union
sensitivities about wage and employment changes left them un-
guarded. The effect was that for quite different reasons it suited
both major parties to focus more on "public spending" than on
more fundamental economic weaknesses.

There are also a number of practical reasons why the nature of
economic policymaking in Britain has not changed much. Unlike
the war-ravaged countries of Europe, Britain did not have to think
as much about how to reconstruct industry after World War II.
Indeed, Britain does not appear to have thought about the domestic
economy at all. Most of the Marshall Plan credits were promptly
deposited in the Bank of England to build up currency reserves
and to stabilize the pound. The preoccupation of both left and
right was to maintain full employment, and for a decade after the
war the Keynesian tools worked quite well. As Dow (1964) put
it, Britain was "sitting on the post-war boom until it blew itself
out." There were few economic signs to worry government. In the
1950s real earnings increased by half, unemployment was negligible, and excess demand promised to fuel the economy for years
to come. Labour was so occupied with social reform that even
their wage freeze in 1948 brought few protests from the unions.
Labour was as embarrassed by the necessity to devalue in 1949
as it was in 1967. Economic growth was still strong enough to
sustain the Conservative image of success in the 1950s and the
economy was further fueled by a massive housing program. Indeed, Labour and Conservatives sounded so much alike that the
Economist coined the term "Butskellism" after the names of Labour and Conservative chancellors. Political interests were served
by keeping Britain on a fairly steady, if modest, growth path. Both
parties benefited and neither wanted to intervene in industry.

The major economic debate that Labour went through in the
1950s was mostly about defense policy and produced few new
ideas. By about 1960 it seemed that all was not going well. Britain

witnessed the "Erhard miracle" in Germany and saw industrial production surging ahead at high rates in Japan and France. Tranquillity was shattered by Shonfield's attack on British economic policy (1958). He pointed to the low levels of investment in industry, the declining share of manufactured goods in British exports, the inability of government to direct funds to innovative industries, and the tendency to export capital rather than to invest at home. There was a gradual realization that Britain could be fully employed and poor. Even more alarming, but not well identified, was the evidence that growth can be converted into consumption at much faster rates than into new production and enhanced productivity. Britain was discovering inflation. In a revealing statement some years later, Sir Douglas Wass, permanent secretary of the Treasury, recalled that "the words 'economic growth' were not mentioned in any official document so far as I can recall before about 1960" (quoted in Keegan and Pennant-Rea, 1979, p. 16).

Britain was the nineteenth-century economic miracle. From 1811 to 1881, national income trebled while prices actually halved, making a sixfold real increase in national wealth. Taxes remained almost unchanged and the burden of taxation was reduced by two-thirds. Toward the end of the century, however, Britain's economic position began to decline and in many ways has continued to do so ever since. A series of bad harvests in the 1870s triggered a depression that lingered on for over a decade only to be followed by the economic dislocations imposed by the Boer War, the First World War, and a severely deflated economy followed by depression between the wars. Although the British standard of living has risen fivefold over the past century, the economic problems confronting government have multiplied just as rapidly. More important in understanding the growing importance of government, World Wars I and II brought large spurts in public spending that for a number of reasons made restoring the *status quo ante* impossible. A major study of the growth of public expenditure in Britain (Peacock and Wiseman, 1961) attributes most government growth to the massive changes in British society that followed each of these upheavals.

Perhaps the firmest imprint on postwar economic policymaking was made during World War II. Although Churchill had much more economic experience than many British prime ministers, he was fully occupied with the war. In 1941, he formed an Economic Section of the Cabinet, which became a highly centralized command post for the domestic economy. Because the costs of a war of survival are not to be questioned, the chancellor of the exchequer became "the Prime Minister of the Home Front" and was given immense arbitrary power. All the Labour Party leaders were included in the coalition government, and the experience they gained in running a war economy had an important bearing on their policies after the war. Not only did they begin to design how British society would be remodeled after the war (see Chapter 6), but they formed a deceptively simple notion of the ease with which resources, spending, and even governmental machinery could be shifted from one objective to another. By this time it was also forgotten that Keynes had called Britain's financial experts "ninnies," and he became the architect of Britain's postwar financial and fiscal policy. At the time his views were attractive to both parties: he promised full employment to Labour and a stable pound to the Conservatives.

Although Labour's postwar government accounts for a large increase in public spending (from about a fourth to a third of GDP), they found themselves in the same economic dilemma that prevented Labour in 1964 and again in 1974 from making structural changes in the economy. Of course, the dimensions and even the causes of these dilemmas change over time, but the interesting political point is that all three Labour governments have encountered economies that threaten to expand too fast. In 1945 this was not a major political choice because Labour had many social reforms in mind, most of which could be accomplished simply by expanding public spending, so that more fundamental questions were seldom asked. The economic constraints of wartime policymaking were not suitable for peacetime, but shortages meant that rationing and import controls continued and restrained the economy while public spending increased. Labour soon confronted a mounting trade deficit that threatened to become £7.5 billion a year (Dow, 1964, p. 22). Labor shortages and excess demand were the major problems. Devaluation and a wage freeze were the solutions. Labour had no industrial policy other than the controversial Clause IV of their charter, which advocates public ownership of production. But the real political dilemma, as Klein points out (1976), is that it was left to Labour to restrain the economy, while the Conservatives reaped the short-term political benefits of inflationary policies.

Whatever the underlying value differences between the left and right, economic policymaking in Britain has tended to dampen ideological differences. The growth of the welfare state thus creates a certain paradox or, more exactly, a number of paradoxes. As public spending increases and government assumes a larger role in the economy (whether it is used in the "right" way in an economic sense is irrelevant), governments seem to be able to make smaller changes in policy as electoral swings change ruling parties. This is partly due to the fact that economic cycles do not correspond to political cycles. If things are going well (or, more realistically for Britain, better), a new government has little incentive to change the economic course of the nation. If things are going worse, then the size and complexity of the constantly growing public budget delays decisive action, and distracts leaders from more serious economic weaknesses. Because spending programs and social benefits have statutory permanence, no party can make changes without being charged with dismantling or resurrecting the welfare state.

The complexity of the transformation brought about by the growth of public spending cannot be fully outlined here, but it is important to see that "public sector" can be a misleading phrase. The size of the public budget says little about how resources and the economy are in fact organized. Sweden, for example, is a "high spender," but the economy is still largely in private hands. In Japan, on the other hand, public spending is extremely low, but firms provide a wide range of services and benefits for their employees. Public spending in Britain, more than in most countries, cannot be analyzed without considering the organizational and institutional constraints in which government is embedded. As the halcyon days of the 1950s dimmed, Britain began to wonder how to influence the economy through public spending, but this was only the tip of the iceberg.

Agenda

By 1960, the government was aware that increased public spending had important effects on the economy, but the new course of action continued to separate official economic policymaking from the implications and possible effects of public spending on economic growth itself. Keynesian thinking was still influential, and neither party wished to formulate more aggressive policies that would presuppose closer coordination with industrial and commercial decisions in the private sector. Thus, the appointment of the Plowden Committee was recognition that stabilization objectives might be hurt by erratic and unplanned public spending, not that economic policymaking itself should be radically changed. For this reason, the Plowden Report (1961, cmnd. 1432) is not a radical departure from the past.

The Macmillan government had already prodded the civil service to try and find out how the huge sums expended by government might be more sensibly used. A White Paper on Public Expenditure (1960, cmnd. 1203) had already noted that ill-timed and sudden changes in public spending could adversely affect the economy and that government should estimate future capital expenditure by sector. There was also a strangely prescient report on monetary policy, the Radcliffe Report (1959, cmnd. 827), which raised the then almost heretical possibility that interest rates might no longer be an effective instrument of public policy and therefore were no longer useful in guiding investment priorities. These early efforts were very likely counterproductive in stimulating wider-ranging examination of British economic policy. They drove the Treasury and the Bank of England into an even closer alliance to defend what was (and in many ways still is) regarded as their turf, namely, the formulation of short-term (three months to a year) and medium-term (one to three years) policy. The Treasury was clever enough to see that anything said about the long term would never affect them.

Like Fulton, the Plowden Report illustrates how easily Whitehall can protect itself. As Mackenzie wrote in an amusing guide to the Report (*Guardian*, May 25, 1963), there were two important principles: "no dirty linen in public; outside critics are bores." Plowden himself had been head of the Treasury's Economic Planning Board from 1947 to 1953, and five of the eight other members were "insiders." The Treasury had initially fought the review, and accepted only on the grounds that it be made by a Treasury committee, not by a more general government inquiry that might imply a recalcitrant or inadequate Treasury. In fact, it appears that the conclusions had "already been accepted" (Chester, 1963). Being a Whitehall committee, the Plowden Committee met in private and the full report and proceedings were never published. But the crucial significance in terms of economic policymaking was even more negative because the Report reinforced and justified a view of public spending that even further insulated government policies from economic realities.

The Treasury made sure that the Plowden Report placed the control of public spending on familiar ground. How ill-prepared Britain was for the approaching economic turmoil is suggested by the fact that Gladstone would easily have understood the Plowden Report and approved its implicit assumption that public and private interests are easily distinguished. The basic observations (see Reading 3-1) were sound and no doubt a milestone in planning public expenditure. The Report noted that fully half of future public expenditure was known a year in advance and that this could form the basis for a rolling forecast of public spending. The economic significance of nationalized industries, then investing about £7 billion a year, was recognized as a public spending problem, but not linked to the economy. The tone of the Report was definitely managerial: more cost analysis should be done, but Parliament was not the proper body to carry it through; nationalized industries should be brought into economic planning, but mainly by better accounting to the Treasury; and the budget should be more concisely and clearly organized to achieve efficiency, not to redress the inability of Parliament and ministers to know what they were doing with public money.

As Brittan points out (1971, pp. 234–35), nearly all the instruments of economic policy that government continues to use were created during the chancellorship of Lloyd (1960–62): the "pay pause" to control wages; the "forward look" to anticipate public spending; the "economic regulator" to permit the chancellor to vary consumer taxes between budgets; the National Economic Development Council to work toward tripartite economic planning (government, labor, and business); discretionary tax relief in the form of lightening the surtax (luxury tax) to tap income incentives; a first step toward making the nationalized industries earn their own way (provide their own investment); and a National Incomes Commission to begin to assess the relation of prices and wages. But even though so much of this represented Prime Minister Macmillan's own relatively advanced ideas about the problems of British economy policymaking, as the American economic slump of 1962 ricocheted off the British economy Macmillan became disillusioned with Lloyd and dismissed him. Macmillan suspected Britain's heavy commitment to defend sterling, favored a more substantial capital gains tax, and deplored the inadequacy of government statistics by comparing them to "last year's Bradshaw" (the railroad timetable).

There are several ominous changes contained within the Conservatives' array of economic policy tools. The first and probably the most important was the inherent contradiction of setting out to plan public spending at a time when intervention in the economy was happening more frequently and economic cycles were becoming shorter and more severe. Deeper economic problems were already evident even if government did not know what to do. It was known, for example, that the economic "boom" of 1960–61 had had little effect on industrial productivity (Brittan, 1971, p. 248). The ability of the economy to expand and contract without increasing productivity was then attributed to "labor hoarding" (the reluctance of employers to release workers and therefore to overman as a hedge against future growth) and excess capacity in industry that discouraged innovation and investment. There were even discussions of a payroll tax to discourage investment in service industries, which appeared in 1966 as Labour's Selective Employment Tax (SET). For a decade these early signs of deep-seated economic trouble were ignored because the economy as a whole still performed reasonably well. Compared to past budgets, that of 1963 set a high growth rate of 4 percent, which was nearly achieved from 1962 to 1966. Politically prudent ministers know when to leave well enough alone, and Whitehall had little to offer because planning public spending kept them fully occupied.

A second change is how manipulation of "stop-and-go" measures, provided by the battery of tools mentioned above, made governmental "control" less certain and more intricate. The new agencies (NEDC, NIC, etc.) linked to main economic actors outside Westminster did not prosper. Public spending actually passed 40 percent of GDP in 1960 well before government began to get down to economic planning and sophisticated forecasting in a serious way. Within Whitehall the debate about public spending and its economic implications was muted by appointing the Fulton Commission (see Chapter 2) in the hope that, if the public service could be made more efficient, then government would spend its money more effectively, maybe even spend less. Such a relationship has never been demonstrated. "Stop-and-go" techniques provide their own litany of why things go wrong and have been minutely examined by economists, usually with very different conclusions (see Blackaby, ed., 1978; Beckerman, ed., 1972; Stewart, 1977). However one comes out in this complex economic debate, ministers had numerous reasons, as did Whitehall, for *not* thinking about more intractable economic issues. My point is not that Macmillan and Wilson were unaware of the deterioration of the British economy, for they clearly were. The point is that there were *political* reasons why neither sought to break down sectoral, organizational, and financial barriers in order to respond to clear indications of economic vulnerability.

Expansionist policies contributed to keeping the Conservatives in power for thirteen years (1951–64), so there were few reasons for them to point to the continuing decline of British industry. Wilson's approach was in many ways even more distracting and possibly more futile. Stewart (1977, p. 32) calls Wilson a "civil servant manqué," most visible in Wilson's confidence in rational solutions (even if irrationally arrived at), changing the machinery of government, and desperate measures to prop up old solutions. Wilson's 1964 electoral promise to expose the society to the "white heat of technology" seemed very heady stuff. Much less clear was the readiness of either management or the unions to submit to this searing experience. The new Department of Economic Affairs, and later the addition of "Productivity" to the title of the Department of Employment and the creation of a Ministry of Technology, may have impressed Whitehall, but their influence on the Trades Union Congress (TUC) (see Chapter 4) and the Confederation of British Industry (CBI) was marginal.

Like most prime ministers, Wilson thought an incomes policy would become the critical link between government and industry. The irony was that this put him on a collision course with the unions, as we shall see in Chapter 4. Within government, his policies were in many ways only refinements of Conservative initiatives (Clarke, 1978, p. 132). The main vehicle was to be the Department of Economic Affairs under the energetic George Brown (later Lord George Brown). The Treasury was of course furious to see long-term forecasting outside its realm, nor did the ambitious new chancellor, Callaghan, have any intention of seeing his empire diminished. The saga of the Department of Economic Affairs, best told by Brown himself (1971), is a superb illustration of the bewildering organizational problems of contemporary economic policymaking. The new department's main purpose was to prepare a National Plan, which emerged in 1965 only to be scuttled a few months later, when new economic restrictions and dislocations destroyed its assumptions.

Alongside (and sometimes ranged against) the weak economic planning agency were the Industrial Reorganization Corporation (IRC), an agency to encourage industrial mergers in order to increase efficiency, and the Prices and Incomes Board to deal with wage and price policy. The dilemmas of the Prices and Incomes Board have been forcefully described by its chairman, Aubrey Jones (1973), who saw how the competition for votes in wage settlements easily became synonymous with inflation. In any event, the economy went through three cycles of "stop-and-go" in six years ("cooling off" in 1966; "reflating" in 1967; and "squeeze" in 1968). The net effect brought the Opposition to note that Wilson was the "best Conservative Prime Minister the Party did not have" (Brittan, 1971, p. 337). In the first three years of Labour rule from 1964, unemployment increased by 2 percent, there was a wage freeze in 1966, and millions were spent to avoid devaluation. Even so, there was not the sheer panic of the seventies. In 1968, Callaghan expected a budget surplus of £200 million (turned into a £700 million deficit by the Suez war) and could still talk confidently of a 3 percent growth rate.

Though it cannot be described in detail, the most constructive efforts by the Labour government were to continue the review of nationalized industries begun by the Conservatives. Labour saw that releasing some of the £1.7 billion annual investment then required by nationalized industry (half provided by government) could support new services even while the economy declined. Less attention was given to the fact that in 1967 this sum was also equivalent to the total investment in private manufacturing industry. However difficult it was (and remains) to devise an effective industrial policy, it was clear that the £10 billions of assets held by nationalized industries could be better employed and that the rate of return ought to be sufficient to replace the capital invested in public companies. A White Paper (1968, cmnd. 3437) told the nationalized corporations to achieve an 8 percent rate of return. The problem illustrates the fading distinction between "public" and "private" as well as the dilemmas of deciding what "efficiency" is when ministers can veto price increases, allocate capital, review investment plans, and appoint directors. But perhaps the most curious thing was that a government committed to influencing patterns of ownership and capitalist habits took so long to use the weapons that were already in its hands. As we shall see, by the 1970s Labour had more imaginative and enterprising ideas of what industrial policy is all about.

Process

The process of aligning economic policymaking with economic problems went relatively slowly in Britain. On the one hand, the macroeconomic principles enshrined in Treasury procedures and relied upon by chancellors were hard to displace with untried theory and methods. There was, for example, no medium-term model of the economy until 1968 (Worswick and Blackaby, eds., 1974). The Plowden Report had set in motion the machinery to provide an annual public expenditure survey under the Treasury's Public Expenditure Survey Committee, but economic dislocations of the sixties combined with Treasury reluctance to see such a document made public so that it was not regularly published until 1969. Although the Treasury had won the war with Wilson once a separate planning operation collapsed, they had lost many skirmishes, such as the IRC and SET, which they opposed. So long as economic policymaking was still regarded as something that takes place wholly within government, an idea that suited British politicians and was easily reconciled with British political practice, the Treasury was always likely to come out ahead. Whether the country came out ahead is another question.

The severe blows to the economy and heavy public borrowing in 1965 had a shock effect that was soon reflected in budgets if not in more profound ways. Having cost the country roughly a billion in resources by devaluation (Brittan, 1971, p. 369), Callaghan left the Treasury to go to another hot spot, the Home Office (see Chapter 7). The new chancellor, Jenkins, sacrificed numerous Labour sacred cows in the 1968 and 1969 budgets: the world role of the pound was abandoned; there were miniscule increases in public spending; and family allowances were to be recovered by tax increases. For the first time there was a glimmer of intent to match increased public spending with increased taxation. There were to be no capital gains or personal income tax increases, but several consumer taxes went up. Many of the underlying weaknesses still showed through. Manufactured exports increased, for example, but imports increased even more, suggesting that Britain was not competing with foreign goods and that British industry was not taking up the economic opportunities purchased at such a high price for the country.

Even so, Jenkins' tough measures again reversed the economic stereotypes of the two major parties. The balance of payments showed a surplus of £700 million in 1969 and remained in surplus through 1972, giving Heath breathing time in the next government. Both Labour and Conservatives might regard 1969 and 1970 as years of political catastrophe, but the public borrowing requirement was actually negative, representing a "turn-around" of roughly £2.5 billion in the public debt. Despite all the discouragements and reversals of the past decade, it appeared that the British economy could perform.

To see how this opportunity was missed, one must look to the Conservative government of 1970. The transition illustrates how the complications of economic policymaking are difficult to fit into the pattern of electoral and party politics. Labour policies under Jenkins were quite compatible with Conservative views. The excess to which Heath and his chancellor, Barber, went in order to differentiate their party from Labour's conversion to cautious policies in the late sixties shows how a two-party system can fashion disastrous economic policy for good political reasons. As Brittan suggests (1977, p. 30), Heath's devotion to marketplace solutions has probably been exaggerated, in part because of the political rhetoric of his own ministers. What made him unbelievable were the enormous reversals in his economic choices in the short space of two years.

Heath came to power pledged to reject all forms of wage control, but by late 1972 conditions had become so bad that he imposed statutory limits on wage increases. He seemed to have learned little from Wilson's disastrous efforts to create a voluntary wage policy and his later defeat when he confronted the unions (see Chapter 4). Like most Conservative governments, his reduced income taxes but did not reduce public spending, paving the way for new government deficits. Public spending increased over 10 percent each year from 1970 to 1973, twice the rate of increase of Labour government spending in 1968 to 1970. In 1973–74, public spending increased nearly 20 percent, the largest increase since World War II although larger increases were to come from the next Labour government. No wonder that by 1974 many Conservative voters were wondering if they could afford Mr. Heath.

Perhaps most damaging were new gyrations of economic policy and an entirely new round of musical chairs as agencies were reshuffled. Heath shared Wilson's belief in "rational" government organization, which Brittan (1977, p. 28) so aptly labeled "half-conscious Fabianism." Like Labour, Conservatives underestimated how reconstructing government bears on expectations and preferences of key economic actors outside government. How one can still underestimate this once public spending reaches half or more of national income is a mystery. More elaborate procedures of economic policymaking in France, Germany, and even socialist Sweden produce fewer shocks of this kind. Labour's Prices and Incomes Board was wound up and their Industrial Reorganization Corporation abolished. There was a determined effort to hive off public agencies as, for example, the training activity of the Department of Employment, which became a supposedly more energetic and innovative semipublic agency, the Manpower Services Commission. By the end of Heath's government many of these steps were reversed, most notably by establishing a separate Pay Board and Price Commission after the reversal on incomes policy. One could add to this a controversial and expensive reorganization of local government (see Chapter 5) and the National Health Service. Despite Heath's dogged determination to make government disappear, it only seemed to become more complex.

The greatest irony of Heath's government was the 1972 Industry Act, which later became the foundation of Labour's more aggressive industrial policies. The secretary of state for industry received sweeping powers to intervene directly in industry where he saw opportunities to improve the British economy. Labour had oddly enough taken a more cautious approach with the IRC, whose merger strategy provided less leverage over industrial decisions. Pledged not to support lame-duck industries, the Conservatives provided a huge subsidy to one shipbuilding firm (Goven) and shortly afterwards bailed out Rolls-Royce. From these efforts came the first steps, after nearly two decades of "fine-tuning," to deal directly with industrial policy. Why it took the British policymaking machinery so long to make such a transition is perhaps a more important question than how it emerged from decisions of competing parties. In the more prosperous European countries, machinery of this kind can be traced back to postwar reconstruction. Intervening in industrial choices was never strange in France, Germany, and Sweden.

The Heath government is a watershed in British economic policymaking in another important way. Brittan has characterized the latter years of the Conservative government as "spending ourselves into prosperity." Under Heath, there was a huge increase in the money supply as he and Barber turned to expansionary policies after 1972. It was, as Keegan and Pennan-Rea point out (1979, p.

183), a huge gamble to see if growth could overtake inflation. Too much has probably been made of Heath's labor relations troubles (see Chapter 4), though he deserved most of them. Earnings went up more rapidly than at any previous time, but so also did inflation. Somehow the British industrial structure was not responding to the opportunities that Heath, like Wilson before him, had labored to create at such enormous cost. The manufacturing share of exports continued to decline. Investment in British industry rose only feebly and from 1974 plummeted. What one was witnessing was the growing inability of "stop-and-go" to affect the economy, much less strike at underlying economic and industrial problems.

Consequences

The politics of policymaking can get stranded on rather barren ideological ground. Labour and Conservatives claimed to have different objectives over the past two decades. Labour wanted more income redistribution and more public ownership. Conservatives wanted to restore the price mechanism and reduce taxes. Both were caught in a trap that both helped construct. To preserve political consensus there was remarkable agreement between the two major parties that social benefits should increase (see Chapter 6); that a voluntary incomes policy was needed; that the pound should be defended even as British industrial competitiveness declined; and that planning public spending could be an effective adjunct to economic policies even though isolated from major economic actors. Many of the economic misfortunes can be attributed to the *agreement* of the major parties, not to their differences. These agreements can be traced to the needs of cabinet government and adversarial politics.

How could they agree so much? Many of the reasons for this have already been outlined: the prevalence of Keynesian thinking the political demands on the economy created by elections, and the concentration on getting it "right" within government by improving forecasting and the like (see Chapter 2). More interesting is how little imagination went into figuring out how each party would achieve those objectives that *differentiated* them rather than those that gave continuity to British politics. Economic adversity and disappointment affected both parties more or less equally. Both had to struggle with immense problems, and this may be a sufficient explanation of why more innovation in government was not forth coming. This is a bare-bones explanation, however, which says little about the forces imbedded in British political institutions that discourage such efforts. The period from 1964 to 1974 was in many ways a period of limbo, when both parties were content, though furiously occupied, to "fiddle" the British economy without ever deciding why performance was so erratic.

By 1976 there were signs that political differences might effectively penetrate economic policymaking. To glimpse how this began one must step back into the disarray of the Labour Party after the 1970 defeat and recall the contradictory position of Labour trying to impose statutory controls on unions in 1969. While there is little love lost between the Labour Party stalwarts of the TUC and the left wing of the Labour Party (see Chapter 4), Heath's absurd attack on nearly everything held dear by both groups brought about a period of self-examination, a luxury that most politicians cannot afford. The vehicle for reconstructing the party and repelling the Conservative attack on cherished Labour programs was the Economic Liaison Committee of the Labour Parliamentary Party, TUC, and the National Executive leaders.

The story of the internal fight over economic policy had been well told by Hatfield (1978), and can only be summarized here. Its origins date from Posner and Pryke's analysis (1966) of how nationalization burdened government with lame-duck firms and unprofitable industries. From this grew the notion that government should directly benefit from more profitable enterprises, the model being the Italian Industrial Reconstruction Institute. Essentially, the new idea was that the public, meaning government, should own profitable enterprises and even use their profits (plus whatever else could be drained from private firms through taxation) to invest in new and promising companies. The discussion had particularly important implications for public spending for it presupposed recognition that "soaking the rich" would not basically alter the economy. What one needed to tap was how some persons became rich, namely their privileged claim to economic growth that was exercised through ownership of stock. Capitalism could be put to work for socialism.

The new strategy faced formidable obstacles. First, it was by no means clear that the unions would accept the vision of a transformed economy as a substitute for wage increases. To construct an incomes policy Callaghan, the convenor of the Liaison Group, accepted union wage demands (see Chapter 4), which aligned him against the full implementation of the radical proposals. Second, in order to pursue such a policy, government must bridge the boundaries between private firms and public interest, which has never been easy to do in Britain. The device was to be "planning agreements," inspired by German success, that would give government full information about profits, investment plans, and other internal information on selected industries. In a word, companies were to provide the ammunition for their own execution. Such information was (and remains) fully protected under British law. Third, the self-financing of nationalized industry would be pursued with a vengeance, one of the strange ways in which the thinking of the Labour left and the Conservative right converge. Heath's statutory price restraints had fallen much more heavily on nationalized industry, where government could directly fix prices, than on private industry. The effect had been that by the mid-seventies nationalized industries were running record deficits and eating up more rather than less public money. The new strategy was to use viable public corporations to raise public capital, possibly even to sell some assets and shares, and to press harder to make all of them profitable in order to soften the blow of additional public spending that Labour naturally also wanted to continue.

As it turned out, this package was never fully enacted, but the proposals mark the beginning of a radically new view of how the economy relates to the political system in the advanced welfare state. Although Benn, the secretary of state for industry, received much publicity for these ideas in 1974, they are the product of a decade's failure to move toward Labour's avowed aims and involved a number of Labour advisors. The rationale for new legislation actually came from the Conservatives' 1972 Industry Act. The irony went full circle; the excesses of the previous Conservative government made it politically possible to implement these plans. But they were unacceptable to Wilson and Callaghan, who in 1974 personally rewrote the Industry Act into a mere shadow of the original version. At this point we can begin to glimpse how the welfare state may actually prevent radical change. Underlying the refusal were the huge spending promises, estimated at £5 billion, that Labour officials had made to the unions to purchase future wage restraint (see Chapter 4). By the time Labour regained power, inflation had reached 25 percent and an adverse interna tional economy was draining off British resources faster than ever before. Even if the new chancellor, Healey, had been sympathetic to the Labour backbenchers, there was little he could do in 1974.

A decade's concentration on planning public spending was rendered almost worthless in a few months. In addition to huge public spending commitments, the oil crisis and further decline produced huge borrowing requirements (borrowing went from £2.7 billion to £6.7 billion in the first six months of office). As Maynard and Walker point out (see Reading 3-4), public expenditure was increasing more than twice as fast (5 percent) as output (about 2.2 percent). The consequent inflationary spiral, inherited from the Heath government, reached astronomical rates of over 25 percent in 1975. "Fine-tuning" has somehow catapulted the country from Heath's three-day week to money that disappeared on the way to the bank. The public expenditure forecast was a shambles, and the Treasury was encouraged (no doubt with ministerial urgings) to "fiddle" even more with economic reporting. It is a sad commentary that a decade of developing public expenditure planning ended in 1975 with the most draconian and indiscriminate of spending controls, "cash limit" budgeting (see Chapter 2). The immense power concentrated in Westminster is revealed in the haste with which such controls were imposed, but the real question is why the same powers had been used with so little effect to strengthen the economy in the preceding years.

Wilson, of course, had always had an eye on industrial decline, but conditions in 1975 demanded an admission that public spending would be sacrificed to industrial needs. Economic stringency imposed what adversarial politics could not build. Few were deceived by the opening words of Wilson's "Industrial Strategy" that said the problems were "short-term." The White Paper makes very clear what was in store for the British people (see Reading 3-2). Possibly an even greater irony for Wilson, who had spent so much time building planning machinery, was that the new strategy rested on consultation organized by the National Economic Development Office (NEDO), a Conservative invention. Within NEDO, "sector working parties" were to test ideas and proposals in ways that government seemed unable to do. The working parties of concerned industrial, commercial, and labor leaders were collectively to criticize and evaluate economic policies, and NEDO was to make an annual evaluation of Britain's industrial progress. Though Britain had several sophisticated economic models, some sponsored by the Treasury, this was the first time an organized critique had taken place outside government.

Inflation destroyed the credibility of public spending forecasting and forced British leaders to seek new ways to link economic policy to industrial decisions. Though a pallid representation of the proposals of the Labour left wing, the 1975 Industry Act created the National Enterprise Board (NEB), a label intentionally selected to embarrass Conservatives, who had begun massive injections of public funds directly into private companies. The NEB was allocated £700 million (later increased to a billion) but only £275 million were authorized for the first year. Wilson clearly intended to keep the left's more ambitious proposals on a tight leash, and in 1975 Benn was moved from the Department of Industry. Under conditions of severe economic distress, the NEB was forced to go on more industrial rescue operations, including huge investments in British Leyland. Even so, excluding the lame-duck industries, the pre-tax profit of the NEB's first year (1977) was £34 million and the return on capital a respectable 11 percent (*Economist*, May 6, 1978).

Such proposals as a state investment bank, an institution that France and Germany had used for many years, were ignored until the controversial Equity Capital for Industry was established in 1976. But the belated effort to create a government-influenced banking sector not only was small but was also without the network of public and private agencies that strengthen continental state investment banks. As the left wing of the Labour Party pressed for nationalization of clearing (commercial) banks and insurance companies, Callaghan headed off more complex forms of state involvement in the private sector decisions by appointing Harold Wilson (now Sir Harold) to head a Committee on Financial Institutions to study why the City failed to take more interest in industrial development. Efforts to consolidate the British social security system (see Chapter 6) precluded raiding private pension and insurance funds to acquire capital. When Labour stepped down in 1979, only one planning agreement had been made, and this was with Chrysler UK, which had received a large loan from the NEB (*Times*, July 28, 1978).

Inflation forced the British government to do what apparently could not be accomplished during periods of slow growth. Labour still wanted to provide more services, but existing spending and just keeping up with inflationary increases left Westminster hard pressed. The first steps toward combatting inflation were announced in "The Attack on Inflation" (see Reading 3-3). Flat-rate wage increases were worked out with the TUC, but did not last. More food subsidies, rent support, and pension increases were needed to protect the poor. The full force of this dilemma came home in 1976, when Healey slashed over £3 billion from the budget while increasing consumer taxes and National Insurance contributions to protect benefits. To further complicate the conventional interpretation of Labour, taxes on dividends were reduced and personal income tax allowances were increased as an incentive to increased productivity. In such ways, economic cycles confound any simple interpretation of party politics and economic policy. Labour was compelled to do what we might expect to be the Conservatives' task.

At high levels of public spending, inflation means that benefits are reduced if left in constant money terms and can only be increased by more taxation or larger contributions to the various welfare programs. Such choices are always difficult, but the most interesting aspect of Britain's dilemma in 1976 and later was how poorly equipped the government was to make these choices (see Reading 3-4). To some extent this was because the public expenditure forecasts create ministerial and public expectations that more money will always be forthcoming. There are also odd inflationary effects built into public spending, which tends to be labor-intensive and therefore to suffer higher cost increases than those in the economy generally (the "relative price effect"). A great many increases in spending are required by statute, and Britain did not evolve the intricate bargaining machinery of France and Germany that weighs social benefits and inflation against tax and income changes. One can blame Whitehall, but it is also clear that there are few ministerial incentives in the British policymaking process to construct such complex machinery. Government preserved and extended its economic role from 1965 to 1975, but public employment increased at unprecedented rates, manufactured exports continued to fall, inflation reached new heights, and industrial productivity constantly dropped (see Bacon and Eltis, 1978). It is not so much that poor decisions were being made in the established territory of government, but that the crucible of government could survive these ever-mounting crises without wondering if it was asking the right questions.

One positive outcome of the turmoil of 1975 and 1976 has been that economic policymaking was forced to find new ways to manipulate public money. Massive cuts helped demolish boundaries between Whitehall's jealously guarded programs. For example, both Labour and Conservatives agreed that nationalized industries should pay their own way. Labour published a White Paper in 1975 (cmnd. 6315) that recognized that "generalized inefficiency" hampered industry as much as low investment. The government then asked the National Economic Development Office to examine the future of nationalized industries, itself a surprising decision because NEDO cannot be influenced, discredited, or ignored as easily as review bodies within the Whitehall empire. The NEDO report (1976) suggested a new layer of "buffer" organizations between ministers and public corporation directors, hoping to achieve in the public sector the "concertation" found in European economies for both private and public decisions. The subsequent White Paper (1978, cmnd. 7131) found these ideas unacceptable. The government reasserted that nationalized industries would have a reasonable rate of return (placed at 5 percent) and asked that their accounts come closer to private practice by including the "opportunity cost of capital." In such ways the public sector even under Labour was driven to incorporate "private" standards. More important, the new policy indicates how a large public sector, if hard pressed, can devise "horizontal" transfers (see Reading 3-6). Between 1975 and 1977, government reduced nationalized industry subsidies by £1.4 billion (*Financial Times*, Jan. 18, 1979).

A concluding word should be said about the political effects of "stop-and-go" decisionmaking. All the advanced industrial nations have had to devise such instruments to stabilize prices and to live in a precarious world economy. What differentiates Britain from other European countries and Japan is how slowly such changes in economic policymaking took place and how reluctant leaders were to reexamine the British economy. The temptation to place responsibility on the Treasury will not do even though there is evidence that the Treasury resisted proposals that might diminish its influence. But we must also ask, influence over what? From the perspective of Heclo and Wildavsky (1974) the Treasury was doing a good job, but this conclusion arises from assessing the Treasury as an actor *within* government. No matter how the economy changes, on these terms, the Treasury will always prevail. Cash limits and firmer public borrowing limitations after 1975 did the same. The more important questions concern ways of using public spending to combat underlying economic and industrial weaknesses (see Reading 3-5). Perhaps the most curious fact about the politics of economic policymaking in Britain is that *no one* is responsible.

The explanation goes much deeper than Treasury pride or even ministerial competition. The political system does not create incentives to rethink economic policy. Ministers have an eye on the next election and Treasury officials are preoccupied, often with good reason, with the short term. "Stop-and-go" encourages and justifies this kind of thinking. In this sense the pattern of economic policymaking and concentrating on public spending fit well with the immediate political interests of Westminster and Whitehall. Ward and Neild argue (1978) that public spending has been so vulnerable to short-term, politically inspired change that it bears no relationship to changes in economic activity. For over two decades government was provided "soft options" by declining military expenditure, erratic control of public capital formation, and deceptive calculation of public spending targets in volume terms. The inability of the British economic system to develop long-term economic goals seems deeply imbedded in institutional and constitutional rigidities that serve politicians well, but serve the country poorly. Were erratic change only found in periods of growth and relative prosperity they might be more easily attributed to economic causes.

One is left with the conclusion that British economic policymaking never truly controlled public spending, nor did it build links into the private sector as did France and Germany. In a way Britain devised the welfare state, but never thought much about what to do with it. The market economy of the radical right was unacceptable, and they were easily discredited because their attacks on the public sector often made no sense. The ideas of the radical left were slow to take shape and do not solve the problems of a "siege economy." Import controls, nationalization of private pension funds and insurance companies, wealth taxes, and withdrawal from the world economy promise more political turmoil without assuring economic prosperity. This said, British radicals of the late twentieth century, rather like the radicals of the late eighteenth century, have raised some perplexing questions about Britain's economic future *because* their views also presuppose political changes. What has Britain gained from providing firms with about £2 billion a year in industrial investment grants, depreciation allowances, and the like? Why must some £2.5 billion in income tax concessions accumulate in private pension funds and insurance without being more effectively directed to improving the British economy (Holland, 1976)? One need not share Holland's marxist predispositions to see the economic contradictions that underly his observations.

Adversarial politics has not done well at keeping public spending down or in building bridges between the public sector and the economy's industrial base. Except for Wilson's stillborn Plan of 1965, neither ministers nor the Treasury ever asked that this be done. Inflation did what political will could not do. As Stout (1975, p. 118) says, "Inflation is the smoke in the continuing battle between separate more or less powerful groups for incompatible shares in the national product." Inflation brought politics to bear on the whole economy in ways that Westminster and Whitehall avoided for over twenty years. Perhaps it is not coincidental that signs of renewed political struggle over economic choices occurred when the strength of the two-party system was in question, and over 1979 and 1980 (see Reading 3-6) created severe strains within both major parties. The unfortunate thing is that the British economy apparently needed to deteriorate so severely before the political system began to recognize the complexities of economic policymaking in the welfare state.

Readings

3-1. LONG-TERM SURVEYS OF PUBLIC EXPENDITURE AND RESOURCES*

The initial steps toward relating public spending to the economy were to assemble the various components of government expenditure in a comprehensive way. The Plowden Report pointed the way toward such planning of public expenditure in 1961.

13. The development and use by Government of long-term surveys of expenditure and resources is the core of our proposals. This involves techniques of management and measurement that are in their infancy, and there are serious practical considerations involved. If policy were based upon these surveys before the underlying ideas had been thoroughly digested both by the Treasury and by the Departments, their use might do more harm than good. The

Control of Public Expenditure (Plowden Report, cmnd. 1432; London: HMSO, July 1961).

surveys are at an experimental stage, which is full of technical and administrative pitfalls. However, the Treasury has been actively developing these techniques in recent years; and it should now be possible to make substantial progress, provided that the practical considerations are kept fully in mind, and that no more weight is put on this work than it can technically bear.

14. In some areas of public expenditure, we understand that "forward looks" are prepared regularly covering a period of four or five years ahead. In defence, this is now done annually. These exercises are important for the management of the defence effort itself, to get a proper balance and to establish a sound basis for planning. In civil public investment, including that of the local authorities and the nationalised industries, there have for some years now been regular forecasts for several years ahead (cf. Public Investment in Great Britain (Cmnd. 1203) of November, 1960). Similar work has been done in current expenditure of certain social services, notably education and pensions. Where the Government and other public authorities are employing people and placing orders themselves, this work of forward planning and estimating should be a normal function of management: without it, indeed, it is difficult to carry out a purposeful development of the various public services with limited financial resources. Where on the other hand the Government are paying out grants and subsidies, such as those to agriculture and national assistance, which depend upon the state of the market or upon recipients' earnings from other sources, an additional element of uncertainty is introduced, and the idea of a long-term forecast loses some of its meaning.

15. We mention this as one illustration of the conceptual and technical problems involved in making these surveys; another is the necessity to work in terms of a definition of "public expenditure" that, in addition to Government expenditure above and below the line, embraces local authorities' total expenditure, the gross receipts and outgoings of the national insurance funds, and the whole investment of nationalized industries, whether financed from earnings or from the Exchequer; a total now exceeding £10,000 million a year. To take three examples, the Government cannot usefully consider the future needs for education, pensions or electric power stations without bringing in a much wider range of expenditure by public authorities than is represented by the Government's expenditure alone. The future cost of education is essentially expenditure by local authorities, which the Exchequer supports

through the general grant: the future cost of pensions is covered by national insurance contributions as well as by the Exchequer supplements to them: the future investment in electric power stations must be considered as a whole, and not just that part of it that is financed from the Exchequer. There is so much financial interlocking throughout the public sector that all the expenditure must be analysed together.

16. The other side of the survey is the prospective development of income or economic resources. This is susceptible to prediction five years ahead only within broad limits. Moreover, public expenditure will itself be affected by the rate of economic growth; and the rate of economic growth will be affected by the size and nature of public expenditure. Nevertheless, we think that it should be possible to form worthwhile judgments about whether a certain prospective size and pattern of public expenditure is likely to stimulate or to retard the growth of gross national product, and is likely to outrun the prospective resources available to finance it.

17. In our view, therefore, it is technically practicable and administratively necessary to develop long-term surveys on these lines. But we must repeat that this work is in its early stages. Its purpose is to help the Government to make good decisions, by providing a better perspective. It will not provide automatic criteria, or create a substitute for the application of judgment. It is therefore doubtful whether any Government will feel able to place these surveys before Parliament and the public. To do this would involve disclosing the Government's long-term intentions for a wide range of public expenditure, and also explaining the survey's assumptions about employment, wages, prices and all the other main elements in the national economy. It would be surprising if any Government were prepared to do this.

3-2. CALLAGHAN'S RESPONSE TO INFLATION*

Deterioration of the economy meant that a decade's effort to plan public expenditure had to be radically overhauled. In mid-1975 the government issued a paper on the threat of inflation and expressed its determination that this battle must override other economic objectives. There was still hope that this could be done without massive unemployment.

*Prime Minister, *The Attack on Inflation* (cmnd. 6151; London: HMSO, July 1975).

1. In his statement on 1 July, the Chancellor of the Exchequer said: "A sharp reduction in the rate of inflation is an over-riding priority for millions of our fellow citizens, particularly the house-wives and pensioners. It is also a pre-condition for the reduction of unemployment and the increase in investment which the Government, the TUC and the CBI all want to see."

Our rate of inflation has been much higher in the 1970s than in earlier periods and recently it has accelerated sharply. In common with many countries we have experienced in the past two years a big increase in the rate at which costs and prices have risen. Like other countries we suffered in 1972–73 the great increase in the cost of imported food and raw materials, and in 1973–74 the even greater increase in oil prices which have together cut back what is available to us to maintain and improve our national standard of living. But whereas most other countries have succeeded in bringing down their rate of inflation, we have not. Our prices are 25 per cent above those of a year ago. The figures for our competitors are nearer 10 per cent.

2. This must not go on. The country insists that inflation must be curbed: the Government are determined to achieve this, and believe they will have the support and co-operation of the whole nation in doing so. But there can be no solution to the problem of inflation which relies on the creation of mass unemployment and under-utilisation of our productive equipment. This would be wasteful, socially evil and against our long-term economic interests. The direct and sensible solution is to reduce our rate of increase in wages and salaries. The Government, the TUC and CBI are agreed that this rate should be brought down to a level which will ensure that by the late summer of next year, the year-on-year increase in prices will be no more than 10 per cent, and that by the end of next year it will be down to single figures. They have also agreed on the pay limit needed to achieve this objective.

3. The problem is not just one for the next year: the Government intend to maintain policies which, over a number of years, will control domestic inflation and prevent any resurgence of the present rates of price increase. We have to get down to inflation rates no higher than those of our competitors and stay there. But the next twelve months will be critical, and for the emergency situation which the country faces now there has to be a straight-forward approach which is seen to be just but rightly gives preference to the lower-paid in a period of national difficulty. This is why

the Government are supporting the TUC's proposal for a universal pay limit of £6 per week.

4. The sacrifices called for will not be easy: this will be particularly true in the early months of the policy because of the price increases already in the pipeline. But the alternative is much worse: a continuation of present rates of inflation would greatly increase unemployment, threaten us with external bankruptcy, and gravely damage the social and economic fabric of the nation. To try to cure inflation by deliberately creating mass unemployment would cause widespread misery, industrial strife and a total degeneration of our productive capacity. The only sensible course is to exercise pay restraint and reduce our domestic inflation without sacrificing our long-term economic goals.

3-3. BELATED EFFORTS TO BUILD AN
INDUSTRIAL STRATEGY*

By late 1975 it was clear that public expenditure planning did not necessarily contribute to solving the most critical economic problems. The government's White Paper in late 1975 acknowledged that the struggle for economic recovery would be long and painful. More important, it reversed earlier emphasis on public expenditure and recognized that industrial strength was the basis of economic policy.

The British people face immense short-term economic problems in unemployment, inflation and the balance of payments deficit. These problems have arisen at regular intervals throughout this century, though rarely in a combination quite so intractable as at present. The exceptional difficulties of Britain's position in the economic recession which grips the whole world is due in large part to the fact that the performance of British industry since the war had been steadily deteriorating under successive Governments in comparison with its competitors. So while we tackle immediate problems, we must also get to grips with the long-term weakness of British Industry, and relate short-term solutions to the requirements of this task.

2. The task we face is nothing less than to reserve the relative decline of British industry which has been continuous for many

*Chancellor of the Exchequer and the Secretary for Industry, *An Approach to Industrial Strategy* (London: HMSO, Nov. 1975).

years. It is not something we can achieve overnight. The full benefits will only emerge in the long term. But we must start the process now.

3. This document sets out the Government's proposals for developing a long-term industrial strategy. We believe that any approach to an industrial strategy must satisfy two conditions. First,
it must be realistic and flexible. Our proposals involve a careful
analysis of the performance and prospects of individual industries
which will be continuously adjusted as experience grows and circumstances change. This analysis does not itself constitute a strategy; it provides a flexible framework within which strategic decisions can be made. Second, it must engage the co-operation and
drive of both management and labour in both the private and public sectors. The Government emphasises the importance of sustaining a private sector of industry which is vigorous, alert, responsible
and profitable. It intends that the public sector should exhibit the
same qualities. We intend to achieve the necessary co-operation
through regular discussions with representatives of both sides of
industry, both at sector and at company level. The decisions which
follow the analysis must be made by companies, unions and Government.

4. The first results of this approach were reflected in the Government's recent measures to encourage investment on a selective
basis. The measures to help investment were chosen after the sort
of sectoral analysis which is set out in this paper. They are moreover related to the problems immediately ahead, since they are
primarily intended to remove obstacles to the growth of some of
our key industries as the world economy recovers. We shall keep
the effects of these measures under review and we shall not hesitate to take any further steps that may be necessary, consistent
with our over-riding objective of conquering inflation. As we begin
to develop a new industrial strategy we shall increasingly be able
to plan our short-term measures within a longer-term industrial
framework so that short- and long-term measures reinforce one
another.

5. For its part, the Government will have to continue maintaining a balance between economic and social objectives which often
have conflicting implications. Nevertheless, the Government intends
to give greater weight, and more consistently than hitherto, to the
need for increasing the national rate of growth through regenerat-
ing our industrial structure and improving efficiency. For the imme-

diate future this will mean giving priority to industrial development over consumption or even our social objectives. There is no other way of developing the industrial base on which the Government's whole programme of economic and social reform depends. The Government will have to ensure the proper co-ordination of macro-economic and micro-economic policies since success will depend on a complex variety of factors needing support at national, industry and firm level. We recognise the need to maintain an adequate level of demand and employment if both sides of industry are to possess the confidence required to carry the necessary changes through.

3-4. EROSION OF PUBLIC SPENDING CONTROLS*

Although Britain began to design a system to forecast public expenditure in 1961, it seemed to operate well only during the period of growth. Maynard and Walker describe how expenditure forecasting eroded as economic dislocations became more severe, eventually leading to the arbitrary control of budgetary cash limits.

The recent attempts to reduce public expenditure and the future cuts which are now being discussed have been caused by the rapid escalation in expenditure, and by the resultant inflation and squeezing of private investment. Recently Wynne Godley has presented evidence to the expenditure committee which shows that, if you compare the public spending increases by all Chancellors from Barber in 1971 to Healey in January 1975, and compare this with what happened, the difference in the two rates of growth of public expenditure is 3 per cent by year: by 1974–75, actual expenditure exceeded planned expenditure by £5,000 million. The immediate causes of this are threefold. Firstly public sector employment has increased. As Bacon and Eltis have shown in their recent articles in the Sunday *Times*, central government employment between 1961 and 1973 increased by 14 per cent, whilst that in local government increased by 53 per cent. Secondly, increased public employment has been accompanied by increases in the levels of remuneration of public sector employees. During the period 1973–

---

*Alan Maynard and Arthur Walker, "Cutting Public Spending," *New Society*, Dec. 4, 1975 (selections). This first appeared in *New Society*, London, the weekly review of the social sciences.

74 to 1974–75, the average increase in the wages and salaries of public sector employees was 29 per cent, some 11 per cent in excess of the rate of change of prices. Earnings differential between the public and private sector are not easy to calculate because the data source, the New Earnings Survey, does not distinguish clearly between the public and private sectors. Thirdly, price control, in particular the rent freeze and food subsidies, has increased the cost of some programmes substantially.

Behind these immediate causes of public expenditure inflation lie the more fundamental problems of the present PES structure. The use of the relative price effect assumption, in planning expenditure, means that the size of the public sector's labour force may increase without control over time. Furthermore, the PES assumption that the government is in a position to fix its wages and prices, in ways that will stay, seems to be erroneous. The increased militancy of the public sector unions, together with the apparent narrowing in private-public sector differentials as a result of government policy, has led to increased employment *and* increased remuneration.

The PES process seems to be logical enough *provided* that the basic assumptions of the model are correct. Unfortunately, experience during the first half of the 1970s must make us question the assumptions. Firstly the labour market assumption that government was the price maker appears to be wrong. The labour force has recognised that there are rewards to union militancy. Secondly the panic response of the Conservative government in 1971, to reflate the economy because it feared social unrest (due to high unemployment in Glasgow in particular) led to an inflation which was combated by price controls, which led to increased government subsidies, and hence to extra expenditure on food and housing in particular. This inflation and labour militancy caused programmes to exceed their cost estimates, and to *ad hoc* adjustments in the budgets to permit programmes to be carried out. Under the PES system such adjustments *are not counted as increases in spending*— although spending increases!

The final response is most unwelcome, as it represents a return to the "ad hockery" existing before the Plowden report. Furthermore, it has a highly unfortunate effect on decision makers. Because their budgets were raised, the decision makers were never exposed to fluctuations in relative prices. The price of labour rose rapidly, but economy in the use of labour was not encouraged because the financial constraint was so flexible. The pressure to compare the relative prices, and also to choose the lowest possible mixture of costs was absent.

What's right and what's wrong with our system of public expenditure? Much of the existing process remains sensible enough if the right assumptions are made. Firstly, the decision maker has to make a reasonable guess about the growth course of GDP over the five year planning period. Yet such accuracy is often absent in the Treasury work. As Godley and Ward have pointed out in successive evidence to the expenditure committee, the growth rate assumptions of the Treasury are often far too optimistic: they frequently tend to show a stupid disregard of our real growth experience over the last 200 years.

The second problem arises from price controls, imposed in response to inflationary pressure induced by excessive stimulation of the economy. Such a policy inevitably requires extra public expenditure and it benefits particular income groups in a random fashion. This is an important defect in the present system. It may make politicians popular, but it has the cost of fueling the inflationary fires when it further inflates expenditure.

Our final area of concern is the labour market assumption. The implicit belief here is that the government *is* able to make the price. Operating via the Pay Research Unit, it accumulated evidence to determine wages in central government in particular. The criteria by which the unit fixes optimal public-private pay differentials are lost in the fog which shrouds so much activity in the Whitehall village. This fog should be removed. Perhaps the expenditure committee could be the wind which disperses it.

Like any model, the PES is worth no more than its assumptions. Public expenditure can be estimated with accuracy only if the growth rate, the rate of inflation and its effects on subsidies, and public sector pay policy are accurately predicted. One alternative is to predict inflation, fix expenditure in money terms, but allow overspending equal to the rate of change of prices and no more. This has the advantage of encouraging decision makers to react to relative prices, and to select the cheapest options. However, as a yearly exercise, this alternative requires one to predict inflation; and, like the present system, it demands that politicians establish the rules and maintain them. Such action may not be possible.

Even if the rules were *not* bent, the inherent efficiency "bonus" is limited by the nature of the public expenditure process. This process offers no incentive to the decision maker to conserve his resources. Each year he spends frugally, but if by January he faces the possibility of being in surplus on 31 March he spends madly to prevent the resources being reclaimed as unspent by central government. Why not give decision makers an incentive to be frugal *by offering them part of the benefits of their frugality?*

Whatever the rules which govern the functioning of public sector activity, the monitoring of public expenditure should be improved. The public expenditure committee, and its specialist advisers, have cast a great deal of light into hitherto murkey areas. However their vigour is reduced by their limited resources for investigation. It must never be forgotten that the government is now allocating over 57 per cent of the GDP. To monitor this process is a gigantic task. It is clear that our present institutions are inadequate. The decisions of bureaucrats and their political masters should be subject to rigorous scrutiny, or we will get the incompetent and undemocratic government we deserve.

3-5. ADVERSE EFFECTS OF PUBLIC EXPENDITURE FORECASTING*

By 1978 it was clear that the Public Expenditure Committee White Paper was in many ways misleading. The assumptions were sometimes overly optimistic and ministers found it difficult to translate into government programs, sometimes producing underspending. David Blake, the Times *economic correspondent, criticizes the 1978 PESC. A year later the Thatcher government postponed the PESC until the budget was ready, in effect merging the two documents in order to achieve stricter controls.*

The Trades Descriptions Act does not really apply to government publications, which is just as well for the authors of the latest White Paper on the Government's Expenditure Plans 1978–79 to 1981–82. Anyone looking at this document hoping to come away with a clear idea of what the Government believes will happen either to public spending in particular or the economy in general is in for a grave disappointment.

Take public spending first. The spending plans for the coming financial year, which starts in April, are reasonably clear. They

*David Blake, "The Government Has the Muscle to Keep Down Public Spending," *The Times* (London), Jan. 13, 1978 (selections).

involve a growth of spending in volume terms—that is in terms of the amount of goods and services which the public sector uses, rather than the amount of money which it pays for them—2.2 per cent above the planned spending for the current financial year.

There the clarity ends. For this year's plans have borne little relationship to what has actually happened. Because of the introduction of the cash limit system, the actual amount the Government is spending this year will be 4½ per cent lower than planned.

So depending on how you look at it, public spending will either increase by the very small amount of 2.2 per cent next year, which is the difference between what is planned for 1978–79 and what was planned for this year; or it will increase by the very large amount of nearly 7 per cent, which is what emerges if one adds up the planned growth and assumes that next year the plans will be met exactly instead of being under-fulfilled.

Nothing in the White Paper provides a basis for knowing which of these two outcomes will actually happen. The signs are, however, that the increase in actual expenditure will tend to be towards the top rather than the bottom end of the range. This is because two years in which central government departments have persistently spent less than they were allowed have left their mark.

There is a much greater willingness beginning to emerge to come close to the ceiling on spending because past experience has shown that the chance of breaching it are not as great as was feared.

In itself, this is probably a good development. There is all the difference in the world between an argument about whether governments should aim to have a high level of spending, which is a proper topic for political debate, and the quite different technical question of whether it is a good thing for governments to spend what they plan to. . . .

There are a number of quite remarkable characteristics about this approach. The first is that although the allowable level of public spending is determined by the growth of the economy there is no sign of a belief that growth in the economy is conditioned by the amount of demand which is caused at least in part by public spending.

The authors of the White Paper are clearly still Keynesian enough to believe that it is the level of demand which determines the level of growth in the economy, but they wisely restrict their comments to saying that they assume that by 1979 private demand will be high enough to achieve 3½ per cent growth without lowering the tone of their paper by saying how great that private demand would have to be.

It all looks as if the Government had started out wanting to convince everybody that it could achieve growth of around 3½ per cent but drew back at the last moment because it found the economic arithmetic unpalatable or implausible or possibly both. . . .

The latest set of spending forecasts is thus linked to a growth prospectus which, if it is not actually fraudulent, is certainly seen as being very doubtful both within the Treasury and outside. Yet Ministers argue, with every appearance of conviction, that these spending plans are different from those of the past because they are in large measure proofed against the need to make panic cuts if growth turns out to be less than expected.

Leave on the one side the question of whether the right response to slow growth is to cut public spending or to raise it; what are the ministers actually talking about?

It might be that not only have the Treasury succeeded in imposing an upper limit of around 2 per cent between now and 1980 (and given even less in 1981) on the growth of spending if fairly optimistic growth forecasts turn out to be correct. They have also built into the system a quite new characteristic which changes the balance of power within negotiations each year.

Less than half of the national increases in spending in 1979 has actually been committed to any programme, so if it were decided to restrict still further the growth of spending the Treasury would not be imposing cuts on cherished departmental projects, they would merely be vetoing a potential increase.

There is, of course, a price to pay for this. Because the actual allowed increase in the programmes is so small (and because transfers continue to rise) capital expenditure has been cut yet again, continuing the bias which exists in the government machine in favour of current expenditure.

But in return for this price, the Treasury has talked of allowing moderate growth in public spending while in fact keeping the lid tightly on; and it has done it without allowing the debate on future uses of North Sea oil revenues to affect the issue.

Whether the end of holding down public spending in this way justifies the means, ending the public spending White Paper's role as the key medium-term economic document is a matter of judgement.

And whether the hole which has been dug by successive cuts will be filled by the private sector's expansion is a matter of fact which we shall just have to find out as we go along.

3-6. MRS. THATCHER'S STRUGGLE WITH EXPENDITURE CUTS*

Mrs. Thatcher hoped to cut public spending by £4 billion, but found it possible to extract only about one billion from her ministers. Under conditions of severe inflation, highly controversial reductions in the real value of social benefits, and an inescapable obligation to provide a huge grant to local government, there seemed little choice but to impose even more severe cuts on nationalized industries. In fact, she found the PESC operation more damaging than helpful and decided to delay publication until the budget was ready, and also to reduce the forecast's time span to three years. Some of these dilemmas that undermine public expenditure planning are discussed by Frances Cairncross.

The White Paper assumes that the nationalized industries move from borrowing £2.3 billion last year to making net repayments of £400 million in 1983–4 (at 1979 prices). That represents a turnround of £2.7 billion. Compare and contrast that with the fact that total public spending is to be cut from £69.9 last year to £67.1 in 1983–4 (at 1979 prices): a reduction of £2.8 billion.

How is it to be done? Sir Geoffrey (Chancellor of the Exchequer) was a trifle vague when he was asked that question by the House of Commons Treasury and Civil Service Committee on Monday.

He thought that about two-fifths of the turnround would come from the elimination or reduction of losses in coal, steel, shipbuilding and railways and about a quarter from the elimination of underpricing in gas and electricity.

Any taxpayer who is joyfully looking forward to paying income tax at 25 per cent by the end of this Administration might just pause to consider what this means. It implies that the price of gas and of electricity will rise faster than inflation over the next three years, and it means that his season ticket from Guildford or his

*Frances Cairncross, "Why the Government's Public Spending Clean-up Means It Will Be Dirtier by Rail," *The Guardian*, April 19, 1980 (selections).

day return to Eastbourne will take a bigger chunk of his income in 1983–4 than it does today.

But there is some force in the point made by the Cambridge Economic Policy Group in their Review this week: "The Government, finding itself unable to make real cuts in expenditure of a kind which would lead to genuine tax reductions, is having recourse to 'cuts' which are not themselves distinguishable from tax increases. . . . In reality increases in . . . nationalised industry prices are tax increases as much as a rise in income tax is."

There are two particular flaws in the way cash limits work which have begun to matter a lot more as the nationalized industries have begun to find the limits a tighter constraint:

First, they operate in a much more rigid way than do the constraints on a commercial company's borrowings. In particular there is no way that an industry that undershoots its cash limit one year can benefit from the saving the next year.

Secondly, some of the industries can raise their prices much more easily than most commercial firms. Indeed, the industries where cash limits have been most effective in helping management to take uncomfortably tough decisions have been those large loss-makers like steel and shipbuilding which compete internationally.

For other industries—for British Rail, for instance, or the Post Office—the cost of an expensive pay claim can always be passed on in higher fares or more expensive postage stamps, or more subtly in dirtier railway carriages or less frequent mail collections.

The more weight is placed on the system of cash limits, the more important it is that the Government find ways of making sure that the consumer does not end up footing the whole bill. It is more important than ever that the nationalized industries should be set performance targets, against which the quality and efficiency of their services can be measured.

4 Industrial Relations: Confusion of Sectoral Policies

As we saw in Chapter 3, economic policymaking in Britain has changed as the problems of managing the public sector and guiding the private sector have multiplied with the development of the welfare state. The growth of the state raises new requirements to integrate and coordinate a number of economic policies so that government is pushed well beyond the tasks of monetary supervision and debt management of nineteenth-century national economic policy. In examining the British response to the growing complexity of industrial relations, we are confronted with the dilemmas of a mixed economy that increases the mutual interdependence of industry, workers, and the state. For a variety of reasons dependence has grown to the point where the conventional distinction between the private and public sector has almost lost its meaning. Roughly a third of the British labor force of nearly 24 million persons is employed by national and local government, nationalized industries, or industries heavily dependent on government support.

Perhaps the central question in examining British efforts to maintain good relations with the labor movement is why such a fundamental change in the political and economic structure of every modern industrial democracy was so poorly understood by government. The paradox becomes more acute when we consider that Britain took the lead in establishing a welfare state following World War II and, at least during the Attlee Labour government (1945–51), had unreserved support from British workers. After the prolonged unemployment that affected Britain between the wars, the primary concern of workers and government was full employment. Keynesian principles reassured workers that the full employment was attainable and the massive social reforms brought tangible benefits. There was no necessity to find a new working relationship between the worker and government. Attlee published his White Paper on incomes and prices without consulting the national labor organization, the Trades Union Congress (TUC), and by his personal appeal could settle a serious dock strike. In 1950 the annual conference of the TUC actually voted to continue the wartime "Order 1305," which provided compulsory collective bargaining.

Since that time labor relations in Britain have steadily deteriorated, and increasingly resulted in confrontation between industry and unions. Indeed, one-party government may be ill-suited for the task of redefining industrial relations in the welfare state because industrial conflict is inescapably shaped by the needs of adversarial politics. There is no alternative for workers but an alliance with one of the two major parties. Consequently, there is virtually no alternative for the more conservative of the parties but to oppose working-class demands. The policy effect is more destructive because *both* major parties are inhibited in looking for new solutions and inevitably constrained when labor-management conflict erupts. This, in turn, can lead to serious misperception of needs and priorities. With startling consistency the first Wilson government (1964–70) and the Heath government (1970–74) sought statutory controls on unions and tried to force them to recognize national policy objectives. Neither government fully realized the changing structure of labor and industrial conflict: the growth of public sector unions, the importance of increased participation in industrial management, and the growing interdependence of incomes policy with social policy generally.

In other industrial democracies like West Germany and Sweden, experiments and legislation have begun to involve workers in management decisions. Even in ideologically torn France, relations between workers and management in public and private enterprises have been reasonably good. Britain, however, has swung between exonerating and punishing unions with little progress toward establishing common goals. Much has been made of the shortcomings of the organization of the British labor movement and the problems of the TUC in controlling its member unions, regulating jurisdictional conflicts, and disciplining rebellious union executives and shop stewards.

As we shall see, the notion that labor problems were *internal* to the labor movement has dominated British official thinking and distracted political leaders. The failure of the economy has forced government to reconsider industrial relations. One does not need to have a marxist perspective to see how the complications of stagflation inextricably affect prices and incomes. The vicious circular effect of wage and price increases is not confined to Britain. All the industrial nations have reconsidered how labor relates to national economic policy. Britain is by no means unique in this respect, but Britain began to suffer economic reversals well before the rest of Europe and Japan, as we saw in Chapter 3; yet it has been among the most reluctant to change the well-worn habits of liberal economic thinking. Why a pioneer in devising the welfare state should be among the last to work out a new system of industrial relations requires an explanation.

Context

The difficulties in generating a national framework for industrial relations policy appear to stem from early constraints placed on the assertion of union power in the political system. Like the rest of Europe, Britain experienced severe labor strife in the late nineteenth century as the country began to experience depression and unemployment. But unlike in most of Europe, industrial conflict did not immediately produce a doctrinaire socialist party. (In the German elections of 1892, for example, the socialists received three million votes and gained fifty seats in the Reichstag.) Despite their alarm at the rise of the working class, British political leaders were more accommodating than most of their continental counterparts. A Royal Commission on Trade Unions of 1867 did much to create favorable public opinion toward the early craft unions. Its report was followed in 1871 by the Trade Union Act, which protects unions against strike damages and is widely regarded as the charter of the British labor movement. Though it was to have a stormy history, the principle was accepted that unions could not be sued for restraint of trade and in 1875 legislation protected peaceful picketing.

During the rash of strikes and the rise of new industrial unions in the early 1890s, another Royal Commission on Labour raised the possibility of building a more elaborate national network of conciliation bodies, similar to those being fashioned at the time in Germany and France. Most of these recommendations were cut out of the 1896 Conciliation Act in favor of preserving a "voluntary" system of bargaining (Pelling, 1976, pp. 176–90). Likewise, the Royal Commission on Trade Disputes, appointed by the Conservatives in 1904 and having no trade union member, favored continuing the "partnership" between labor and management and anticipated a new era of labor peace just as Britain was about to enter a period of unprecedented conflict. The aversion to formulating more comprehensive and effective means of negotiating with the unions has often been attributed to labor's own internal divisions, which were and remain by no means negligible. One can also see, however, that Westminster was not eager to enter into this complex policy problem. In 1919 a National Industrial Conference suggested forming a National Industrial Council (Wigham, 1974, p. 50), which was rejected. Again, in 1929, Balfour's Committee on Industry and Trade examined the country's arbitration procedures only to conclude there was no demand for new institutions. In 1931 the TUC endorsed proposals for "Permanent Conciliation Officers" in each major industrial area, but nothing was done.

If government was reluctant to become heavily involved in labor problems, it is equally true that both unions and employers distrusted national intervention. The roots of this second development run deep in British culture and history (Tholfson, 1977; Bauman, 1972). The craft unions that developed in mid-Victorian England jealously guarded their prerogatives against government as well as against nonmembers and employers. In many respects, they more fervently espoused the liberal creed of self-reliance and self-improvement than did political leaders. The president of the Boilermakers pronounced in 1857: "We are not united to set class against class but to teach one another that we are all brothers" (Kynaston, 1976, p. 19).

The more militant industrial unions of the 1890s were similarly pragmatic. Benjamin Tillett, leader of the London dockers, disdainfully rejected the "hare-brained chatterers and magpies of Continental revolutionists" (Pelling, 1976, p. 117). From this tradition has grown the marxist explanation of a "labor aristocracy" and liberal preoccupations with union barons. Strong union leadership was no less apparent in the efforts to centralize unions in the 1920s than among the middle-class labor leadership of Victorian England (Pelling, 1968, pp. 38–61). Whichever explanation one prefers, the labor movement set itself apart from government and needed strong leaders because of government's inhospitable approach to union problems. The unions needed to be self-sufficient and provided many services for workers. We shall see in Chapter 6 how the Friendly Societies, organized by unions to provide welfare and insurance for workers, opposed the early national insurance schemes of 1911.

With the outbreak of labor unrest during World War I, industrial relations were elevated to a national problem, as outlined by the Reconstruction Committee of cabinet ministers under Lloyd George, the prime minister. Their five reports in 1917 advocated regular contact between management and labor, the organization of district labor councils throughout England, and the improvement of conciliation and arbitration machinery. In the same year the Ministry of Labour was formed. In 1920, union membership reached a new zenith of 8.3 million members. Although unemployment insurance was extended from 3.3 to 12 million workers in 1920, the country was poised for a major confrontation at the very time it was dismantling its capacity to communicate with the unions and workers. The outcome cannot be fully described here, but the General Strike of 1926 did more than any of the earlier defeats to polarize labor relations in Britain. Not only did the government break the strike in nine days, but the uncertainty of union leaders so demoralized workers that union membership fell to 4.3 million members by 1933.

The two-party system leaves the worker with little choice but to work with the Labour Party, although roughly a third (about two-fifths in 1979) vote for the Conservative Party. For all the accusations of conspiracy and special interest politics, the alliance of Labour and the unions was not an easy one to form nor has it been all that comfortable for the TUC. The decision to align the union interests with the Labour Party was the outcome of long negotiations that produced the Labour Representation Committee in 1900. At first the Labour candidates were heavily working class, but the proportion of workers among Labour MPs has steadily declined over the past fifty years. Despite the close relations between the TUC and the Labour Party, the unions are barred like any other pressure group from openly imposing mandates on parliamentary candidates and there is little reason to think that their informal influence on Labour Party leaders is exercised any differently, if more openly, than is the influence of business pressure groups on the Conservative Party. Indeed, it is the alliance itself, which *neither* party can ignore, that may be the major obstacle to reconsidering industrial relations policy in Britain.

From its formation in 1868 the British TUC has been engaged in constant struggle with government. In mid-Victorian England, for example, the Amalgamated Engineers had 200,000 members well before any political party had constructed a national organization. The labor movement remains a powerful and proud organization, a fact that is often clouded over in partisan debate that concentrates on their inescapable alliance with the Labour Party. The TUC and the unions propelled workers into powerful positions and working-class leadership developed. Of the roughly 24 million workers in Britain, nearly half are union members, the highest level of union membership among all the modern democracies. But fashioning a united political group from these members has never been easy. At the turn of the century there were over 1,300 unions for some 2 million members. Now there are about 300 unions, but the 100 affiliated with the TUC represent about 95 percent of total membership. The organizational problems are further complicated from within because huge unions easily dominate in the conduct of TUC business. About half the total membership of the TUC, nearly 6 million persons, are organized in five unions (Price and Bain, 1976).

If the welfare states does nothing else it proclaims an era of bigness (Taylor, 1978). But British trade unions have always been big: in 1978 the TGWU (transport and general workers) had over 2 million members; the AUEW (engineers or manufacturing industries) nearly 1.5 million; the GMWU (general and municipal workers) just under a million. Unlike France and Germany there is no uniform pattern of union organization although most unions have a National Executive whose officials are often elected for life, and regional and branch offices throughout the industrial areas of the country, and convenors (factory agents) and shop stewards at the grassroots. The 300,000 shop stewards tend to be militant union members, but are not part of the formal union organization even though they can exert immense influence on workers (McCarthy, 1966; Hinton, 1973). There are over 100,000 paid union officials, mostly at the branch level. As we shall see, the major thrust of reforms in the 1960s was to bring the voluntaristic and presumably undependable plant-level organization under control, an objective that with varying degrees of frankness was shared by unions, management, and government.

To understand the role of the TUC it is essential to know that it is a loose confederation of powerful independent unions, many of which would be quite secure without the TUC. The presidency of the TUC rotates and is honorific. The general secretary of the

TUC has important influence as a spokesman for labor and is an important liaison between government and the unions, but his views can be easily rejected by major unions and often have been. The 1977 TUC conference, for example, voted down proposals by Jack Jones, a union veteran and himself a militant leader, to try to reconstruct a national incomes policy with the Labour government. The big unions have always kept the General Council on a short leash. At the turn of the century the unions provided only £2,000 to run their national office when their treasuries held over £100 million. The few thousand employees of the TUC are easily outnumbered by the thousands of paid officials who are recruited from their own union ranks and are generally suspicious of the intellectual atmosphere of TUC headquarters. The TUC's General Council, its governing body, tends to be more conservative than the labor movement because places are reserved for more traditional small unions. General policy is laid down by the boisterous and chaotic Annual Congress, where the unions vote in proportion to their membership. Unlike the annual conferences of the parties, the TUC conference obligates TUC leadership.

Much has been made of the undemocratic features of union organization (Forester, 1976; Milligan, 1976). It is true that branch-level electoral apathy has permitted left-wing militant groups within some unions to increase their power way beyond their numbers, but union leaders are hampered in dealing with the threat by their need to sustain the solidarity of large and unwieldy unions. Most company boardrooms do not operate differently from the National Executives of the large unions. The argument against undemocratic unions became part of the case against unions in the 1960s and easily slipped over into the unsubstantiated argument that if workers were truly represented then collective bargaining conflicts and jurisdictional disputes would disappear. It is also easily forgotten that in some conflict-ridden industries, such as mining, technological progress and reorganization has been dramatic (400,000 of 700,000 jobs disappeared from 1958 to 1972), and in some areas torn with jurisdictional disputes, such as electricity production, agreements have been worked out to modernize the industry. Both the size and traditions of some big unions make them reluctant to call strikes: the gas strike of 1975 was the first one ever initiated by the GMWU. Nor has the TUC been afraid of risking its influence by negotiating with unpopular governments. Despite the rough treatment given unions by the Heath government, the TUC entered into talks to avert the 1974 miners' strike, the first in fifty years, that brought down the government. Had Heath not been so relentless he might have avoided the 1974 defeat with the help of the TUC. But British leaders of both parties have been slow to accept the reality of labor's power, meaning both the strengths and weaknesses of the British labor movement.

There is no doubt that labor strife varies with economic cycles. The desire of both the Conservatives and Labour to impose more statutory controls on unions arose with the economic dislocations that plagued Britain from the 1950s onward. The correlation of strike activity with economic decline and its disappearance with full employment and growth is, of course, one of the more obvious reasons why a statutory policy is likely to fail. It cannot adjust rapidly enough to changing economic conditions. What may appear to be a constructive requirement during prosperity may easily become a disruptive and even repressive requirement during decline. Nonetheless, since 1960, British political leaders have been worried about strikes, especially unofficial strikes. The dramatic injustice of some strikes tends to mobilize public opinion and thereby focuses the attention of political leaders. For example, in 1978 an unofficial strike of thirty-two toolmakers of British Leyland Motors threatened the jobs of 250,000 workers in the auto industry.

Interpreting strike statistics is no easy matter and again too much has been made of crude aggregate figures in the British debate on industrial relations (Turner, 1969a). While it is correct that total man days lost reached a new high of 8 million in 1957 and hovered around 3 million during much of the 1960s, it is also correct that with one or two exceptional years the number of stoppages diminished from 1957 until the late years of the Wilson government and the all-out warfare against the Heath government. If British strike figures are adjusted to size of working class, Britain comes out midway between a strife-torn Canada and a placid Switzerland (Department of Employment, 1978). Strikes are also concentrated in large plants, which not only makes sense but should facilitate seeking remedies. Even in the worst recent years (1971–73), stoppages in 150 of the 600,000 plants accounted for a quarter of all stoppages and two-thirds of lost working days. By industrial sector the more prosperous manufacturing factories are relatively strike-free and the declining industries of shipbuilding, mining, and steel have more labor troubles.

British unions are often considered dogmatic and unresponsive because of their insistence on voluntary bargaining arrangements and their suspicion of statutory controls. In fact, like nearly every other large organization in the welfare state, unions are imbedded in all kinds of legal controls. They have quite possibly been correct in thinking that they live in too complex an industrial setting to expect laws to settle all kinds of industrial disputes. On the whole, they have been supported by the employers in this belief. From a political perspective, it must not be forgotten that British workers have lived through several generations of conflict where punitive conditions were imposed on them by Parliament and the courts. The unhappy result is that labor legislation in Britain easily becomes a tug-of-war in an adversarial political system rather than a search for policies that might deal with the intricacies of industrial relations.

The TUC's dependence on Labour to pursue the policies of unions notwithstanding, relations between the TUC and the Labour Party have not been a simple matter. Since 1962, union members must be party members in order to attend the Annual Conference, although the unions provide about nine-tenths of the party's funds. Over the 1960s more militant union leaders found the policy of the TUC's general secretary, "to take the unions out of Trafalgar and into Whitehall," uncomfortable (Minkin, 1974). Members of the TUC General Council no longer sit on the party's National Executive Committee, and gradually the lines between the party and the unions have been more clearly drawn. In many respects, the problem is more acute for Labour than for the TUC. Even Labour's new headquarters were built with a loan from the TUC.

Though much political capital has been made of Labour-TUC dependence, unions do not need MPs to exercise policy influence. The political relationship between unions and Labour may be counterproductive to devising more durable and flexible industrial relations policies. When Labour has a large majority, union influence diminishes; when Labour is weak in Parliament, the unions can exercise excessive influence by controlling a few MPs with strong union attachments. The diminished policymaking powers of Parliament itself mean that the proportion of safe Labour seats made available to TUC and union candidates is not of crucial importance in policymaking, nor are the key union leaders sent to Parliament.

Agenda

The necessity of devising new ways to incorporate unions in national industrial relations policy has been evident since the first serious economic dislocation of 1955, which, as noted in Chapter 3, also stimulated new thinking about economic policymaking. With the Labour Party divided and in opposition a moderate TUC leadership provided a long period of union acquiescence to the party's needs. But this early inflationary spiral showed that new industrial relations policies were needed if wages and prices were to be kept in harmony. The chancellor of the exchequer, Macmillan, was sensitive to this need, and the Conservative White Paper *Economic Implications of Full Employment* (1956) raised the notion that mutual sacrifices would be needed. A more hostile tone appeared in a paper by a group of right-wing Conservatives, *A Giant's Strength* (1958), which advocated statutory controls on unions. Though it was disowned by the Conservative government, it represents the first explicit demand for strong union legislation.

In the flurry of jurisdictional disputes that also occurred at this time there appears one of the first recognitions that the entire structure of industrial relations policymaking was inadequate. In 1954 a court of inquiry (an investigatory body with no powers) was established to study shipbuilding and manufacturing wage claims. In his decision Lord Justice Morris noted that there was no way such inquiries into disputes could "form a view upon their implications for the national economy" (Wigham, 1968, p. 110). In a nutshell this is why courts cannot provide solutions to wage conflicts. The economic implications of strikes, jurisdictional fights, and wage increases constantly shift and cannot be specified clearly in law. The TUC pointed out then, as it did later, that many industries with established arbitration procedures had poor industrial relations, while many with no arbitration machinery had good labor relations records. Binding controls on unions do not seem to be associated with labor peace.

There were desultory talks about forming an industrial parliament and rejuvenating the weak National Joint Advisory Council. The critical issue was revealed by *The Times* when it commented, "The system of government conciliation grew up on the assumption that the Government were not involved and could hold the ring impartially. It may be difficult for it to survive in its present form now that governments habitually have policies of their own on wages" (quoted in Wigham, 1968, p. 119). Important changes were made in this direction. From 1962, George Woodcock, the general secretary of the TUC, worked to bring its organization "into the twentieth century," and shortly afterwards the Confederation of British Industries (CBI) also reorganized. As we saw in Chapter 3, Macmillan's National Economic Development Council, the sole joint body for labor and employers to survive the turbulence of the next decade, provided a forum for tripartite discussion. The complex issue of workers' dismissal rights was addressed in legislation of 1963, and the government was considering legislation to ease the amalgamation of unions when it fell. (Similar legislation was later passed by the Wilson government.) Thus, there were numerous steps toward organizing both unions and employers so they could act more responsibly in dealing with economic and industrial relations policy. Unfortunately, this new awareness as well as the improved organizations could as easily generate irreconcilable conflict. The paradox of British industrial relations policy is that both the Labour and Conservative leaders proceeded to make this outcome virtually unavoidable.

During the 1961 economic crisis Macmillan imposed the first arbitrary "pay pause" since Attlee. In 1962 he formed the National Incomes Commission with investigatory powers over wage settlements. By the 1964 election both parties were feeling impatient and frustrated by the new complications of wage policy. In what was to become a familiar seesaw between the parties, Wilson dismantled the National Incomes Commission and established the National Board of Prices and Incomes, which he regularly undermined over the coming years by making wage deals without consulting it (Jones, 1973). On entering office Wilson made a peace pact with management and the unions (*Statement of Intent*) that promised that bargaining would remain voluntary. But, like Macmillan, Wilson was persuaded that the unions often acted irresponsibly and were unable to make reliable agreements with government. His first impulse was to create a Ministry of Productivity to link wage agreements to productivity, but he then decided to work toward involving labor in national economic policy through the new Department of Economic Affairs. George Brown (later Lord George Brown) devised an "early warning" system on wage demands with TUC cooperation (Panitch, 1976, pp. 85–105), but faced with mounting inflationary pressure, this proved to be no more than a brush-fire operation.

One should not underestimate the immense political and economic pressures on the Wilson government. Because of its small majority, it could not pass major legislation until the 1966 election, and it was fighting new economic crises. Nonetheless, its dual strategy to reorder industrial relations could hardly have been better calculated to aggravate labor strife and union suspicions. It embarked on a concerted effort to force the unions to be responsible, while deflationary national economic policy threatened unemployment. Much has been made of Wilson's secretive habits, but less has been said about why such conflicting decisions are awkward within the British political system. The first part of this problem was assigned to the Royal Commission on Trade Unions and Employers Associations, the Donovan Commission.

From the start the Commission became political and therefore more contentious than anybody hoping to pick its way through the intricacies of British industrial relations could afford to be. One critic suggests that it would have been preferable to have a departmental committee rather than to put "a political hot potato into the hands of a mixed bunch of axe-grinders and pundits" (Kilroy-Silk, 1973, p. 46). Although the Commission had an able research director in W. E. J. McCarthy, its investigations were almost entirely carried on by the Oxford group of industrial relations scholars of whom "Clegg acted as the Father, McCarthy as John the Baptist and the other researchers as their disciples" (Kilroy-Silk, p. 58). In any event, the Donovan Commission is the prototype of the Royal Commission as an instrument of political procrastination.

The terms of reference of the Donovan Commission were broad: "to consider the relations between management and employees and the role of trade unions and employers' associations in promoting the interests of their members and in accelerating the social and economic advance of the nation, with particular reference to the Law affecting the activities of those bodies." As it turned out, the report had as much to say about employers' associations as about unions, suggesting that employers' difficulties in participating effectively in industrial relations policies are probably as great as those of unions. Why the unions have not launched such a counterattack to the frequent charges that they are unable to speak with one voice is probably a tribute to their own acceptance of the mixed economy.

The only person who addressed the larger issue of how these organizations relate to national economic policy generally was Andrew Shonfield, a long-standing critic of British economic policy and industrial relations (1965), who wrote a Memorandum on this neglect (see Reading 4-2). Over the three years that the Commission labored, Britain's economic situation steadily deteriorated and the recommendations were in many ways inappropriate when they finally appeared. By 1970, for example, stoppages were not caused as much by short, unofficial strikes in business as by longer, official strikes of public sector unions. Indeed, as the 1960s progressed and Labour's relations with the TUC eroded, "waiting for Donovan" became a standard quip in Whitehall corridors.

The Commission's Report (see Reading 4-1) primarily addressed two questions: the inadequacy of Britain's collective bargaining arrangements and the internal weaknesses of unions. The first issue was analyzed in terms of the "formal" and "informal" systems of wage bargaining, arguing that the industrywide system of the postwar era had eroded and now operated alongside an informal system of workplace and factory-level bargaining. As many critics pointed out, this conclusion was heavily influenced by the Commission's preoccupation with the most strife-torn and often declining industries. It was estimated that about only 4 million of the then 23 million employed persons in Britain actually worked under a dual system (Turner, 1969b; McCarthy, 1970). In what ways the presumably more orderly formal arrangements for national-level bargaining actually accounted for labor tranquillity in the past was not made very clear. Neither was it explained how the alienation of workers from their unions and other national policy bodies (Goldthorpe, et al., 1969) was to be eradicated. All this produced a wave of articles about the "historicism" of the report that was not wholly unjustified (Crossley, 1968; Flanders and Fox, 1969).

The second major part of the Report dealt with the role of shop stewards, strikes and stoppages, dismissal (redundancy) arrangements, jurisdictional disputes, and a number of problems associated with unofficial strikes and therefore the breakdown of national bargaining relationships. Important as these problems are, many critics thought that there were few guidelines to the most pressing issues except for Shonfield's Dissent (see Reading 4-2). By 1968, for example, it had become fairly clear that "wage drift," the tendency for local piecework and overtime agreements to surpass national wage settlements, had become a major force behind uncontrollable inflation. Britain was also beginning to experience the inflationary effects of "thresholds" build into wage agreements that brought mandatory increases throughout the year whenever inflation exceeded specified limits. What the Commission proposed that Labour seized upon was a Commission on Industrial Relations to make long-term studies of industrial relations problems, but the Donovan Commission was firm in its conviction that bargaining must remain voluntary.

By early 1968 the restructuring of industrial relations had become an election issue. A few months before the Donovan Report, the Conservatives announced their policy, *Fair Deal at Work* (1968), whose proposals are similar to the 1971 Industrial Relations Act. Wilson was equally anxious. The Ministry of Labour was elevated to acquire a secretary of state, Barbara Castle, as pressure for a statutory incomes policy grew. The new Department of Employment and Productivity was designed to replace the now defunct Department of Economic Affairs and, contrary to the Treasury's wishes, was to have some overall influence on economic policy. A kind of super-ministry of economic problems, it took over responsibility for the Prices and Incomes Board, monopolies, mergers, and restrictive trade practices and the Manpower and Productivity Service inherited from regional services of the old Department of Economic Affairs. The new secretary of state was even more suspicious of Whitehall mandarins than Wilson, but it was never clear what the role of the new competitor to the Treasury would be.

When Labour published *In Place of Strife* (Department of Employment, 1969), the depth of bipartisan agreement that unions must name statutory controls became clear. Setting a precedent that has now become commonplace, Castle discussed her White Paper with the TUC before it was endorsed by the cabinet. A further blow to parliamentary proprieties was the decision to set up the Commission on Industrial Relations by Royal Warrant (more or less a permanent Royal Commission) until a statute could be passed. Inspired by the American Taft-Hartley Law, the statute was to give the secretary of state discretionary power to impose a four-week cooling-off period. There followed what has been aptly called the "battle of Downing Street" (Jenkins, 1970).

In Place of Strife proposed fines if unions ignored the Commission on Industrial Relations' findings in jurisdictional disputes, compulsory registration of collective agreements, an obligatory strike ballot for key industries, and the voluntary imposition of legally binding collective agreements, and removed the legal protection of unofficial strike leaders. The curiosity of the Labour Party sponsoring such legislation is only matched by the foolhardy sequel of the Conservatives repeating the same blunders. In the parliamentary vote on the White Paper, fifty-three Labour MPs opposed and forty abstained. The TUC called a special congress to voice their opposition, and once it was clear Labour could not assemble a majority the bill was dead.

Process

The process leading to the 1971 Industrial Relations Act underscores a peculiar problem of the two-party system in making industrial relations policy. While Labour must try hard not to appear to be the tool of unions, the Tories must go to exceptional lengths not to appear to be their enemy. The delicate balance between party interest and workable policy is constantly threatened by the extreme wings of each party. The potentially destructive capabilities of the parliamentary system require that each party forego reversing its adversary's legislation, but do not preclude duplicating errors. The Conservatives have not always treated unions like "a hostile foreign power" (*Times*, March 7, 1978). Moreover, in the early 1970s and again in 1978, polls showed that nearly two-thirds of the British people thought some sort of union regulation was needed.

The Conservatives must work even harder at industrial relations policy than must Labour. In ãny event, *Fair Deal at Work* was not remarkably more punitive than the Labour proposals. Tory liberalism rebelled against the closed shop, but Conservative leaders were sufficiently realistic to know that often both employees and employers favored a closed shop to get labor peace. The device of a "post-entry" closed shop, or "agency shop" as it was called, is not a severe compromise with union objectives. Nor were the proposed bargaining regulations all that destructive to union interests because legally enforceable agreements were voluntary, and remained so in the 1971 law. Unions could not be hauled into court over violations of wage settlements unless they agreed to it. The stumbling block was how to state in legal terms the complex procedures needed to establish these ideas (Fox, 1979; Taylor, 1979). The Conservatives differed from Labour in their understanding of the dilemma concerning restrictive union practices, which essentially meant irresponsible use of strikes. Sir Keith Joseph, a leading Tory planner and strategist for Heath, saw that the worst strikes may often be those that do not occur (Moran, 1977, p. 67) because overgenerous settlements trigger wage and price inflation. Carr was much closer to orthodox Tory liberalism, arguing that both unions and business must conform to the needs of an unfettered marketplace for wage determination, something that neither the TUC nor the CBI wanted.

Perhaps the most important result was that when the Tories took office in 1970 they were overprepared and overeager. Sitting on the Opposition bench for six years has been known to create such anxieties. Neither the TUC nor the CBI expected labor legislation to be rushed through Parliament after the turmoil of the late 1960s. Again Whitehall was subjected to the sweeping away of laboriously built machinery that handled the delicate and complex problems of workers. The Department of Employment lost its second title, Productivity, although productivity bargaining agreements were one of the more solid achievements of the Wilson government and clearly crucial in trying to link wage and price policies. The Prices and Incomes Board was abolished although the 170 reports it had made over the previous six years were fundamentally important in relating industrial and economic policy. The Department of Employment's Manpower Service, the closest thing Whitehall had to a skilled manpower policy group, was demoted. In effect, the state was withdrawing from industrial relations policy.

The 1,970 clauses and nine schedules of the bill were a lawyer's delight and raised severe apprehension in both the CBI, whose views had been consistently rejected in preparing the legislation, and the TUC, which had withdrawn from the consultations when told that no major changes were admissible. The 1971 Industrial Relations Act was one of the few major pieces of legislation passed without considering the concerns of *any* of the groups that would implement it. One of the more curious features of the ensuing struggle is how hard the major interest groups and the civil service tried to advise the government of imminent disaster. The TUC called a special congress whose motions are notable for their restraint and, as might be expected, concentrated on the specific legal constraints that would most seriously curb union power. The point is important, for the TUC and many member unions were not opposed to many features of the 1971 bill: protections of workers' individual rights, more orderly handling of jurisdictional and dismissal disputes, and even closer consultation with government about wage settlements. Like the CBI, the TUC felt strongly that courts are not the place to settle labor problems.

The new law was much too complex to be fully treated here, but the distinguishing feature was the quixotic hope that a formidable array of judicial institutions would remove politics from the conduct of industrial relations. A national Industrial Relations Court was set up to hear claims in violations of the Act. Industrial tribunals (hearing bodies) were brought within the judicial system and were to consider cases on compensation and to issue enforcement orders. Labour's Commission on Industrial Relations was kept, but beefed up to pass judgment on union recognition, the creation of agency shops, and the determination of bargaining units, not unlike the American National Labor Relations Board. Possibly the most critical way in which law entered into industrial relations was through the registrar. Only unions that agreed to register would remain tax-exempt and noncompliance was estimated to cost the unions about £5 million in taxes. But registration also required that the unions have an acceptable array of rules governing their elections, membership, and strike procedures. Unregistered unions lost their immunity liability in industrial disputes, which could include both jurisdictional and sympathy strikes. Further, upper limits were placed on fines for registered unions, but there were none for unregistered unions. Heath's political gamble was that the unions would not maintain solidarity against registration. Many observers felt that he might have won this gamble had not his own doggedness made the issue even more repellent.

Thus, the Act had nothing but destructive effects on the more serious problems of achieving a new relationship between unions and government. More moderate unions, like the GMWU and AUEW, were embarrassed that they found little wrong with it while in more politicized unions militants could maximize labor unrest. Like the debate on local reform described in the next chapter, the law did nothing to recover Parliament's prestige, and the debate was described as a "rambling farrago of political abuse, anecdote and misused statistics" (Moran, 1977, p. 98). The employers, whose legal initiative was needed in order to enforce the agency shop, were acutely embarrassed and were no more eager than the unions to add to Britain's labor troubles. In fact the Act settled only one labor dispute, a railway strike, where the obligatory strike ballot was dutifully carried out only to have the government forced to settle for more than it wished to. One Tory back-bencher remarked, "Ask a silly question and you get a silly answer" (Moran, p. 138). The Department of Employment later calculated that over 3 million days had been lost protesting the bill and a million over the cases brought to the new courts. Resentment over the new law and fears of new wage controls combined so that in 1972 strikes and stoppages reached the highest levels since 1926, with over 23 million lost working days.

But the greater cost of the 1971 Act was that it delayed and obstructed action on the more pressing issue of linking wage policy to union and employer organizations. Under severe inflationary pressures Heath opened tripartite talks with the TUC and CBI in early 1972 and by fall was personally discussing a new incomes policy with the TUC (Panitch, 1976). These talks broke down and a pay freeze was imposed. In early 1973, strong price and wage controls were enacted, the Pay Board and Price Commission were created, and the Department of Employment was again reinforced to be a more effective industrial relations team. The cases that were brought to the National Industrial Relations Court became comic operas. In one case an anonymous donor from industry paid a union's fine so work could be resumed and in another the government's own solicitor general appeared to argue why the case should be dismissed. Heath no doubt fell in 1974 because the disastrous strikes and economic disorder made him appear incapable, but the Act was effectively abandoned from 1972. Ironically, Heath's defeat in 1974 is sometimes attributed to an election eve broadcast by the CBI director on the disastrous effects of the 1971 Industrial Relations Act. The failure was not only that the machinery was inappropriate and ineffective but that parliamentary government had so pathetically failed even to identify what the problem was.

Consequences

Combined with inept and often short-sighted leadership, the parliamentary process had displayed its inability to deal with industrial relations. In its final report the Commission on Industrial Relations repeated the often proclaimed need to have long-range and professional consideration of these complex questions safeguarded "from the hazards of political change and involvement in short-term issues" (quoted in Wigham, 1968, p. 185). While not a wholly satisfactory solution, the alliance of Labour and the TUC fills this need, and the blunders of the early 1970s made sure the alliance would stay intact. Under the care of Callaghan, the TUC-Labour Liaison Committee became the focal point for Labour's plans to restore industrial relations to the *status quo ante*. Thus for the third time in a decade industrial relations machinery was swept away. The new government abolished the Commission on Industrial Relations (their own creation), the Pay Board, and the National Industrial Relations Court. A standing Royal Commission on Distribution of Incomes and Wealth was established.

In fact the legislative agenda fashioned by the new Labour government and the TUC contained nothing on wage policy. The TUC was in a powerful position to extract benefits and proceeded to do so with few concessions to the increasing dilemma of inflation other than a verbal commitment to the Social Contract or voluntary wage restraint (see Reading 4-4). In the meantime, rents were frozen, pensions increased (see Chapter 6), and the Industrial Relations Act repealed. Oddly enough, only 39 percent of the voters supported complete abolition, including a bare majority (55 percent) of Labour voters (Butler and Kavanagh, 1974, p. 141). The Trade Union and Labor Relations Act of 1974 essentially restored industrial relations to their pre-1971 state, but did include a minor concession to workers who were uncomfortable with a closed shop by forbidding dismissal for "religious or other reasonable grounds." An amendment in 1976 removed "reasonable."

As part of the renewed dismantling of the Department of Employment in 1974, a Conciliation and Arbitration Service placed many labor-management problems under quasi-judicial control. In 1975 the Employment Protection Act enlarged and formalized the powers of this service, which became the Advisory Conciliation and Arbitration Service (ACAS). In many respects Britain only rediscovered the problems of a highly diverse but powerful labor movement. Like the CBI, the TUC hoped to see unions merge and stabilize industrial relations. But inflation and economic decline multiplied disputes and inescapably generated more elaborate quasi-judicial machinery, which, in turn, opened appeal to the courts. The successful appeals of several independent unions against ACAS decisions that favored the TUC affiliates revealed the problems of making industrial relations policy in the courts and again aroused union resentment over legal interference (*Times*, Nov. 28, 1978). Beneath this issue is the even more serious dilemma of how the individual rights of the liberal state will be reconciled with the collective rights of large organizations and interests that are a consequence of the welfare state.

The unfortunate effect is that the parliamentary process tends to become a shuttlecock for the expression of short-term union and employer goals while little can be accomplished on the larger front of incomes and economic policy generally. The Employment Protection (Amendment) Act of early 1978, for example, responded to loopholes in closed shop procedures after a union defeat in the Grunwick strike (Rogaly, 1977). Disciplined unions such as those in West Germany can iron out internal disputes without constantly invoking party politics. Even the much weaker French union organizations resolve many troublesome disputes at the plant level in part because the more ideological aims of workers mean that national agreements are likely to raise even more embarrassing political differences. Impressed by German codetermination and other forms of labor participation in Scandinavian countries, Labour hoped that new policies to advance industrial democracy might alleviate these nagging problems and pave the way for better understanding of national economic problems. After a serious row within a divided cabinet and among jealous ministries a Committee of Inquiry on Industrial Democracy (Bullock Committee) was finally created in late 1975 (see Elliott, 1978, pp. 205–20).

When the Committee reported in 1977, the paradoxical result was that the two groups, Labour and the TUC, who might seem most eager to have industrial democracy were less than enthusiastic. The CBI (1977) was implacably opposed, while the TUC retreated from its earlier enthusiastic position (1974). The 1977 TUC Congress endorsed labor participation, but the motion expressed concern that it would weaken collective bargaining. It was also coupled to demands for full disclosure of industrial strategic plans, which is virtually impossible to do with interlocking corporate structures. In 1978 the TUC added public sector participation demands that the prime minister, Callaghan, rejected. By the time the government White Paper appeared in May 1978, Bullock was virtually a lost cause.

Thus Britain emerged from a decade of turbulent policymaking with very little to show. The concessions that Labour had made to unions over 1974–79 only provided reasons for the Conservatives in late 1979 to try once again to undo union gains. The secretary of state for employment, Prior, clearly did not want to repeat the fiasco of the Heath government (see Reading 4-5), but Conservatives were intent on removing some of the excessive powers of unions by outlawing secondary picketing (picketing related firms and thereby shutting down an industry over small disputes) and by qualifying closed shop restrictions (a vote of 80 percent of the workers would be needed). There are few countries where these proposals would seem oppressive, but they quickly set in motion the same intransigience that has plagued British labor-management relations for most of the century.

In a world of economic interdependence and easily transferred economic crises, the task of industrial relations policy becomes more and more to make adjustments to changing industrial opportunities and international pressures. Without an underlying consensus about the aims of economic policy such as exists in Germany or Sweden, industrial relations easily deteriorate into the tug-of-war found in Britain. The welfare state casts government as both employer and defender of the public interest. Strikes that shut down hospitals and fire departments are only the more dramatic evidence of the two-edged sword now wielded by public sector unions. Public employment forces government toward a nonpartisan position, for neither party can afford the public wrath that defeated Wilson and Heath. Public sector wage settlements are often more difficult to negotiate than private sector agreements. The productivity and quality of public service is notoriously difficult to calculate, making objective standards elusive. Unskilled public workers suffer from the enhanced bargaining power of more professional government workers, thereby increasing wage differentials and further aggravating conflict. By 1977 the voluntary wage restraints that Callaghan had organized in 1975 and 1976 deteriorated as professional and white-collar unions rejected flat-rate wage increases that eroded incomes differentials.

As Basnett points out (Reading 4-3), there has never been any such thing as totally free collectively bargaining. Since 1940 there have been very few years when Britain was without some form of wage restraint. As Clegg points out (1976, p. 445), successive governments have tried since 1960 to devise a new industrial relations system and from 1969 their policies became "frantic": "Politics and institutions followed each other in bewildering confusion, and governments of both major parties advertised their failure by swinging from one extreme to the other." In the welfare state there can be no constructive arena for industrial relations unless economic priorities and aims can be agreed upon. Parliament is unable to point the way toward reconciliation, and one-party government only seems to exacerbate and intensify conflict.

Readings

4-1. TRYING ORGANIZATIONAL SOLUTIONS TO INDUSTRIAL CONFLICT*

The Donovan Report on the dual system of collective bargaining saw industrial conflict originating in the incompatibilities of the formal and informal structure of industrial relations. Concentrating on the labor management problems of the private sector, the Report looked to organizational change to relieve conflict.

143. We can now compare the two systems of industrial relations. The formal system assumes industry-wide organisations capable of imposing their decisions on their members. The informal system rests on the wide autonomy of managers in individual companies and factories, and the power of industrial work groups.

144. The formal system assumes that most if not all matters appropriate to collective bargaining can be covered in industry-wide agreements. In the informal system bargaining in the factory is of equal or greater importance.

145. The formal system restricts collective bargaining to a narrow range of issues. The range in the informal system is far wider, including discipline, recruitment, redundancy and work practices.

146. The formal system assumes that pay is determined by industry-wide agreements. In the informal system many important decisions governing pay are taken within the factory.

147. The formal system assumes that collective bargaining is a matter of reaching written agreements. The informal system consists largely in tacit arrangements and understandings, and in custom and practice.

148. For the formal system the business of industrial relations in the factory is joint consultation and the interpretation of collec-

*Royal Commission on Trades Unions and Employers' Associations, *Report* (Donovan Report, cmnd. 3623; London: HMSO, 1968), pp. 36–37.

tive agreements. In the informal system the difference between joint consultation and collective bargaining is blurred, as is the distinction between disputes over interpretation and disputes over new concessions; and the business of industrial relations in the factory is as much a matter of collective bargaining as it is at industry level.

149. The formal and informal system are in conflict. The informal system undermines the regulative effect of industry-wide agreements. The gap between industry-wide agreed rates and actual earnings continues to grow. Procedure agreements fail to cope adequately with disputes arising within factories. Nevertheless, the assumptions of the formal system still exert a powerful influence over men's minds and prevent the informal system from developing into an effective and orderly method of regulation. The assumption that industry-wide agreements control industrial relations leads many companies to neglect their responsibility for their own personnel policies. Factory bargaining remains informal and fragmented, with many issues left to custom and practice. The unreality of industry-wide pay agreements leads to the use of incentive schemes and overtime payments for purposes quite different from those they were designed to serve.

150. Any suggestions that conflict between the two systems can be resolved by forcing the informal system to comply with the assumptions of the formal system should be set aside. Reality cannot be forced to comply with pretences.

4-2. LEGAL RESPONSIBILITIES OF TRADE UNIONS*

In his "Note of Reservation" to the Donovan Report, Shonfield argued that a voluntaristic approach to collective bargaining, even if possible and implemented, is inadequate in a modern industrial society. Like other large organizations, unions have acquired great social and economic power. Their rights and obligations should be spelled out in law.

5. It seems inconceivable in the long run that in a society which is increasingly closely knit, where the provision of services to meet the elementary needs of a civilised daily life depends more and

*Andrew Shonfield, "Note of Reservation," in Royal Commission on Trades Unions and Employers' Associations, *Report* (Donovan Report, cmnd. 3623; London: HMSO, 1968), pp. 289–91.

more on the punctual performance of interrelated work tasks of a collective character, trade unions will be treated as if they had the right to be exempt from all but the most rudimentary legal obligations. This is the traditional view, which has bitten deep into the British system of industrial relations. It is what the TUC in their evidence to the Royal Commission referred to as the principle of 'abstention, of formal indifference' on the part of the state (paragraph 174). The principle has been breached over a widening area, largely as a result of the advance of the welfare state and the effort to guarantee for workpeople by law more rights and benefits—redundancy payments, better industrial training, fairer contracts of employment—than collective bargaining had been able to secure for them. It will be breached further if the recommendations of the Royal Commission, especially on the regulation of dismissals from employment, are accepted.

6. But all the while the myth that the act of regulation is a falling from grace and that each case is to be treated as a regrettable exception, which must not in any circumstances be generalised, continues to influence powerfully the judgment of many of those concerned with industrial relations. Since my own view differs profoundly from this received opinion, it is necessary to say something briefly on the general topic of the place of law in an industrial system.

7. I start from the proposition that the deliberate abstention of the law from the activities of mighty subjects tends to diminish the liberty of the ordinary citizen and to place his welfare at risk. If organisations are powerful enough to act the bully then very special grounds are necessary to justify the decision not to subject their behaviour to legal rules. The legal rules need not be much brought into play in practice; if such organisations enforce their own systems of rules and these work in the public interest there will be little actual labour for the law to do. But the content of the rules and the way that they operate in particular cases must not be allowed to escape from close public surveillance. I therefore regard the principle which is stated in paragraph 471 of the Report to be characteristic of the British system, that collective bargaining should remain "outside the law," to be wrong. The special grounds for treating trade unions in this way which seem to have influenced the 19th and early 20th century legislators, who laid down the framework of rules which govern British industrial relations to-

day, were essentially that trade unionism was an unpleasant conspiracy of a kind which would be reprehensible if practised by anyone else but which had to be tolerated in this particular instance as the only available means of conducting relations between employers and the representatives of workpeople. However, it was felt to be wrong for the law to do anything to support such a conspiracy, e.g. by making any of the agreements among the conspirators enforceable as ordinary legal contracts. The only course was to leave the trade unions to their own devices.

8. Historically the doctrine of the "licensed conspiracy" served a useful social purpose. The trade unions were weak and vulnerable at the time, and the respectable prejudice against them, which was shared by judges, would almost certainly have meant that legal decisions on matters affecting their affairs would have tended to inhibit their growth. The removal of these matters from the purview of the courts therefore helped the British trade unions to establish themselves as the large and influential bodies which they are today. But now that they have evolved to this dominant role, it would be highly anomalous if the legal prejudices of an earlier generation were to continue to be used to encourage them to avoid undertaking ordinary contractual obligations in their relations with employers or to permit their actions to escape the public regulation which has come to be accepted as the common lot of corporate bodies wielding economic power.

9. It is true that the trade union is in the last resort a fighting organisation; its business is to be equipped to be able to make a nuisance of itself in pursuit of the interests of its members. The reform suggested here is not intended to reduce its capacity to fight. But the trade union is also a regulative body: it makes rules about the way in which certain economic activities are to be conducted and about who is to be allowed to conduct them. Where these rules appear to run counter to the welfare of the community, e.g. in sustaining restrictive work practices which make things more expensive than they need be, they should be subjected to public scrutiny. And the trade union concerned should be placed under an obligation to justify these rules, if it wishes to maintain them, by reference to a set of criteria established by legislation which take account of the public interest as well as the interest of the particular group of workers directly involved. A specific proposal on the control of restrictive practices is made later in this note.

4-3. PUBLIC SECTOR EMPLOYMENT, INCOMES POLICY, AND INFLATION*

By 1977, labor-management relations had been substantially changed because industrial conflict had become a much greater threat to the society and because of the growth of public sector employment. David Basnett, general secretary of the GMWU, outlines the links to incomes policy and inflation. He points out how new problems will require new initiatives from both unions and government.

The current firemen's dispute has highlighted, in a dramatic and potentially tragic way, the problems and inadequacies of wage determination in public services. I do not wish to comment in detail on that dispute but on the basic problems which apply not only to firemen, but to local authority manual workers, town hall administrators, civil servants, policemen and teachers as well. The unwanted confrontation with the firemen has simply underlined the anomalous position of all public servants under any incomes policy.

There are over six million workers in the public services, employees of national and local government and its agencies, with another 1½ m workers in nationalised industries and Government-owned companies. The public services sector has been the country's fastest growing area of employment. It has the most developed and systematic structure of industrial relations, but also the most centralised. It is the most intensively unionised, about 80 per cent of public employees being union members, against a national average of 50 per cent. Yet fundamental issues of industrial relations and elementary problems of collective bargaining have yet to be resolved.

Decisions on the pay of public servants inevitably become a matter for political decision and public discussion. The pay claims of public service workers become a test of whichever incomes policy prevails at the time. Every last penny and every last percentage point in their settlements becomes a test of the Government's 'machismo'.

There are at least four broad types of incomes policy, and in all of them the public sector bears the brunt of enforcement.

*David Basnett, "A Way Out of Warfare over Pay," *Sunday Times* (London), Dec. 4, 1977 (selections).

1. Statutory incomes policies, like Labour's of the 1960s or Heath's three-stage counter-inflation policy. Under them the public sector, with centralised wage bargaining and rigid control, is bound to stick more rigorously to the policy than the private sector, where substantial wage drift occurs.

2. Agreed voluntary policies, like the agreements of the past two years between the Labour Government and the TUC. In these cases again, public services cannot get around the agreed ceiling (though on the other hand they can be expected to get the maximum rise permitted by the policy without a great deal of difficulty).

3. Unilateral non-statutory policies, like the present 10 per cent limit where, apart from the 12-month rule, there is no agreement between the TUC and the Government on a wages formula. Settlements in the private sector have already shown more flexibility, though not those in the public sector.

4. Allegedly no policy, like the early years of the Heath Government, when the guinea pigs for its $n - 1$ approach, in which each settlement was supposed to be one per cent lower than the one before, were the public services. As a result, groups such as local authority workers, teachers, civil servants and hospital workers were, often for the first time, driven to industrial action.

It is an inevitable fact of life that there will always be a formal or informal incomes policy for the public services, where there can never be totally "free collective bargaining."

I am not arguing that public service workers are inevitably and invariably worse treated by Government than are workers employed in the private sector. The treatment of the public services varies according to the economic and political climate that currently prevails. What I am arguing is that incomes policies are operated with far greater rigidity towards the public sector than towards the private.

Government, in its role as employer, regards the current norms or pay ceilings as far more important than the more mundane, but ultimately more important, problems of industrial relations which are the bread and butter of collective bargaining throughout the rest of the economy; such things as wage structures, manning levels, productivity, incentives and differentials. The problems which this lack of flexibility on pay brings are further compounded by the extremely centralised nature of the negotiating machinery in the public services.

4-4. DIFFICULT CHOICES FOR THE TUC*

In addition to the many differences among unions in organization and objectives, there is an even more perplexing problem of how the TUC can align itself in a strong two-party system. With high unemployment and economic decline, the political choice for the TUC becomes even more ambiguous. Jack Peel, director of public relations, Directorate of Employment and Social Affairs, EEC, describes these dilemmas.

Governments may come and go but the TUC, like Tennyson's brook, goes on forever. The implications of this permanence are unlikely to be heard from the rostrum at Brighton this week, but they should be considered. In the grip of pre-election fever the TUC is likely to be cosier and more conspiratorial than usual.

Understandably, the loud noises will be orchestrated in support of the Labour Government, thus stifling what might have been trenchant criticism of incomes policy and high unemployment.

Whatever the outcome of the election the TUC will remain a powerful and influential pressure group. For the TUC to prefer Labour is one thing—but it would be wise not to give too many hostages to fortune. To be able to work with any government implies moderation, strong leadership and a minimum of political sabre rattling.

In the heavy atmosphere of this week's debate it may shock younger delegates to learn that in postwar years the TUC General Council has sometimes worked more smoothly and efficiently with a Tory rather than Labour administration.

The historical and political affinity between Labour and the trade unions has meant that both sides have tended to take each other for granted. They have expected too much from each other and their relationships have been tetchy and sometimes turbulent, as in 1969 on the White Paper *In Place of Strife*.

Relationships between the TUC and Conservative governments have generally been cooler and more formal, though impeccably correct. Neither side has taken chances and progress has been made as a consequence. This pattern was soured on the Conserva-

*Jack Peel, "Awkward Questions for the Unions," *The Times* (London), Sept. 5, 1978 (selections).

tive side by the devastating argument over the Industrial Relations Act and sweetened for Labour by the crisis-induced social contract—both issues bringing instinctive though opposite reactions from the TUC.

Paradoxically, a Labour victory at the next election could bring bigger heartaches for the TUC than Conservative success. Labour is determined to continue some form of incomes policy as a continuing arrangement and is also committed to legislation or industrial democracy.

On both of these issues TUC-affiliated unions are divided. To take them seriously would mean fresh responsibilities for trade unions, including full reform of wage structures and a new breed of bargainers. It would indeed involve change in the adversary style of trade unions and a challenge to their *whole raison d'être*.

If the Conservatives win the election, they are likely to take a softer line on both points; though the need for some form of incomes policy should be above the party battle. The Tories will certainly not try to put the unions in a legislative straitjacket, bearing in mind the disaster over the Industrial Relations Act.

Surprisingly, the real danger to the TUC is not from a rampaging Conservative government, but from within its own ranks—from those trade unionists who are willing to allow it remain a prisoner of its history in order to avoid the trauma of change.

It is painfully evident that free collective bargaining does not provide social justice between different groups of workers and never can because of its inherent crudity. Justice must surely come from order, not anarchy. However daunting the task, the TUC should try to plan fairer wages structures within an overall framework of economic reality devised by the Government and both sides of industry.

Clearly the expectation of responsible behaviour must be balanced with a meeting of material needs so that the best behaved do not always have to be equated with the lowest paid. Moderates have always seemed to be penalized for their reasonableness in British trade unions.

Over the years the TUC has forced the pace of change and made a firm and beneficial impact on governments and society, but primarily as a weapon of defence—not as a positive instrument of change. Britain's problems are now so urgent and complex that unions must believe in change themselves in order to be effective in changing society.

You would not normally put a teetotaller in charge of a drinking contest. In the same way if unions press for drastic changes in the social order, they should accept that they are part of the society they are trying to change, and adjust their thinking and actions accordingly.

Conservatism is hardly the best breeding ground for radicalism. Britain gave birth to football and trade unionism and is still regarded with a basic reverence in both fields by countries which have overtaken us. To regain the World Cup, so to speak the TUC will have to look to its laurels.

4-5. CONSERVATIVES SEEK TO RESTRAIN TRADE UNIONS*

When the Thatcher government was returned in 1979, the Conservatives were committed to restricting some of the most disruptive union practices. Much to the discontent of more reactionary elements of the Party, Prior designed a compromise bill concentrating on secondary effects of strikes and on union elections and avoiding the worst of the Conservative's disastrous 1971 Act. A Guardian *editorial speculates on the next stage of Britain's tortuous industrial-labor relations.*

In a wholly understandable attempt to avoid comparison with Ted Heath's ill-fated efforts to sort out the unions, Mr. James Prior, the Employment Secretary, has discreetly disguised his Industrial Relations Bill as an "Employment Bill" on the Commons order paper. More importantly, Mr. Prior has also abandoned the scatter-shot approach of the former prime minister. This time around, the Conservatives are going for limited restrictions on secondary and flying picketing and the operation of the closed shop. They are making "coercive recruitment" of union members an offence which would leave union officials open to action for civil damages—if an employer chooses to pursue the matter. Finally, Mr. Prior is offering public money to those unions who wish to conduct secret strike ballots or secret elections for union posts.

Even so the trumpets have sounded at Congress House, where Mr. Len Murray has already prophesied that the Bill will turn British industrial relations into a "battle-ground." Some union activists are even talking of a rerun of the round of illegal strikes,

*"Objections, but No Kneejerks" (editorial), *The Guardian*, Dec. 8, 1979 (selections).

refusals to recognise courts of law, to pay fines or obey injunctions, the arrests, the imprisonments, the politically motivated protest strikes, which subverted the Heath legislation, and did much to destroy his Government. A few activists—not many but certainly some—will spend this weekend reading the small print in the Bill and preparing quite deliberately to engineer confrontations. The majority of trade unionists, in the silence of their homes, might well be asking instead whether the Bill is really as bad as kneejerk reaction would have us believe.

The question breaks down into three parts. Is the Bill fair? Is it workable? Is it relevant? After all the chaos of last winter, with widespread secondary and flying picketing—the obstruction of companies and services not directly involved in disputes by pickets, many of whom were not directly involved in the particular disputes themselves—and the ruthless enforcement of closed shops in recent years, there is no doubt that some order is needed.

If the TUC is unwilling or unable to deal with the excesses—however occasional—of its members, then it should not be unduly surprised if the State intervenes. More so when a government has just been returned on a manifesto which included specific pledges to deal with exactly the issues Mr. Prior is now attempting to tackle.

So it is hard to object in principle to the Bill. In practice, in the shoddy, shabby world of industrial compromise, will it work? The Government has gone to some lengths to see that it will. Learning from bitter experience, ministers have avoided creating new criminal offences and new industrial relations courts to try them. Thus secondary picketing will not be a crime to be controlled by policemen. Instead an employer who feels sufficiently damaged by secondary pickets can seek an injunction. And only if that injunction is ignored, can the pickets eventually be liable to contempt charges or actions for damages.

To summarize. Is the Bill fair? In context, yes. Is it workable? Mostly, with a little bit of luck. Is it relevant? To the civilised conduct of disputes, just about. But to our fundamental industrial ills, inflationary wage bargaining, ill disciplined, competitive unions, unconstitutional and unofficial stoppages, a deep desire to maintain restrictive practices, the Employment Bill offers no solutions at all. Mr. Prior is wise enough to recognise this. So are most of his colleagues. It is far from clear that the unions, or Conservative rank and file voters, will show the same sophistication.

5 Local and Regional Policies: The Rejection of Territorial Politics

The concentration of policymaking powers in Westminster and Whitehall, described in Chapter 1, has severely limited the capacity of the British political system to deal with localized policy conflicts and choices. Nearly every other modern democratic state has well-defined organizational links to lower-level governments. This organizational network becomes the conduit for localized influence of various kinds on the center and, in turn, also serves the center in establishing its policy goals at lower levels of the political system, monitoring results, and adjusting procedures. In West Germany or the United States this network is constitutionally established within the federal system, while in France the unified administrative system provides these contacts with subordinate areas and regions. Contrary to the expectation that spatial and locational aspects of policymaking would decline with the growth of government, these considerations now appear to loom larger in importance because of the complexities of policymaking and policy implementation in the welfare state.

The difficulties that Britain has experienced in making and executing territorially defined policies are best seen by examining an apparent paradox in the history of British policymaking for lower-level governments. On the one hand, the former local government system is of paramount importance in the execution and management of national policy. The central bureaucracy of Britain, described in Chapter 2, is relatively isolated for a unitary state and has few territorial outposts. Whitehall could not survive without the nearly 3 million local government officials who provide education, housing, and many social services. British local government accounts for roughly a third of all public spending and employs about 10 percent of the working population. On the other hand,

Westminster seems able to ignore the policy role of local government with impunity. No modern government can exist without making spatial and locational decisions. What differentiates Britain from France, which also has a unitary system, is how easily national policymakers can act without careful consultation with local government and how easily national objectives are imposed on this vast subnational structure.

The paradox of center-local policy and politics in Britain is accentuated because local and regional policies are so crucial to the British system, while the policymaking links between subordinate areas and the center are so poorly developed compared to other welfare states. There is nothing approaching the *réseau*, or network, that characterizes French center-local relationships, and obviously none of the constitutionally legitimized conflict of federal systems. British aversion toward territorial politics is deeply rooted in her constitutional and institutional history. In historic regional conflicts, such as the seventeenth-century wars with Scotland or the nineteenth-century rebellion in Ireland, the English have been prepared to make territorial compromises that would be unacceptable in most European countries. Indeed the extent to which Scotland retains an identity and a separate governmental machinery, and the quasi-federal arrangement worked out for Northern Ireland, suggest that it is not simply constitutional or institutional inflexibility that produces the detachment between central and local policymaking in the British system. When forced to deal with strong territorial dissent, Britain has been fairly resourceful and not confined by old dogmas. Nonetheless, the question remains whether policymaking in the finely tuned and complex welfare state can effectively proceed if national crises are required to bring about territorial involvement in the policy process.

Context

Perhaps the major territorial crises are not a good indicator of underlying attitudes toward the solution of spatial and locational policy problems because Britain is geographically isolated and dissidence never posed the threat to national hegemony that it did for the continental countries, where political rivals were quick to seize upon separatist movements. Likewise, the historical unification of Britain proceeded without foreign intervention (at least since Mary Queen of Scots), so territorial politics could be treated with more detachment, if no less brutality, than in the rest of Europe. As a secondary effect, these historical conditions meant that, in the evolution of British government, the center never needed to have as close touch with localities as, for example, France needed in both the *ancien régime* and during its stormy progress toward republican government. Britain's historical advantage may now be a policymaking disadvantage, however, for it precluded the need for close and continuous contact with local leaders, provincial cities, and regional forces that permeates the history of other Western European countries and Japan.

Even within England there was not the same need to construct machinery for center-local bargaining over policy objectives that can be found in most European countries. The emergence of the liberal state in eighteenth-century England is probably another example of the advantages of being an early innovator. The relatively harmonious upper-class interests that dominated both parliamentary and local life have in fact been used by one distinguished historian to explain Britain's early political stability (Plumb, 1969). More difficult to explain is how the common interests of the aristocracy and gentry could continue to dominate local government until nearly the twentieth century. Because the British franchise steadily expanded throughout the nineteenth century, it is sometimes assumed that democratic government made equally steady inroads into policymaking at both levels of government.

But the inadequacy of Victorian local government did not arrest the flow of new responsibilities and functions to the local level. Starting from the reorganization of the Poor Law Unions in 1834, a stream of new responsibilities were assigned to newly created local bodies for health, education, police, and sanitation. National leaders were justifiably suspicious of leaving these important functions to the mercy of the turbulent local politics and the clumsy local administration of the time. The result was the rapid proliferation of *ad hoc* local boards, governed by separate statutes and responsible to national inspectors. The British local government system was, quite simply, unfit to govern. Until 1888 there were about twenty different types of local authorities and over 30,000 diverse units of local government similar to the French system of communes. Although the Local Government Act of 1888 installed democratic control and orderly government at the local level, the British local councils found themselves burdened with immense responsibilities that had accumulated over the century. In a way, it is this heavy functional responsibility of British local government that has prevented it from having a policy impact at higher levels of government and, thereby, developing the more complex network of intervention and bargaining with the center that we find in nearly every other country.

There are basically two ways that local actors can gain access to national decisionmaking: infiltration of the administrative procedures linking levels of government or exploitation of electoral and legislative politics to project local preferences onto the national scene. A number of circumstances determine which of these routes will be taken to influence national policymaking as it affects localities. In France, for example, the *réseau* integrates the administration with local designs and politics. In the United States, logrolling and patronage politics have made it relatively easy for local politicians to gain access to Congress and the executive. In Britain neither of these avenues was open to local politicians. The relatively disciplined and nationally oriented party politics of the late nineteenth century left little room for local political leaders to exploit their territorial power bases to gain entry to Parliament. On the administrative side, the counties and boroughs prided themselves on their self-reliance and autonomy. In the meantime strong national ministries grew and came to dominate policymaking in the major policy areas. To some extent the competitiveness of national politics, including tensions created by the rise of the Labour Party after the turn of the century, produced a steady stream of national legislation that simply kept local government too busy to engage in direct bargaining with Westminster and Whitehall.

An important organizational element in this pattern was that local government never had a single advocate at the center. Central responsibility for local affairs was divided among the central departments bearing the responsibilities for local services. Ambitious cabinet ministers did not (and still do not) want to see their positions qualified, nor does cabinet government, as noted in Chapter 1, facilitate central coordination. Until 1951 there was no central department bearing the name "Local Government," and then it was ensconced within the Ministry of Housing and Local Government, whose primary political aim was to fulfill the Conservative election pledge of more housing. From 1888, local matters had gravitated toward the Ministry of Health, whose concern for sanitation and public health had provided the impetus for local reform in the nineteenth century. Nor did the old counties and boroughs manage to speak with a collective voice at the national level. Although the local government associations dated from late Victorian England, there were (and remain) separate associations for counties, boroughs, and districts (the second tier of county government). The main objective of the associations was to maneuver private bills through Parliament in order to exempt individual cities, districts, or counties from parliamentary or administrative constraints.

In a way that is structurally similar to the sectoral problem of labor relations, discussed in Chapter 4, national politics and administration in Britain have managed to keep local government, and with it the territorial and locational complications of policymaking, at arm's length. Just as national government never developed the organization and contacts needed to engage labor and management more directly in pressing issues of economic policy and labor relations, so also the local and regional extensions of the political system are not very directly *engaged* in the policymaking process. Some aspects of local policy are intensely debated, such as comprehensive schools or public housing, but these issues are defined by *national* parties. Neither political nor administrative intergovernmental links enable localities to have a consistent or influential role in deciding more general policies. Where severe differences occur in center-local negotiations, there are few alternatives to confrontation. As we have seen in the case of both economic policymaking and labor relations, the system does not seem to anticipate policy conflicts very well nor does it easily involve adversaries to avoid conflicts. Most of these problems are recognized in Britain and in fact are the theme of a Central Policy Review Staff study (1977) of center-local relations.

In the era of the welfare state Britain is not alone in inheriting a local government structure that was designed to operate in the laissez-faire setting of the liberal state. More to the point, the system never served as an effective national policymaking instrument, nor is there much evidence that national politicians or officials wanted it to be such. Until 1972 (the Act actually came into force in 1974) there were in fact four different local government structures: the Greater London Council with thirty-two metropolitan boroughs; the fifty-eight counties of England and Wales with a two-tier structure embracing 259 "non-county" boroughs, 522 urban districts, and 469 rural districts; eighty-three unitary and more urban county boroughs; and the Scottish local governments still organized around "burghs" and connected to the Scottish Office. If one extends the definition to the United Kingdom, the local government of Northern Ireland provides a fifth component. Each of these components had different functional authority, and, of course, their various functions were frequently amended by statute to make local government law in Britain a tangle that only the most experienced could understand.

For those at the helm of government the British local government system was (and in many respects remains) a bewildering array of choices. The system eludes easy attachment to national objectives (see Reading 5-3). In 1971 the largest county, Lancashire, contained over 2.5 million persons, while the smallest, Radnorshire, had less than 20,000 persons. The largest county borough, Birmingham, had more than a million persons, but the smallest, Canterbury, a bit more than 35,000 persons. Similar variations existed in their size and their resources (property values). From a policymaking perspective, the system defied generalization, thereby making it virtually impossible to pass a law in other than fairly specific, functional terms with any hope of having uniform effects throughout the system. The complex structure also meant that local governments were so diverse that they had great difficulty resolving their own common spatial problems, such as finding land for housing, and even greater difficulty forming any kind of political coalition to extract concessions from the center.

The de-politicization of British local government is more apparent than real, but in a curious way center-local politics are not geared to policymaking. Perhaps the best illustration of this is the formulation of local government problems provided by the Royal Commission on Local Government in England, which reported in 1969 (Reading 5-1). In few other countries could the complexities of center-local policymaking be so easily reduced to a series of dichotomized choices. The structure itself pits rural areas (counties) against cities (boroughs), creating the historic issue of "town versus country." The territorial organization of France disperses this issue while the more overt patronage politics of the United States assures that each territory (states and cities) can extract benefits from the system. The extent to which the town versus country issue fits the underlying parliamentary and party structure of British politics does not seem wholly accidental. It also helps explain why British local governments feel less need to act in concert because the political structure itself reflects their urban-rural division.

Even the highly complex functional role of local government in Britain has often been reduced to "democracy versus efficiency," suggesting a more straightforward choice than any other democratic political system would consider possible. In their most wildly rational moments the French have seldom underestimated the organizational pitfalls between formulating an objective and implementing a policy. British preoccupation with efficiency in local government matters has a long history, but it also reveals a startling naiveté about the complexity of policy itself, particularly when execution and evaluation must take place under such diverse circumstances. The testimony of the various central government departments to the Royal Commission is replete with evidence on how much the optimum size, resources, and facilities of areas for local services vary from one function to another. But a highly centralized system rules out the possibilities of using local bargaining and cooperation as a way of constructing solutions and defining areas. Nor are intermediate solutions such as setting minimum levels of local services and benefits acceptable to central policymakers.

The curious effect is that Westminster and Whitehall can neither let go of local government nor very easily bend it to fit central designs. In some policy areas such as education the Department of Education exercises minute control over schools. In other areas such as public housing there is less detailed control, but almost immovable controls on financing and rents. The unavoidable diversity of controls means that government in fact is rather poorly armed to influence local choices in any comprehensive way. Most of the formal weapons are *post hoc* like the audit and budget review. The less formal controls that emanate from Whitehall in the form of circulars, consultation papers, and general advice have no standard form or meaning. All this tends to place more influence in the hands of national and local administrators, who understand the mysteries of center-local relationships in each policy area. A byproduct of this system is that the functional committees of the local councils exercise immense influence over local policymaking. One of the striking paradoxes of the 1972 reorganization was that Parliament hoped to eliminate uncoordinated and unresponsive decisionmaking within local government while these remain critical policymaking problems within Whitehall itself.

Agenda

A more detailed examination of the history of local and regional reform in Britain would show that it has never really been "off" the political agenda. The subnational structure of government has a strange nagging quality in every political system and somehow never seems to go away. How and when major change occurs, however, provide distinct junctions of politics and policy. The British are distinguished among the welfare states in trying to bring about a global reform of the local government system between 1965, when the issue was given priority, and 1974, when the new system went into effect. Lest one be too critical of the shortcomings of British politics, it must first be recognized that it is the concentration of power in Westminster that made this ambitious enterprise possible. The only major welfare state that has approached the scale of the British reorganization is Sweden, though West Germany, France, and others have programs to consolidate local government. The simple act of making a frontal attack on so complex a structure tells us a great deal about the prestige and influence of Westminster.

Since World War II, the British knew that the local government system had to be changed. The Attlee Labour government (1945–51) had a massive majority and could easily have changed the system, but it was understandably heavily occupied with the national reforms that Labour wanted to enact. Such things as the nationalization of health sent shock waves through local government but, in spending terms and other functions, local government remained a major segment of the political system. Between 1951 and 1964 the Conservatives concentrated on the housing responsibilities of local government, and on overhauling the grant system, a goal they achieved in the Local Government Act of 1958. But in terms of bringing spatial policies in line with functional needs not much was accomplished.

The procrastination in itself is not particularly surprising. Nearly every prime minister since Peel has expressed his distaste for interfering with local government. In Britain the reasons are twofold. First, the national institutions are heavily dependent on *not* having local politics and policy compromise the status of cabinet and parliamentary government. Important new localized activities, most notably the aggressive program to build new towns after 1948 and renewed assistance to depressed areas, were organized outside the formal local government system. Both cabinet members and Members of Parliament knew then as now that local government is a Pandora's box. Areal conflicts, some of them dating from Victorian England, disrupt local constituency associations, make poor electoral ammunition, and divide parliamentary parties. Unlike France and the United States, national party organizations do not depend heavily on the party leaders within local government, and they, in turn, are so busy with their daily problems that reorganization is not popular with local militants. In short, there is very little political mileage and a great deal of political conflict in local reform.

Second, it was quite clear that raising local reform would create severe cross-pressures within both major parties. For twenty years Whitehall had a series of boundary commissions at work to try to work out sensible territorial compromises. The main lesson had been learned with the first post-war inquiry under Sir Malcolm Trustam Eve, who wound up doing battle with the local government hydra with one arm tied behind his back. After months of fruitless negotiation and investigation he simply resigned because the government would not give him permission to reallocate the functions of local government as he tried to adjust the areas. The reluctance of central policymakers to permit both dimensions of local government, functions and areas, to enter into the struggle for local reform is an important explanation of why most reforms fail. Labour wanted to intervene directly in the delivery of services and benefits and was most concerned with individual equity. To concede more functional choices to lower levels of government would threaten their most cherished goal. The Conservatives adopted a similarly functionalist view of local government for more traditional reasons. Local governments with more initiative at the national level would be a threat to their conception of representation and constitutional order.

Since there were no clearly defined national party interests that could be tied to local reform, local government reorganization would probably not have become a national issue were it not for the decision of a rather impetuous minister, Richard Crossman. The Labour government of 1964 had a small majority and there were serious divisions within the cabinet. Like earlier prime ministers, Wilson had no great interest in local government, nor did most of the Labour leaders. The reform efforts of the previous Conservative government, however, had led to the appointment of a Committee on Local Government Management under Sir John Maud (now Lord Redcliffe-Maud) and a Committee on the Staffing of Local Government under Sir George Mallaby. Both groups were occupied with local government as an efficiency problem. Their existence meant that the minister for housing and local government could easily postpone a more general inquiry, and Crossman was most interested in public housing, a much more lively political issue. For reasons that are still not entirely clear (Jones, 1966), Crossman decided to drop his bombshell in September 1965, when he announced the government's intention to form a major Royal Commission on Local Government. The decision appears to have been only briefly discussed in cabinet, though Crossman was close to Wilson and they had undoubtedly talked the idea over privately.

In the fall meeting of the Association of Municipal Corporations (the boroughs' national association, now the Association of Municipal Authorities) Crossman charged that "the whole structure of local government is out of date, that our county boroughs and county councils as at present organized are archaic institutions" (Crossman, 1965). He spoke out vehemently against the Conservatives' 1958 legislation that kept town and country distinct. The decision drifted for a few months until the Boundary Commission's recommendations for Lancashire appeared, which might have cost Labour as many as twenty parliamentary seats (Crossman, 1975, pp. 439–41). With the additional political incentive of an excuse to delay parliamentary redistricting, Wilson and Crossman proceeded to appoint a Royal Commission. There was virtually no discussion in cabinet, and after a rather desultory search for a Commission chairman it appeared best to link the Royal Commission to the existing Committee on Local Government Management by making Sir John Maud chairman. Conforming to the segmented structure of British local government, separate inquiries were launched for Scotland and Northern Ireland. Wales was a special case, for the anamolies of its local organization had long been recognized and posed special problems to Labour, who did not want to upset their Celtic stronghold. Such a disjointed approach to spatial problems is itself evidence of the concentration of policymaking power in British government.

The curiosities of Royal Commissions have been noted in Chapter 1, but the Royal Commission on Local Government in England had good credentials (Stanyer, 1973). All but two of the eleven members had extensive local government experience and four came from the old Committee on Local Government Management. Its research director and his assistant, Jim Sharpe and Bruce Wood, were knowledgable and imaginative students of British local government. The most overtly political act in forming the Commission was to include Derek Senior, whose strong support for a regionalized solution was known and sure to make a unanimous recommendation impossible, which of course would make it easier for the prime minister and cabinet to ignore a Commission's advice. As it turned out, the Commission spent much of its time arguing with Senior, who eventually submitted a dissent that is longer than the report itself.

Like many charges to Royal Commissions, the Local Government Commission had a charge so broad as to be ambiguous: "to consider the structure of Local Government in England, outside Greater London, in relation to its existing functions; and to make recommendations for authorities and boundaries, and for functions and their division, having regard to the size and character of areas in which these can be most effectively exercised and the need to sustain a viable system of local democracy." But, again like most charges to Royal Commissions, the exclusions are most important. The Royal Commission by its constitution omitted about a third of the British population: London, Scotland, Wales, and Northern Ireland. They were free to examine the distribution of functions *within* the local government system, but not in relation to central government. Though their report contains a brief discussion of center-local relationships, the activities of Whitehall remained sacrosanct. This qualification as well as the sheer complexity of totally redrawing the local government map meant that the Commission, though not barred from examining the vexing problem of local finance, could do little on finance, which was later studied by the Committee of Inquiry on Local Finance (the Layfield Committee, 1976).

The Commission was free to consider regional government, but its recommendations for weak provincial councils, which are surprisingly similar to French regional councils, were among the first to be disowned by both parties. By 1969, when the Commission was ready to report, Scottish nationalism was the real threat to the Labour Party. To defuse this issue Wilson was thinking of appointing a Royal Commission on the Constitution, which he did in late 1969, thereby making further delay possible. In 1973 the Constitutional Commission Report contained an entirely new set of regional proposals that were similarly unacceptable to both parties. It is not surprising that the most explosive issues become political decisions. What distinguishes Britain from France, for example, is the ease with which local and regional policy can be divorced from local politics. Neither party wants to see England regionalized or, more accurately, to see the independence of the regional outposts of the central departments threatened by local political leaders. Essentially, the Royal Commission, like all previous inquiries into local government, could examine the system "from below," but not "from above."

Process

The Royal Commission on Local Government recommended that England be divided into sixty-one local government areas, all but three unitary governments. A number of long overdue changes were suggested, such as abolishing the aldermancy, simplifying election procedures, and modernizing local management. The Commission was especially concerned with the participatory aspects of local government: why good candidates could not be found for local elections; why turnout is so low (about a third of the eligible voters usually turn out); and why citizens have little interest in local affairs. The national debate that many hoped would follow never took place, primarily because Britain was plunged into a national election a few months later. The Commission's own surveys (Research Study 9, 1969, p. 128) showed that 65 percent of the people were satisfied with their local government area, and an unfortunate 7 percent wanted even smaller areas.

The Labour government did have time to produce a White Paper (1970) on the Report that begins to reveal qualifications that were eventually to emasculate the recommendations. Labour added two additional two-tiered units to the three conceded by the Commission, thereby reducing the desired unitary authorities from fifty-eight to fifty-one. Fearing that the lower-tier units would abuse their educational powers under the suggested redistribution of powers, counties were given additional educational responsibilities. Local democracy got very short shrift and the "local councils," which were to be little more than advisory neighborhood groups, were rejected. The main problem was (and remains) that Labour's voting strength in the urban areas created a curious dilemma for the party. To achieve its national redistributive aims Labour must either circumvent localities or consolidate small local governments, both of which offend local sensitivities. Electoral logic led Labour to favor larger local units in the 1960s; a decade later their strategy was reversed.

In a dramatic illustration of how adversarial policymaking can upset policy choices, the Conservatives took over reorganization after the 1970 elections. Their spokesman, Peter Walker, who became the secretary of state for the environment, said in 1969 that the Conservatives favored smaller units and two-tiered local government for the whole country. After only eight months in office Walker produced a White Paper (1971) that essentially reversed the intent of the Royal Commission and the Labour government. The more urban areas, the metropolitan counties (the Conservatives also restored the traditional language), were increased to six, but their size was reduced so that they included 12 million people rather than the 16 million persons under the Commission's proposals. The more drastic change was to restore two-tiered government for the rest of the country by creating districts in the more rural or nonmetropolitan counties. In the more urban areas the districts had more powers, but in the rural areas the county had more power. The curious effect was to stand the 1888 arrangements on their heads. Now the urban areas were compromised, with more potential internal conflict, and the rural counties had more centralized powers. Throughout the system the Conservatives imposed their aim of keeping local government small scale and internally checked by the districts.

As argued above, British cabinet and parliamentary government dislikes territorial politics, and the debate on the Local Government Act of 1972 made it quite clear why this is so. Party lines became scrambled and the debate concerned itself largely with rescuing the many small towns and cities that were demoted from boroughs to districts in order to consolidate areas (Wood, 1975). Over 1,800 amendments were made, and some of the more determined local authorities found themselves arguing the case for their preservation for the seventh time in four years. The details of this debate are not essential to uncovering the peculiarities of territorial politics in the British system. The aim of the reform was primarily to find a better functional organization for local government, but the territorial conflicts that surfaced in Parliament tended to undermine and often to reverse the more "rational" system envisaged by Labour. Though the variations in size and population among English local governments were reduced, the thirty-nine nonmetropolitan counties with 296 districts varied from Cornwall and Somerset with under 400,000 persons to Hampshire and Kent with over 1.3 million. Within the six metropolitan counties the thirty-five new districts varied from under 200,000 to more than a million persons in Birmingham. To these differences should be added Welsh local government, with eight counties and thirty-seven districts, and the Scottish system of nine "regions" and forty-nine districts, which created a regional-city system similar to Derek Senior's proposals.

Although there is little evidence that economies of scale can be made in local government, there is also little doubt that democracies would save money if local administration and policymaking were not subject to the vicissitudes of local politics. This said, it is also correct that the consolidation in Britain was expensive even though it is difficult to distinguish the continued soaring costs of the system from the inflationary spiral that followed the reorganization. One county estimated that the changes cost half a million pounds and in at least one case a new municipal headquarters simply landed in another local government area. The more interesting thing is that these obvious costs were apparently not even calculated. Another set of unanticipated costs, which the new areas had to absorb immediately, were large salary increases for most local officials. Salaries are tied to union agreements and based on population. Making local authorities larger mandated increases as well as paying the additional skilled professional staff needed to achieve what was hoped to be more comprehensive, long-term local planning.

The more interesting aspects of the change are those things that did not enter into the studies and debate. Increasing efficiency had been stressed since the Committee on Local Management and was closely related to eliminating compartmentalized decisionmaking in local government committees. Both Labour and Conservatives favored having a "chief executive" who would have overall managerial authority. With considerable variation, most local governments now have a degree of corporate management though the center has few comparable plans and, some would argue, is poorly equipped to use whatever long-term forecasts and plans emerge from imaginative local councils. In any event, how to make this organizational change was an afterthought, and a general model for new local authority management only emerged in the midst of the transition (Bains Report, 1972). At the root of this problem is the reluctance of central departments to release their individual grip, however firm or weak, on local policies in their areas of responsibility. Truly comprehensive and coordinated local authorities are a threat to central departments as well as to national political leaders. In France, by contrast, such organized and coordinated attacks on Paris are commonplace and often as not are assisted by administrative officials. Such complications would be next to treason in British center-local politics.

The territorial complications of the reorganization were enormous, but it may still be asked why so little attention was paid to finances. From early Victorian England to the present it is clear that local taxation and grants were the very stuff of center-local policymaking. In the 1960s, Britain had already been through several inflationary spirals that had disastrous effects on local budgets. Though wage-based inflationary pressures were less evident then, the huge manpower bills falling on local government were known and by then the growing power of local government unions, particularly those organizing semiskilled and manual local workers (the National Association of Local Government Officials and the National Union of Public Employees), were also known. Two-thirds of the local government bill is salaries and wages. The reasons for this oversight are partly explained in Chapter 4, for labor relations have steadily become a matter for central negotiation. Nonetheless, the government had to appoint a Committee of Inquiry on Local Finance once inflation threatened to bankrupt the country and the 4 to 5 percent growth rate of local spending had to stop.

Even more indicative of the national political constraints operating on British local government is the consistently bipartisan attitude against regional government. Throughout the past decade there was proliferation of regional agencies attached to diverse central departments: Area and Regional Health Authorities, Regional Water Authorities, Regional Transport Boards, Regional Planning Councils, Sports Councils, Arts Councils, to name only a few (Ashford, 1976; Hambleton, 1977). Though local authorities are sometimes asked to send representatives to these bodies, this entire overarching policymaking machinery has few organized links to the local level. The regional agencies testify to the complexities of making and executing policy in the welfare state, but unlike the intergovernmental machinery of nearly every other government in Britain they are relatively immune to local demands and isolated from locally defined preferences. One is again struck by how British government gives priority to functional needs, at least as they are defined in Whitehall and Westminster. Every welfare state has such problems, but Britain is extreme in the extent to which it has insulated such growth against local influence. No other government has been so successful in keeping functional and territorial choices distinct, which may be the major weakness of center-local policymaking in Britain.

Consequences

The reorganization of local government between 1972 and 1974 left Britain with a much more consolidated local government system than is found in most welfare states. Even before reform there were only about 1,400 local government units; after reorganization there were about 450. There were about 44,000 local councillors and there are now about 24,000. In contrast, the over-articulated French communal structure has over 450,000 councillors. There has been considerable reduction in the number of local council committees, the councils themselves are smaller, and local elections are more democratic. Even with the complications introduced by the Conservatives, Britain has one of the most streamlined local government systems in Europe, but in what respects does it seem to work better or even differently from the old system (Rhodes, 1974)?

An alleged goal was to strengthen local democracy. Consolidation inevitably means that fewer representatives are needed and voter turnout has not changed appreciably. A recent survey of the composition of local councils (Robinson Report, 1977) suggests that the more elderly, male, and middle-class citizens still take on local office from a sense of civic responsibility, not to change the tempo or aims of local government. Although it has not been fully evaluated, modern management took many forms and can estrange councillors from local affairs. The hope that the fearsome workload of being a councillor might be reduced, thereby encouraging others to participate, has not been fulfilled. There is some evidence that councillors still prefer the old committees; introducing more highly professional staff also produced new internal strains. Some of the functions are more cumbersome than before because powers such as planning that once rested with the top tier of local government are now shared with districts. These are all internal criteria of success and do not deal with the more difficult question of how well the new system connects to national problems and policy-making (Reading 5-2).

As we have seen, the British political system has always been cautious about letting local politics and policy intrude on higher-level decisions. But the meshing of locally expressed needs with national policy would be one of the major criteria by which we tell how effective local government is. Only a year after reorganization the first wave of criticism came with the double-digit inflation of 1975 (see Reading 5-3). In the 1960s an optimistic belief in rationality and growth combined with Labour and Conservative preferences for efficient government so that territorial consolidation seemed the most important change. The Conservatives accepted more "modern" local government in hopes of protecting the counties and, at least under Heath, efficiency was a prime objective. Labour correctly associated larger areas with ease of redistributing services and resources. For different reasons both agreed on larger areas, but both also felt that tampering with existing financial links between center and local government was too risky (Pesheck, 1976). The Conservatives were pledged to restrain local taxes, and Labour feared that further diversion of national resources to local government (which was the only place they could come from given the inelasticity of the property tax) would threaten nationally administered programs and policies.

Given this century-old impasse between national and local politics, there was no choice but to permit the transfer (Rate Support Grant) to increase by leaps and bounds. Grants came close to reaching two-thirds of operating expenses and were increasing at over 4 percent per year. To enable center and local government to bargain more coherently over this huge transfer, the historic division of town and county had to be overcome. As we have seen, the reform failed to do this. The grant is negotiated informally with the local government associations, but they, in turn, are still divided between the Association of Municipal Authorities, most often controlled by Labour; the County Councils Association, perpetually under Conservative influence; and the Association of District Councils, which under the new system is severely torn between districts located in rural and urban areas. The subordination of local government to national political needs had the curious effect of leaving the center with no one who could speak for local government as a whole. The inability of localities to speak with a collective voice imposes certain costs on Westminster, especially when national and local interests collide.

In this respect, there was virtually no change in the British local government system. The power of the central government to extract compliance with specific changes like comprehensive education may be exaggerated, but when major conflicts of interest occur Westminster has its way. In 1974, a Manpower Watch was installed to make sure that local government hired only the most essential additional staff. The Treasury imposed the most severe of budgetary controls, cash limits, on local government. Local governments were made responsible not only for wage increases beyond national guidelines for their own staff, but also for their contractors as well (Reading 5-4). A hastily assembled Committee of Inquiry (the Layfield Committee) produced a closely reasoned report arguing in favor of a local income tax, but for the reasons outlined neither party would concede this kind of policymaking leverage to local government. As a concession to local outrage, the Department of the Environment organized a National Consultative Council, where about fifty national and local officials meet to discuss expenditure needs. For the first time in history ministers are asked to defend their policies before local government, no small concession. But the Treasury still prepares national expenditure plans, described in Chapter 3, with no local consultation. Their year-end forecasts can override whatever agreements may emerge from the new Council.

Leaving local government financially vulnerable is a way of controlling it. To some extent every local government system is subject to national financial controls over local government, but in no democratic country is such control so firmly in the hands of central government. In the absence of a more clearly defined bargaining relationship between central and local government, center-local policymaking takes on a "stop-and-go" quality that is not unlike the same problem that plagued national economic policy, described in Chapter 3, and industrial relations, described in Chapter 4. Responding to the problems of the 1960s, the Layfield proposals would provide more expenditure for local authorities, but by the time the Committee reported in 1976 the problem was reversed

(Foster, 1977). Unable or unwilling to devise a more flexible system of local government finance, the Thatcher government proposed in 1979, with virtually no consultation or warning, that the entire grant system be replaced with a centrally calculated subsidy (see Reading 5-5). Even though the local councils were heavily controlled by the Conservatives, and uniformly opposed change, the power of a determined cabinet is sufficient to force such abruptly announced and hastily designed reforms.

A more serious difficulty of the British pattern of center-local policymaking stems from the needs of the welfare state. For the center to sustain the image of autonomous and self-reliant local government while also trying to meet increasingly specific demands poses a dilemma. This weakness is compounded when local government itself reflects the functional compartmentalization found at the center. Increasingly programs require careful local coordination and cooperation among local government areas. The problems of the elderly, child care, immigrants, pollution, and inner city decay presuppose that activities can be locally coordinated and focused in various ways. The earlier British program for inner cities, the Urban Development Programme, was crippled by these difficulties, and the more recent Inner City Programme, aimed more directly at declining cities, was difficult to launch (Bately and Edwards, 1978). In the absence of a more articulated network to involve cities in design and implementation, such programs seem to be arbitrarily imposed from above and tend to become political footballs on the national scene. While politicization of policy at the national level emphasizes the redistributional character of most programs, it also tends to make decisions highly partisan when there may in fact be little reason to do so.

No democratic political system can operate without partisan politics. A more significant question is how partisanship may or may not help solve problems. One of the unexpected effects of the 1972 reorganization was that many urban areas felt "swallowed up" in the larger areas. Many of the old boroughs had substantial organizations of their own and were proud of the services they provided. They were also frequently Labour-run cities that found themselves under Conservative county governments. The two-tiered system, especially in the metropolitan areas, placed obstacles before these districts and they soon banded together to ask the central government to restore the greater powers they once had. In the fall of 1977 the secretary of state for the environment,

Peter Shore, gave a widely noted speech on "organic change." A Labour Party consultative document soon followed (1977), which also linked the change to eventual elimination of the counties and a new form of regional government. Full reorganization only five years after the turmoil and expense of the 1972 changes was unthinkable. What Shore advocated was restoring to some twenty cities increased authority over planning, social services, education, and housing (1979, cmnd. 7457).

Creating larger local areas seemed less appealing to the Labour Party once they found many of their urban strongholds encased in Conservative counties. In fact the Labour Party now wants to go much further, partly under the impulse of the left wing of the Party, which has long considered the reorganization a betrayal of their aims. Despite the distrust of politically controlled regional government in Britain, the left favors stronger regional councils and abolition of the counties entirely. Of course, they are referring to England, not to Scotland and Wales, where the devolution debates often found the Labour left and the Conservative right voting together. The details of these proposals have not been spelled out, but they appear quite similar to the ideas of Derek Senior a decade ago. In a not too indirect fashion the proposals link to the massive transfer to local government. The Labour left wing has no qualms about transferring more money to localities, but it wants to be sure that it is used to redistribute income. The massive grant is a rather clumsy instrument for these purposes just as it is a clumsy device to further any specific program. Significantly, resistance to these proposals came not from local government, though for obvious reasons the counties are opposed, but from within Whitehall. The Department of Education and the Department of Health and Social Services do not wish to see their influence and programs jeopardized by aggressive efforts from the Department of the Environment to redirect local assistance.

The irony of center-local policymaking in Britain is that the system seems to keep fighting the same battles over and over again even though the problems have changed. The enormous importance of local councils in providing goods and services does not seem to give them political leverage and, if it were to do so, such influence might threaten national parties and Parliament, which are insulated from local politics. In 1979, the Conservative secretary of state for the environment, Michael Heseltine, was prepared to remove many detailed controls (1979, cmnd. 7634), but he paid little attention to the protests of the local government associations as he prepared even more arbitrary controls. Oddly enough, Conservative strength in local councils meant that all the local government associations were under Conservative control, but this made little difference to well-armed central policymakers (see Reading 5-5).

The local governments are no more united in confronting Westminster and Whitehall than they were a century ago, nor were they given any incentives to stop feuding among themselves. There are many reasons to think that national politicians and officials are pleased to avoid the conflicts and protracted negotiation that characterize nearly every other local government system in democratic countries. What is less clear is whether the concentration of power at the center suits the needs of the welfare state. The interlocking character of spatial and functional policies has resurfaced with the proposals of the Labour left. As the state does more, it also tries to steer public spending toward more narrowly defined problems and to more needy people. The exclusion of territorial politics from the pattern of center-local relations means that Britain has never developed the network needed to involve localities in this process.

The result tends to be a heroic national struggle to accomplish changes that other countries quietly make by recognizing the mutual dependence of national and local government. National struggles are unavoidably cast in partisan rhetoric, though when many local problems are examined more closely the national partisan alignment may not be appropriate to their needs. Moreover, the solutions offered to these silent partners are likely to be phrased in singular terms, seeking to remove one area of center-local conflict while completely neglecting another. Political stability has been protected by low-keyed local intervention into national policymaking. Local governments have prospered by not being distracted by the intrigue and pressure that French communes and American cities constantly direct toward their capital cities. Whether this detachment will serve Britain well as the welfare state needs more closely integrated and more finely tuned policies remains to be seen.

Readings

5-1. THE DIVISION OF TOWN AND COUNTRY*

The division of town and country was among the most important internal divisions in the British local government system, and was singled out by the Royal Commission. But the choice between functional responsibility and political responsiveness was still conceived as a local problem. Later changes by both Labour and Conservative leaders perpetuated this division.

27. The questions that have dominated all our work are these. What is, and what ought to be, the purpose which local government serves; and what, at the present day, is its scope? Our terms of reference require us to consider the structure of local government in England (outside Greater London) in relation to its existing functions; and it was therefore on existing functions that we concentrated our attention. These are of immense scope and significance, covering as they do responsibility for the police, for the fire service, for almost all education other than university, for the health and welfare of mothers and infants, the old and sick, for children in need of care, for public health, for housing, for sport and recreation, for museums, art galleries and libraries, for the physical environment and the use of land, for highways, traffic and transport, and for many other matters too numerous to mention. . . . But in considering the structure which will best enable local authorities to discharge these responsibilities, we have kept in mind the whole potential of local government, given the existing functions as the substance of what it does. This substance we see as an all-round responsibility for the safety, health and well-being, both material and cultural, of people in different localities, in so far as these objectives can be achieved by local action and local initiative, within a framework of national policies. It is in this light that we have considered the purpose and scope of local government.

28. Our terms of reference also require us to bear in mind the need to sustain a viable system of local democracy: that is, a system

*Royal Commission on Local Government in England, *Report*, vol. 1 (cmnd. 4040; London: HMSO, 1969).

under which government by the people is a reality. This we take to be of importance at least equal to the importance of securing efficiency in the provision of services. Local government is not to be seen merely as a provider of services. If that were all, it would be right to consider whether some of the services could not be more efficiently provided by other means. The importance of local government lies in the fact that it is the means by which people can provide services for themselves; can take an active and constructive part in the business of government; and can decide for themselves, within the limits of what national policies and local resources allow, what kind of services they want and what kind of environment they prefer. More than this, through their local representatives people throughout the country can, and in practice do, build up the policies which national government adopts—by focussing attention on local problems, by their various ideas of what government should seek to do, by local initiatives and local reactions. Many of the powers and responsibilities which local authorities now possess, many of the methods now in general use, owe their existence to pioneering by individual local authorities. Local government is the only representative political institution in the country outside Parliament; and being, by its nature, in closer touch than Parliament or Ministers can be with local conditions, local needs, local opinions, it is an essential part of the fabric of democratic government. Central government tends, by its nature, to be bureaucratic. It is only by the combination of local representative institutions with the central institutions of Parliament, Ministers and Departments, that a genuine national democracy can be sustained.

29. We recognise that some services are best provided by the national government: where the provision is or ought to be standardised throughout the country, or where the decisions involved can be taken only at the national level, or where a service requires an exceptional degree of technical expertise and allows little scope for local choice. Even here, however, there is a role for local government in assessing the impact of national policies on places and on people, and in bringing pressure to bear on the national government for changes in policy or in administration, or for particular decisions. And wherever local choice, local opinion and intimate knowledge of the effects of government action or inaction are important, a service is best provided by local government, however much it may have to be influenced by national decisions about

the level of service to be provided and the order of priorities to be observed.

30.   We conclude then that the purpose of local government is to provide a democratic means both of focussing national attention on local problems affecting the safety, health and well-being of the people, and of discharging, in relation to these things, all the responsibilities of government which can be discharged at a level below that of the national government. But in discharging these responsibilities local government must, of course, act in agreement with the national government when national interests are involved. . . .

5-2. RELATIONS BETWEEN CENTRAL AND LOCAL GOVERNMENT*

The reorganization has produced relatively little discussion on how central government may complicate, possibly obstruct, local government in the British system. In 1977 the CPRS produced a report on the weaknesses and confusions that may handicap local government, in particular because of the functional compartmentalization of local controls in Whitehall.

9.1.   As this report has already argued, most of Whitehall's contacts with local authorities relate to a single service. This is perhaps not wholly true of local authorities collectively; their representatives may, for example, be addressed by the Chancellor of the Exchequer or the permanent secretary of DOE about problems of economic management or local authority spending. It is much truer of local authorities individually. Central government does not in fact know what the overall position is in individual local authorities. It cannot assess the cumulative impact of policies: for example, the possible effect on a particular area of some new statutory requirement or expenditure cut, taking account of existing requirements, the totality of local needs and local expenditure and the links between these. Should a local authority develop a corporate response to its problems, central government is not organised to evaluate this. To express it simply in terms of structure, there is nowhere in Whitehall where representatives of a local authority as a whole—i.e. majority leaders, chief executives, corporate planners

*Central Policy Review Staff, *Relations between Central Government and Local Authorities* (London: HMSO, 1977).

and, in some contexts, treasurers—feel they can discuss problems which go beyond the boundaries of a single service. This contrasts with the ease with which, say, a chief education officer can discuss his problems with the DES. There is not even an identifiable address to which a local authority can apply if it wants informal advice or guidance on its corporate plan or planning techniques. The DOE insists that all this is its role, and one which it is glad to play; but, for whatever reason, many people in local authorities do not see the DOE in this light.

9.2. We have already described the differences in departments' organisation outside their London headquarters. One result is that central government equally lacks any corporate focus at sub-national level. DOE's regional network and the DES Inspectorate or DHSS Social Work Service are very different kinds of organisations and cannot deal with each other on equal terms. Reliance on a professional inspectorate is likely to reinforce the inward-looking tendencies of a particular service. (At present some people in social work seem to be pressing for the SWS to abandon its advisory role and to become an unambiguous inspectorate, which could more effectively support social work departments in their relationships with other services and with treasurer's departments.)

9.3. Regional Economic Planning Boards (REPBs) try to develop an integrated central government view of regional problems in the economic field, but the social department's role here is limited and now always adequately performed. Since last year DHSS has been regularly represented on most of the REPBs by people from their Regional Planning Division in London. This seems to work quite well (although one REPB secretariat described DHSS attendance as "spasmodic"). DES is normally represented by a member of the Inspectorate, drawn from the appropriate regional office. Though the Inspectorate can supply first-hand information about educational matters in particular areas, they are not, by the nature of their job, qualified to discuss broad questions of resource allocation or a DES policy more generally. When such questions come up either they seek advice from DES, or a representative from the department attends. At least one Regional Economic Planning Council has suggested that DES' regional presence is inadequate. The Home Office is intermittently represented, usually by someone from its Urban Deprivation Unit, when relevant questions are on the agenda. But if such a question came up unexpectedly, there would not normally be a Home Office representative to comment on it. It is also worth noting that there are no formal links between the REPBs and the local authorities in their regions. Individual local authority members sit on Regional Economic Planning Councils, but they do so in a personal capacity and not as representatives of any local authority.

9.4. If central government finds it virtually impossible to focus on a single authority in the round, this is even more true for units smaller than a local authority. The GLC, which is experimenting in developing programmes for dealing with deprivation in two small areas, pointed out to us the difficulty of getting people in central government departments to think seriously about the relevance of national programmes for the areas in question.

5-3. LABOUR TRIES TO RESTORE POWER TO THE DISTRICTS*

In the last days of the Callaghan Labour government (1976–79) local reorganization again became a political issue because a number of Labour strongholds felt constrained under metropolitan authorities. The Labour proposal was to restore powers to these districts, and possibly to abolish counties. A Times *editorial stressed the disruption of another change and suggested that there are no permanent solutions given the complexity of local government tasks.*

Bristol, now effectively a mere district in the county of Avon, was for hundreds of years one of the most august municipal powers in the kingdom, with a sway and independence second only to that of London. Such an overthrow is not forgotten or forgiven quickly —it certainly has not been in the short four years since Bristol and many other large cities were stripped of most of their powers. So when Mr. Peter Shore speaks there today to the Labour local government conference he could hardly ask for a more appropriate occasion if he were to announce that some of its lost glory was to be restored. To judge from the tone of statements he made last year, he would be glad to do so. There is a growing outcry for emancipation from the larger cities that were swallowed up in 1974. The reorganization, a Tory creation, has never found much favour in Labour ranks. But it does not seem that Mr. Shore has

*"Not the Time for Another Upheaval" (editorial), *The Times* (London), Jan. 28, 1978.

managed to persuade his colleagues in Cabinet that it is yet time for major changes.

Few who were involved in the last reorganization would regard the prospect of a new one with anything less than dread. Local government is only just beginning to recover from that upheaval. Much of the chaos seems to have been less the result of the admitted flaws in the plan than an inevitable accompaniment to radical alterations in a structure so large and complex. Before the new system could settle down, fresh tumult broke out over public spending restrictions. The reform has not yet had an adequate chance to show how it would work under ordinary conditions.

Another upheaval at this stage could only be justified if it promised unmistakable and widespread benefits. It cannot be said that the councils calling for the restoration of their powers have come anywhere near showing that such benefits would follow. When there were ten of them, all with historic names, it might have been tempting to feel that the upheaval might not be so very great after all. But there are 32 now. There is no threshold of size below which towns cease to resent the domination of counties over them, or to suppose that they could run things better themselves.

The old county boroughs, which were more or less self-sufficient in local matters, generally ran their affairs with efficiency and great civic pride (the sense of identity in a community is a factor that was taken too little into account in 1974). But they were too small to sustain some modern services and they were often at war with their neighbouring counties, which, lacking their resources of ratable value, tended to be relatively backwards in their standards of provision. This tension between town and country is something ingrained, and the new system contains it better than the old one, though less well than it might have done.

The aggrieved districts do not ask for all their powers back. Their main demands are for education and for social services. The ten largest have populations not very far from the level of 250,000 that the Redcliffe-Maud report considered the minimum capable of providing those services efficiently. Since those days our sense of the advantages of scale has in any case become a little less acute. The case for moving education, where account must also be taken of the difficulty of the county in making adequate provision if it were to lose the city schools, is less strong than the case for moving social services. The latter gain in many ways from being organized in such a way that they are responsive to the needs of individuals and small communities. They also need to work in close contact with housing services, which are a district responsibility.

There is no ideal size for a council: it is either too big for some functions and too small for others. Even in social services some matters, like residential homes, need a wider catchment area even than most counties. For that matter, an authority with 200,000 inhabitants can run its affairs as coldly and remotely as one many times larger. Some sources of discontent, like the blurred responsibilities in planning affairs, are inherent in the two-tier system with which we are landed, for better or worse. Mr. Shore speaks reassuringly of having nothing more drastic in mind than "organic change", but change on the scale that is being discussed may well be more than the organism can stand. In most of the fields that have been mentioned, the answer is more likely to lie in administrative delegation and co-operation between councils than in basic structural reform.

5-4. CONSERVATIVES AROUSE NEW FEARS OF INTERVENTION*

The latent tendencies toward centralization in British local government were fully exposed when the secretary of state for the environment launched his new Local Government and Planning Bill in the fall of 1979. Although the intricate proposed law was drastically cut in order to fit into a crowded parliamentary agenda, it still promised to provide stiff new controls on local authorities. These same controls will undoubtedly later be used by a Labour government to further subject center-local relations to adversarial demands. David Hencke of The Guardian *outlines the new proposals.*

Britain's ratepayers are on the brink of seeing a major revolution in the way their local services are financed and run. If the proposals outlined in the 13 documents leaked to the Guardian from the departments of education and environment go ahead, local authority services will become the arm of the central bureaucracy.

For the first time an individual council will be able to be picked out and penalised by central government. Enormous powers will

*David Hencke, "How Heseltine Plans to Nationalise Local Government," *The Guardian*, March 24, 1980 (selections).

be given to Mr. Michael Heseltine, the Environment Secretary, to force authorities to cut services or raise their rates considerably.

Civil servants will also be able to examine in detail for the first time, the cost of individual services and put pressure on authorities to standardize costs. The tool to be used to implement the revolution is called the block grant. Its introduction has sparked off protests from both Tory and Labour council leaders and united people like Mr. Geoffrey Rippon, a former Tory Environment Minister, and Mr. Roy Hattersley, Labour's present Environmental spokesman in Opposition.

The block grant is a new way of distributing the rate support grant—some £8000 million of cash used to pay 60 per cent of the costs of services like education, housing and social services. The present system uses complex estimates of authorities' needs and rateable resources.

Tory Ministers were, however, determined to control waste, inefficiency and overspending in both Labour and Tory authorities. They looked for a system which could both be understandable and give ministers powers to attack the overspenders. The result, though, looks like failing on the first point and giving draconian powers to implement the second.

In order to be able to assess accurately how local authorities spend money, Mr. Michael Heseltine, the Environment Secretary, is giving civil servants enormous powers to investigate the cost of every service up and down the country. Just as other parts of the Department of the Environment are being told to reduce form filling, speed up planning applications and cut bureaucracy, civil servants covering local authority costs are being given massive new burdens.

Under the block grant, Mr Heseltine is being offered new powers to control the income authorities receive from rates and to force them either to push up rates or to axe services.

Using a new system called "multipliers," Mr. Heseltine will be able to deduct excess income from individual councils if he believes they can generate more than average income to provide services.

Thus an authority will not be able to escape penalties by virtue of its high rate base. This will affect wealthy Tory shires and the Greater London Council as well as Labour authorities.

The cornerstone of the system will thus be a massive investigation of every local authority service by civil servants combined with the implementation of a complex set of ground rules to work out whether an authority has overspent.

The Labour Opposition has only been given one four-page document explaining its effects. The Guardian's 13 documents run to thousands of words explaining in detail how the new grant will work, yet they are not officially available to MPs or the press except by breaking Section Two of the Official Secrets Act.

5-5. CENTER-LOCAL RELATIONS AGAIN IN CONFUSION*

After more than ten years of costly and disruptive restructuring, the Heseltine proposals promise to revive many of the old controversies that have plagued center-local relationships. Localities are alarmed at the undefined powers being assumed by Whitehall, and national government appeared to have a only vague ideas about many key ideas contained in the Bill. Moreover, the new powers would be an invitation to any subsequent Labour government to engage in the same kind of arbitrary control. The prestigious Society of Local Authority Chief Executives outline their fears for the future.

The paradox of the Bill is that while defining in detail the requirements that the local authorities have to meet, the powers to be given to the Secretary of State are defined in very general terms. No clear limits are set to the powers, nor is the basis on which they are to be exercised clarified. Parliament is in danger of passing legislation without being clear how it will be used.

The Secretary of State will determine standard expenditure for each authority, but the basis on which it will be done is not yet settled. It would be remarkable if Parliament agreed to a proposal which would deeply affect the distribution of public money, when the basis of the proposal is not settled.

The schedule of rate poundage (and the multipliers) can be set in a variety of ways to penalise (or to reward) local authorities for their decisions on expenditure. It can be used to penalise severely underspending or overspending. The Government intends to use those powers in a limited way, but no limits are set in the Act.

*Society of Local Authority Chief Executives in collaboration with INLOGOV, *The Local Government Bill No. 2: An Appraisal Prepared by SOLACE,* January 1980 (selections).

No clear basis is laid down for the exercise of many of the other powers given to the Secretary of State or other Ministers. He may specify any rate of return on capital for direct labour organisations. He will be able to decide (rather than the local authority) whether any land held by the local authority is being sufficiently used. He can declare any areas as urban development areas.

Parliament is being asked to provide powers without clear boundaries. True, in some cases this will be subject to resolution of one or both Houses, but legislation should itself clarify the basis on which the powers are being given. Only then can Parliament judge whether the legislation is justified.

To leave uncertain and subject to arbitrary and changeable decisions key elements in the structure that links central and local government is to weaken local authorities. Certainty and stability are necessary elements in building up local responsibility. The proposed legislation is legislation for uncertainty.

The Way Ahead

The Government is proposing far-reaching changes in its relations with individual local authorities. These changes place very substantial powers in the hands of the Secretary of State. The Bill gives little indication as to how those powers will be used. The Bill opens up the prospect of continuing uncertainty for local authorities.

The one point that can be made with certainty is that on the key issues in the Bill, whenever a choice has had to be made, the Government has chosen control and influence by central government over individual local authorities, rather than reliance on local accountability within a national framework. That inevitably replaces local political control by new bureaucratic procedures.

There is nothing in the pattern of local government expenditure to justify a move by Government from concern with aggregate local government expenditure to concern for the position in particular authorities. The influence at national level of existing controls over capital expenditure, grant, advice and consultation have resulted in local government expenditure—both capital and revenue—being broadly in accordance with Government's wishes. There is no reason, in existing experiences, for a change in basic principle.

The Government intends to use the new powers in a limited way because they will be concerned with particular problems such as the open-ended resources element. But legislation is about powers—to be used by any future Secretary of State—not about the intentions of the present Secretary of State.

The Government has adopted to deal with a limited problem an approach recommended by the civil servants—first to the Layfield Committee, then to the Labour Government and now to the Conservative Government—the approach of unitary (now renamed block) grant. That is not an appropriate solution to limited problems. Bureaucratic consistency may seem a virtue—but it can limit the political will to produce simple solutions to simple problems.

The Secretary of State has declared his belief "that an effectively functioning local democracy can monitor the activities of local councils far better than civil servants in Marshal Street". That is the belief that now needs to be applied in practice.

It is a time for reconsideration. It is a time for discussion and consultation between local government and central government. If there are problems, then solutions, appropriate to the scale of the problems, should be explored. There is no case for legislation on the scale now proposed.

6 Social Security: Complexity Overcomes Politics

Few areas of policymaking in the welfare state present more complex choices than the provision of social security. Few would advocate returning to the austere welfare policies of the nineteenth-century liberal state, but, paradoxically, the more successful the welfare state becomes in its major endeavor, the removal of uncertainty from the lives of its citizens, and later the relief of inequality, the more difficult it has become for political systems to guide and influence these very choices. As we shall see in the case of Britain, the precedents in expanding social security are obligations to the future and do not easily accommodate the new needs and preferences. The complexity of reform means that changes require many years and frequently extend beyond the life of a single Parliament; the reform of British pensions has been a major preoccupation for the past twenty years. Added to these inflexibilities are the constraints of the tax system and decisions about where the burden of social security should fall and, especially over the past decade, how social security obligations can be reconciled with inflationary pressures. In the most advanced welfare states, most notably the Scandinavian countries, the planning and organization of social security has become virtually the equivalent to national economic planning.

Because Britain so dramatically proclaimed the arrival of social security "from the cradle to the grave" (Churchill's phrase) in 1942, it is often assumed that Britain is among the more advanced welfare states. While it is true that public expenditure as a percentage of gross domestic product (45 percent in 1975) follows closely behind public spending in the Netherlands, Sweden, and Norway, Britain's social security spending is more equally distributed, but not comparable to the amounts provided in these

199

states or even to benefits distributed by several countries where government plays a smaller role in the economy. In 1972, Britain's public expenditure on income maintenance programs (pensions, child allowances, unemployment and sickness benefits) was 7.7 percent of the gross domestic product, a figure that was slightly exceeded by the United States and surpassed by nearly 5 percent by the more conservative governments of France and Germany (OECD, 1976, p. 17). As we have seen in Chapter 3, Britain has spent a large share of public funds on debt service, stabilizing the pound, and industrial nationalization.

If we take a broader and therefore possibly fairer definition of a country's readiness to provide social benefits, namely education, income maintenance, and health (housing could also be included), Britain's performance is no more impressive. Among the eighteen advanced industrial democracies included in the OECD sample, Britain devotes 12.6 percent of the gross domestic product to such a "total welfare" estimate, but is surpassed by ten countries in this group and is below the average (13.2 percent). The reasons for this disparity are much too complex to be fully accounted for here, but are deeply imbedded in the history of British social welfare. The period of most rapid economic growth in Britain is remarkably bare of major social reforms. Neither the Tories nor the Liberal rulers of Victorian England seemed to place a high priority on welfare, though both were aware of the growing political strength of the working class. There was important landmark legislation, much ahead of the rest of Europe at the time, in the early Victorian factory legislation, regulation of hours, and protection of women and children workers, but these acts stemmed from Victorian morality more than from a vision of a more just society. Indeed, Lord Brougham, one of the more radical Whig reformers of the time, was adamant in his belief that no child should ever benefit from public funds.

Context

The shaping of public awareness of poverty is historically and culturally distinct for every country. Again Britain seems to have suffered the disadvantages of the innovator, for the economic ideas that prevailed in Victorian England were derived from Ricardo, whose Iron Law of Wages posed the constant threat that the poor would absorb all the national income. His thoughts were translated into institutional form by Bentham, whose *Constitutional Code* proposed a Ministry of Indigence Relief. Its main task was to see that the poor were taught the habits of self-reliance and productive endeavor in workhouses, essentially the aim of the Poor Law Reform of 1834 (Bruce, 1968; Fraser, 1973). The emphasis of social reform in Victorian England was on public health, which became a national responsibility, while welfare policies remained the responsibility of local government. In fact, the inequitable and unreliable forms of poor relief provided by the localities were only partially removed in 1929 (see Chapter 5), even though the beginnings of insurance against sickness, unemployment, and disability for wage earners date from the National Insurance Act of 1911.

The notion of "deserving" and "undeserving" poor dominated British thinking about social welfare for more than a century, and was incorporated into many of the twentieth-century welfare reforms. The "deserving" poor were those who had held jobs in more prosperous times, a definition that was reinforced by economic conditions. During the 1920s, there were repeated efforts to provide unemployment relief, a problem that was aggravated by Britain's deflationary economic policies following World War I and that became worse after the depression struck in full force in the early 1930s. The 1930 Unemployment Act, for example, created a category of "transitional benefits," a euphemism for assistance during prolonged unemployment, which became means-tested in the following year. The depression meant that many employed became paupers in the traditional British sense, but there were no efforts to erase the deserving-undeserving distinction by devising a more flexible social welfare system.

As for the other policy dilemmas discussed in earlier chapters, the underlying tensions over defining social welfare were reflected, and to a considerable extent reinforced, by organizational differences within the government. Both the Ministry of Health and the Ministry of Labour were post–World War I concessions to the working class, the former spurred on by the shockingly poor health of British citizens revealed in war preparations, and the latter a response to the growing problems of dealing with modern unions (see Chapter 4). Deeply involved in Victorian struggles over administering poor relief, the Ministry of Health acquired responsibility for the poor and the Ministry of Labour became the champion of the employed. Although the capable minister of health, Neville Chamberlain, wanted the old distinction between paupers and unemployed removed, the Ministry of Labour was heavily engaged with industrial unrest. Caught between national needs and an inflexible local relief system, the Ministry of Health was not eager to "carry the can" for the unemployed in a period of severe economic dislocation nor was Winston Churchill, the chancellor of the exchequer, eager to risk heavy charges on an already strained national budget. The unsatisfactory result was to form local Public Assistance Committees.

The Unemployment Assistance Board (UAB) emerged from this organizational tangle in 1934. Although the old Poor Law distinction was officially abolished in 1929 (in many procedural ways it lived on), the state had to take responsibility for massive unemployment. The UAB was a compromise between the Treasury and the Ministry of Labour, intended to prevent the total swamping of the severely strained national insurance system more than to provide a new concept of social welfare (Walley, 1972). As we have noted, the depression reinforced the long-standing distinction between the poor and the unemployed while demonstrating that the welfare system was unworkable. The permanently unemployed were exempt from the principle of "less eligibility" that had given lower benefits to the poverty-stricken since 1834. The UAB is the predecessor to the post-war National Assistance Board (NAB) and the Supplementary Benefits Commission (SBC). The important immediate point is that even at this early date the goals of British social welfare policy were divided. However stringent and businesslike, a new welfare bureaucracy rapidly developed.

The shock of reality was provided by Booth's and Rowntree's studies of the poor. Booth's investigations of the London poor (1889–1903, 17 vols.) were one of the first irrefutable applications of statistical analysis to a major social problem and demonstrated that nearly a third of those living in the London slums subsisted on even less than the miserable relief given to paupers. There followed Rowntree's study of York (1901), which provided the first workable definition of poverty. He devised and designed a standard list of daily requirements similar to the minimal needs still used by American welfare agencies. It was the work of these men that led to the appointment of the Royal Commission on the Poor Laws in 1905 and the beginning of direct state intervention and state financing to help the poor. But the notion that poverty still represented a "personal failing" survived in the Commission's Report, and the Minority Report, written by Sidney Webb, looked to social engineering to make the labor market work efficiently (Fraser, 1973, p. 148). For the immediate future the Commission had no new ideas except to carefully administer (means-test) special benefits for the poor, preferably through private charitable agencies.

For immediate purposes it is important to underscore that consideration of the principles and complexities of parliamentary social policy worked no better then than now. Heclo (1974, p. 89) notes that the new concepts contained in the 1911 Act were never debated in Parliament, mostly because the left was so badly split. When expanded unemployment insurance was created in 1920, the proposal was before the cabinet only four days before it went to Parliament. A secret Treasury committee worked in the early 1920s to devise "all-in-insurance" that might have wiped out the demeaning distinction between pauperism and poverty, but the funds were not available, much less the political will. The first Labour government of 1924 had three secret committees, none apparently in touch with the other, trying to devise new pension plans. The 1925 Pensions Act was also prepared in secrecy and not even revealed to the cabinet until the budget debate (Walley, 1972, p. 60). The growing pool of permanently unemployed showed that the long-standing distinction between the able-bodied poor and paupers was senseless. Nonetheless, "transition" payments under the 1930 Unemployment Act were still means-tested. The borderlines between poverty and pauperism were breached only because the economic failure made it impossible to keep paupers and unemployed apart. The UAB soon had 800,000 persons on its lists and, as would happen repeatedly, was soon compelled to pay benefits at the highest rates rather than distinguish degrees of need.

One cannot avoid the conclusion that the democratic political process was ill suited then, as now, to work through the intricacies of designing and implementing social welfare policy. Though every liberal democracy of the time had these problems, they were accentuated in Britain by adversarial politics, which provided neither the patience needed to construct new institutions nor the forbearance essential to their implementation. The last public effort to construct social policy was the Royal Commission on Unemployment Insurance of 1930 (Walley, 1972, p. 45). There were and quite possibly remain too many partisan and electoral pressures on politicians for them to deal with the complexities of social policy. Their response tends to be either so heavy-handed as to appear insensitive to human needs or so indiscriminate or vague that costs soar beyond expectation. The experience of the first all-inclusive insurance schemes, the post–World War II Beveridge Plan, repeats this pattern.

In 1942, Sir William Beveridge's proposals appeared to point the way to revolutionary changes that promised a society free of want. Within the bounds of contemporary history the Beveridge Plan has become the demarcation point for the British welfare state. It is an irony of politics more than a criticism of his work that Beveridge did not want the assignment and that the British leaders did not expect to have an entirely new welfare policy imposed on them. The Committee was "intended mainly to shield ministers from political embarrassment, and was not expected even to report until the end of the war" (Harris, 1979a). The report (1942) was actually written by Beveridge alone. The team of civil servants who initially worked with him tactfully withdrew, as civil servants are expected to do in the British system, once the full political and social importance of his proposals were known.

Within a few months of publication the Beveridge Report had sold half a million copies. In fact, the proposals were much less radical than they appeared. Beveridge's thinking can be traced back to his early work on national insurance for Lloyd George in 1907 and a book he wrote in 1924. The proposals were anything but new although they did bring together in one plan a number of advances in British social policy. Sickness, accident, unemployment, and old age insurance were all to be brought into one system providing flat-rate benefits. Among the first flaws to be discovered was that the Labour Party had endorsed a system that was highly regressive because the flat-rate benefits were financed with flat-rate contributions. The Report accepted the principle of tripartite contribution, meaning payments from employees, employers, and the government. Important as this principle is in establishing modern social welfare schemes, Beveridge did not foresee that sharing the cost of social welfare could become a political football, much less what immense administrative complexities might arise in assessing, collecting, and disbursing funds from three sources.

Perhaps the most important departure from British welfare traditions was to try to abandon the subsistence and means-tested notion of assistance that had lingered on since the Elizabethan

Poor Laws. Like a good Victorian, Beveridge thought the potential humiliation of welfare could be eliminated by contriving a self-sufficient insurance plan. As one conservative critic of his plan notes, national insurance was to become "an enormous Friendly Society" (Seldon, 1963). Contributions were to build up over twenty years and payments would be made from carefully managed funds. The fatal flaws in this expectation were to assume that as incomes rose politicians could resist the temptation to pay more liberal benefits (which they did not) and that the flat-rate contributions could keep benefits at reasonable levels under severe inflation or severe unemployment. For the first few years of the system this was not a problem because full employment kept contributions high and payments low. Like many British officials of the time, Beveridge feared unemployment most of all and his scheme allowed for 8.5 percent unemployment rates. With such generous actuarial assumptions, the funds soon exceeded expectations. By 1958, political pressures to dip into the burgeoning funds were irresistible, a decade before Beveridge's plan had foreseen self-sufficiency.

Sir John Walley (1972, p. 74–77) has provided the most trenchant criticism of the Beveridge Plan on grounds of its administrative naiveté. The effectiveness of the "safety net" that Beveridge hoped to construct between poverty and welfare depended on several other programs being successfully implemented. There was first the National Health Service, which would protect low-income families against the ravaging effects of serious illness. As it worked out, the nationalization of health was an extremely acrimonious process, thereby distracting the Labour Party from the second component, the retirement insurance plan. Because of the huge accumulation of pension contributions, financial inroads into the new insurance funds became attractive. The third "pillar" of the Beveridge Plan was family allowances, which many welfare experts had argued for several decades would be the easiest way to redistribute income and to relieve the most serious inequities of the British welfare policies (Rathbone, 1924). The Family Allowances Act of 1945 was the first of Beveridge's proposals to become law (at much lower rates than he wanted) because it appeared to the Treasury to be one way of preserving the old distinction of "less eligibility." Making family support a flat-rate payment system regardless of employment protected the margin between benefits and lowest wages (Harris, 1979b). In this and other ways the old distinction between the "deserving" and "un-deserving" poor was transmitted from the old to the new system.

The National Insurance Act of 1946 incorporated most of Beveridge's proposals, dividing beneficiaries into six categories. Perhaps the most damaging aspect of the categorization was to facilitate opting out for married women so that a generation later, when women represented nearly two-fifths of the employed population, they were severely disadvantaged. The last component of the Beveridge Plan, the National Assistance Act of 1948, was, and remains, the most controversial element of British welfare policy. The shadow of the Poor Laws was cast over the new scheme by the conviction that Beveridge and most officials still held that assistance should "be felt to be something less desirable than insurance benefits." Yet the possibility remained that prolonged unemployment would create groups without resources and that victims of poverty such as widows, the permanently disabled, and children would require special help. For these purposes the National Assistance Board, the predecessor to the contemporary Supplementary Benefits Commission, was created to administer non-contributory, tax-financed, and means-tested benefits. Beveridge, of course, hoped and planned that the numbers of persons reduced to "subsistence levels" would be small, but for many reasons this number grew to over 3 million persons by 1978.

To be fair, the continued implication of inferiority for those who were not earners, and thereby did not contribute to insurance, was the thing that Beveridge and nearly all social welfare reformers most wanted to remove from the British welfare system. In practice, it is extremely difficult to do if any form of contributory welfare, even if state subsidized, is used. The new Board perpetuated the "wage stop," which meant that the maximum non-contributory benefit should not exceed the lowest wage (later to become the average annual wage of unskilled labor). Oddly enough, the "wage stop" was ended in 1975 by Sir Keith Joseph, the Conservative Party welfare expert, not because he disapproved of the principle, but because it stood in the way of converting the system of direct welfare to an indirect system using the tax credits.

The second form of discrimination between the poor and unemployed was the "four-week rule," which still exists under American welfare rules though it is virtually impossible to enforce. After a month of unemployment, benefits can be reduced if an unemployed person refuses an unskilled job. Although the "poverty trap" had not been discovered in 1942, there was also the possibility that among those of greatest need earnings could fall short of benefits to be obtained while not working. Unraveling this dilemma is a more complex problem than can be attempted here, but the issue remains the most politically volatile aspect of social policy in every welfare state. The distinguishing feature of this issue in Britain is that it paralyzed the social policy debate for so long. As social welfare reaches increasingly higher levels, which we have every reason to think will be the case in all the welfare states, the terms of reference in many countries changed to income maintenance, not relief. In Britain it took twenty years to shift the debate from poverty to income maintenance.

Agenda

In the 1950s, Britain had what was considered one of the most advanced welfare plans among the advanced industrial democracies. Ostensibly the major issues had been settled and a workable national program to cover a wide range of social problems had been implemented. But a fundamental characteristic of the welfare state, especially in the area of social welfare policy, is continued political concern with the less privileged and handicapped. The first battle had been won, but new skirmishes soon began. The weaknesses of the Beveridge Plan became apparent as political leaders sought ways to make improvements and as the political parties discovered needs that were either neglected or excluded from the Beveridge Plan. The curious result was that in the decade from roughly 1958 to 1968 it became clear that the entire scheme needed overhauling and was in many basic respects inadequate.

At the root of political discontent with the new scheme is the fact that need, equality, and welfare change their meaning over time (Fieghen, 1978). In the relatively prosperous Britain of the time it was inevitable that demands would arise to redistribute additional national income to the poor and neglected. The rallying cry came from R. M. Titmuss, a professor of social administration, who became a major figure in formulating Labour Party welfare policy and the focal point for nearly all proposals for reform and reorganization over the next two decades. His book (1962) summarized the transformation: welfare is not compensation for officially defined inadequacies of the labor market or specific needs, but is itself a form of income redistribution. In effect, welfare policies are not a program of the modern state, but a justification of the modern state. Obviously such views quickly politicized the welfare issues and were in many ways ideally suited to feed partisan politics. Whether this formulation takes into account the complexities and dilemmas that increasing welfare actually imposes on government and administration is, of course, another question.

In any event, the broad consensus that created the Beveridge Plan was shattered. Titmuss argued that the basic unit for assessing welfare needs and benefits, the individual, was inappropriate and should be replaced with the family; that many conditions of advanced industrial society provided special benefits for the rich, such as tax advantages, fringe benefits, and access to wealth accumulation, that were denied the worker even if direct payments increased; and that welfare policies should not only be more aggressively redistributive but should focus on those particular groups and persons who were most severely deprived. These ideas fell on fertile ground, for the Labour Party was reshaping itself during the long period of Conservative rule and the new generation of Labour leaders were looking for ways to invigorate a party that appeared divided and dull.

In 1955 a Labour Party committee on social welfare was formed including Titmuss and two of his protegés, Brian Abel-Smith and Peter Townsend. They rejected the "two-nation" hypothesis that had inspired British welfare policy since Elizabethan times. Oddly enough, they received little help from the TUC, which found both earnings-related contributions and emphasis on need a potential threat to union influence over wage policy. Many union members belonged to company insurance schemes to supplement flat-rate benefits and to meet special needs. When Titmuss pointed out that 6.5 million persons received unfair welfare advantages by receiving £100 million in tax concessions, he was in fact confronting union power as well as private sector insurance plans. In some ways Britain was reliving the tensions between the Ministry of Labour and the Ministry of Health that had plagued welfare reform a generation before.

The political champion for completely rethinking welfare policy became Richard Crossman, who later became the first secretary of state for social services in a giant ministry to accomplish these changes. Crossman was convinced that the Titmuss group was not only correct but made good political sense. Even Beveridge's modest plans called for 3 percent of the gross national product to be devoted to welfare, but no government until then had collected more than 2 percent (Abel-Smith, 1963). Under the initial plan, the Treasury had agreed to put £100 million per year in the National Insurance Fund, but with favorable economic conditions the Fund had become a lender to government. In the Labour Party's search for a new role, expanded welfare became a natural objective. Crossman helped obtain TUC support and in 1957 the Party announced its new scheme. It was the first foray over the shortcomings of the Beveridge plan that would eventually lead to a new system.

Under Labour's 1957 proposals, flat-rate pensions would be substantially increased, an appeal to the nearly 6 million pensioners (and voters) who became the focal point of welfare reform. The major break with the past was to open the way for earnings-related pensions of up to half of average annual earnings. As a consolation to the private insurance industry, the scheme permitted "contracting out," but also promised more aggressive investment of insurance savings, which Macmillan quickly attacked as "nationalization by stealth." The most difficult task for Labour was to get acceptance of unequal benefits, but it was obvious that flat-rate benefits would perpetually limit national insurance to the wage of the lowest-paid worker, one of the many ways that the Poor Law mentality infiltrated reform. The Conservatives were aware of the shortcomings of the Beveridge Plan and predictably looked to better management of the National Insurance Fund and more attractive private pension plans to improve welfare. The solution (the Boyd-Carpenter plan) introduced variable contributions and benefits in 1961 and encouraged "contracting out." Because state pensions were not adjusted to inflation, the better private plans would be more attractive.

By the early 1960s, the main issues surrounding the future of social welfare policy were defined. First, it had become clear that pensions, and probably most other social welfare benefits, would have to adjust to increased earnings (be "dynamized" in British terms). Second, there was the intensely political question of whether variable contributions should be directed toward private insurance schemes or be captured by the state. Pursuing redistributive policies with a person's lifetime savings is of course much more delicate than redistributing corporate profits from prosperous to failing firms. By 1978 there were nearly 9 million persons insured under 65,000 private retirement schemes and 16 million contributing to the National Insurance Fund. Third, there was the more conventional spending. On this front the temptation almost always proved too great for a two-party system because increasing benefits provides immediate and visible payoffs. In six of the seven elections from 1950 to 1970 (see Reading 6-2) pension increases were promised. Spending money could always be used to attract votes, but how to raise the funds and finance welfare was from 1960 onward left to the bureaucracy and the "welfare lobby."

Special mention should be made of the welfare lobbyists, for they were (and remain) powerful and vocal and could not be ignored as local government associations, for example, could be. The company insurance plans, many in nationalized industries, are represented by the National Association of Pension Funds, and the private insurance companies by the Life Officers Association. Their sheer financial power made them crucial in any reform. In 1978, private pensions funds totaled about £34 billion. Their tax allowance and deductions amounted to roughly £2 billion a year when the Treasury subsidy to national insurance was £1.3 billion. Ranged against them were increasingly effective client organizations, such as the Child Poverty Action Group (CPAG), representing groups that had been neglected. Perhaps the most important force on the left, especially as the welfare problems became more and more complex, was the "Titmuss gang," as Crossman called them, who produced a study showing that the elderly were living in miserable conditions (Townsend and Wedderburn, 1965; Abel-Smith and Townsend, 1965). In fact, Titmuss later admitted that they did their job too well: other pronounced inequities, the treatment of widows and one-parent families, for example, were neglected in order to concentrate on the most obvious injustice, the plight of the elderly.

When Labour returned to power in 1964, except for the TUC there was probably no pressure group with influence comparable to that of the Titmuss group. While pension payoffs were attractive electoral ammunition, everyone knew they were superficial responses to an immensely complex problem, and, even worse, they often exacerbated inequities with other forms of assistance. Democratic participation was clearly inadequate to the task of reform. Though it was an issue in the 1964 elections, only 2 percent of the electorate were aware of new plans, but two-thirds understood that Labour would increase pensions (Heclo, 1974, p. 274). One of the ironies of modern parliamentary government is that, with a majority of only three, the new Wilson government could do nothing until the 1966 election increased its majority. Perhaps an even greater irony is that Wilson's first step toward reform, the 1966 Social Security Act, was prepared in complete secrecy and was never publicly examined (Walley, 1972, p. 114). Whether consensus existed, much less approved new measures, seemed to be increasingly irrelevant to policymaking in the modern welfare state.

Process

Labour came to power in 1964 amid promises that some sort of income guarantee would soon be forthcoming. The Queen's Speech noted that "radical changes in the national schemes of social security are essential to bring them in line with modern needs." The immediate increases in existing benefits cost over £300 million in a period when Britain was beginning to suffer serious economic problems. It appeared that by 1969 a 10 percent increase in existing benefits would cost over £400 million (Hall et al., pp. 442–43). Much to the glee of Conservative Opposition leaders, the details of Labour's social security reform were not ready, but simply spending more under the existing rules (which of course the Conservatives had helped fashion) was virtually impossible. Labour had not only promised more than it could deliver, but, even worse, was caught in a spiral of welfare increases that in themselves could prevent structural change.

The Social Security Act of 1966 was at best a temporary solution to this dilemma. As the poverty lobby had demonstrated, at least a fourth of the retired depended on additional payments from the National Assistance Board to survive. In 1965 there were 1.2 million pensioners receiving additional means-tested benefits and many suspected that under the stigma of poverty perhaps another half million were too proud to come forward to claim benefits. The Act hoped to reduce this stigma by changing the name of the National Assistance Board to the Supplementary Benefits Commission. Over 300,000 pensioners were added to Supplementary Benefits in the first few months of the new system. A second change was to create a single Ministry of Social Security, which included the Ministry of Pensions and National Insurance and the new Commission. A third and more controversial change was to put "scale rates" or the amounts given for the various means-tested supplementary benefits directly under government, thereby making them more accessible to political influence. The principle of earnings-related benefits was extended to cover unemployment, sickness, and widows' benefits, and there were more liberal "disregards" or permissible earnings while receiving supplementary benefits. Though a makeshift piece of legislation, the Act was on the whole acceptable to the Conservatives and indirectly established a minimum income guarantee, namely, the permissible supplementary benefit rate of payment for the poor.

The Act ostensibly responded to the most severe immediate need by putting public welfare within one organization. Beveridge thought additional assistance was a last resort that a properly administered national insurance scheme would not often need. From 1948 to 1965 the number of persons receiving supplementary benefits actually doubled to over 2 million persons. What Britain had in the mid-1960s was an incoherent jumble of four welfare systems: the remnants of the flat-rate benefits and contributions dating from the Beveridge Plan; the adjustments to costs and benefits introduced in a piecemeal fashion over the previous decade in the form of earnings-related payments and contributions; a rapidly increasing and totally subsidized maze of means-tested benefits under the Supplementary Benefits Commission; and a private pension and insurance system that had grown immensely over the decade. It had become virtually impossible to assess the effects of benefits, but it was also clear that many needy persons still went without help. More important, as the entire system became fragmented and less financially viable it was more vulnerable to an economy-minded Treasury. What was needed was a system that would draw together the full savings potential of both private and public insurance schemes, leaving government, it was hoped, to deal more rationally with those who had no support.

Given the adverse economic situation of the late 1960s, the Labour White Papers on Superannuation (1966 and 1969) were a courageous decision, in many ways the most innovative act taken by the harassed and divided Wilson government. Without the determined and buoyant leadership of Crossman, it seems unlikely that anything would have been done. He was instrumental in having Titmuss appointed to the new Supplementary Benefits Commission and brought Abel-Smith into the government as his special advisor. In preparation for a major attack on welfare problems, a super-ministry had been formed, the Department of Health and Social Security (DHSS), from the Ministries of Health and Pensions. Crossman became the first secretary of state of the expanded ministry, and his *Diaries* (1977) show how much he enjoyed being in charge of a major working agency of government.

The new plan differed in important respects from the 1957 proposal, most notably by taking a more constructive view of private pensions. A 1966 study by the Ministry of Pensions had shown that although 80 percent of the now nearly 8 million retired received national pensions, nearly half also had other private pensions. Without private or occupational pensions these people would almost certainly fall below the national assistance scale of subsistence income. Titmuss and his colleagues had vividly painted the specter of "two nations of old age," the marginal existence of those depending on supplementary benefits and the relatively secure retired, whose state pensions were supplemented by occupational pension plans. If nothing were done to construct an integrated retirement plan, the country certainly faced immense pension increases over the next two decades, when the elderly were estimated to become nearly 30 percent of the population.

The economic calculations are too complex to outline in full (see Atkinson, 1969 and 1974), but the main principles are fairly clear. Pension benefits and contributions were to be related to earnings. A redistributive element was included by increasing the proportion of earnings guaranteed to lower-income groups. Most important, pensions were to be "inflation-proofed" through statutory upgrading based on price and earning indices, whichever rose more rapidly. Women were to be treated on the same basis as men. The new system would introduce what was basically a two-tier scheme with the flat-rate pensions continued under a pay-as-you-go plan contained in the National Insurance Fund and earnings-related pensions coming from a new Social Insurance Fund. Over a twenty-year period the conversion to fully earnings-related pensions would be complete.

Perhaps the most ingenious aspect of the new system was working out an "abatement" proposal with the private and occupational pension plans. The aim was to make the plan attractive for those who could to save for their own retirement in private schemes, while also making state pensions high enough to provide a decent living in old age. The compromise had actually been worked out some years before with the private sector schemes and provided a cash rebate from the state system to assist private plans that agreed to meet higher standards. Those who received state-subsidized pensions under private auspices would receive reduced state pensions, thereby sharing the costs. Crossman distinguished himself from earlier Labour ministers of social security by keeping in close touch with private insurance companies, the TUC, and the CBI as the compromise was worked out. On the day the White Paper was released there was favorable comment from the Life Officers Association, although Titmuss clearly still had reservations (1969). In any event, an acceptable "partnership" was found between public and private pensions, and there was no more talk of using state pension funds to compete with private insurance investments.

Like many of the intricate problems confronting the welfare state, working out an integrated pension plan had little to do with Parliament or the public. The main problems occurred within the confines of Whitehall, where the Treasury delayed introducing the new legislation because of economic uncertainties (Crossman, 1977, p. 258, 616, 714). In the cabinet committee for the plan most of the questions were about its effects on civil service pensions. In Parliament the new bill had to compete with a storm that had arisen over *In Place of Strife* (see Chapter 4). Once it reached committee stage in the House of Commons there was relatively little Conservative opposition, another instance of highly complex policies becoming bipartisan proposals. As Heclo points out (1974, p. 279), the delay shows how British socialists compare unfavorably with their Swedish counterparts, who called a special election to mobilize opinion for improved retirement plans. With the new plan on the brink of implementation, Wilson called the 1970 election. As happened in the case of local government reform (see Chapter 5), the Conservatives returned to office to complete a task begun by Labour.

Harassed by economic difficulties, the Conservatives produced a new proposal, *Strategy for Pensions* (1971), which partially restored the distinction between state and occupational pensions. The new government calculated that closing the gap between supplementary benefit scales and state pensions would cost nearly a billion pounds. Earnings-related pensions for the elderly, disabled, and widows were to be removed, restoring the attraction of larger pensions from the private insurers for those who could afford them. Pensions were to be organized around a threefold distinction: flat-rate pensions on a pay-as-you-go basis with graduated contributions; a funded "reserve" providing graduated benefits for workers who could afford making graduated contributions; and a new agency, the Occupational Pension Board, to oversee "contracting out" and to work toward bringing inferior private pensions schemes up to national standards. Their plan did accept Labour's redistributive approach to pensions, but oddly enough exceeded the financial power to be placed with government under Labour proposals. In twenty-five years (the full fund would require forty years to accumulate), the "reserve" would be approximately £5 billion, vastly larger than any private insurance fund. It was, of course, radical ideas of this kind that made Heath suspect to more conventional Conservatives.

The important advance made by the Conservatives was to increase benefits for families. In 1970 they introduced Family Income Supplement (FIS), a means-tested payment to low-income families. Beveridge had included family allowances in his plan, but they were never as central to the British welfare system as they are, for example, in France. Though the Conservative social welfare secretary of state, Sir Keith Joseph, declared war on the "poverty gap," the FIS appeared to widen the gap by increasing the benefits low-paid workers would lose when employed. Though the details cannot be outlined here, the attempt to align welfare with personal incomes rather than to rely on nontaxable payments for predetermined and means-tested needs distinguishes the Conservative approach to poverty. In 1973, Sir Keith proposed an elaborate plan to merge a variety of family support programs so that tax allowances could be more directly linked to need, a step toward a tax credit welfare system. Though extremely difficult to implement, Conservatives have favored tax credits over welfare payments (see Reading 6-4). Like so many earlier reforms, Sir Keith's plans collapsed with the Heath government in 1974 and it was left to the Labour Party finally to accomplish the major reorganization of British pensions.

Consequences

The aim of Labour's 1969 proposals was to move from the minimal definition of social welfare under national insurance to the broader one of alleviating poverty through income maintenance. While the Conservatives had accepted this objective, the 1973 Act kept public and private pensions distinct. The "reserve" scheme provided smaller pensions to fewer people than did the Labour scheme and it was not related to earnings. After the first 1974 election, Labour announced that it would implement only parts of the Social Security Act of 1973 and would bring forth its own plan. The new proposals were energetically propelled through Parliament by Barbara Castle, the new secretary of state for social services and a militant Labour leader. The Social Security Act of 1975 is the result of nearly twenty years of study and gradual change, starting from Labour's first 1957 proposals. It was not strongly resisted by the Conservative Party, which also promised that it would not seek revision of the Act if it returned to power. Thus, the design of an integrated retirement scheme was essentially bipartisan. Polls showed that only one worker out of a thousand understood the new legislation, which, given its complex provisions, is not too surprising.

The most important part of the 1975 Social Security Act was to drive home the "partnership" between state and private pensions that had been crucial to the 1969 proposals (see Reddin, 1977). Keeping the two-tier pension, both "contracting out" and state-insured employees and employers contribute above minimum earnings (initially set at £17.50 per week). Employer contributions (initially 10 percent) were higher than in previous schemes. Above the minimal earnings level the state insured continued to pay at the basic rate, while rates for the "contracted out" dropped by nearly half. However, private pension plans for the "contracted out" have to meet standards laid down by the Occupational Pensions Board and pensions were to be earnings-related. The aim was to provide all insured with roughly half their highest earnings at retirement, not a particularly generous benefit compared with pension plans in many other European countries. Of the 8.4 million retired in 1976 over 5.5 million were still living at the supplementary benefits "poverty level." Coming into effect in mid-1978 (implementation was delayed a year to facilitate "contracting out" and to work out relations with private pensions), the new scheme will not be fully effective until 1998 (see Reading 6-3).

The compromise with the private sector may seem surprising unless one takes into account that Labour wanted to see its objectives achieved at a particularly unpropitious moment. The massive benefits provided by the welfare state mean that marginal changes can be immensely expensive. Labour's White Paper on the new plan, *Better Pensions* (1974), acknowledged that there were 2.5 million retired and 0.5 million widows receiving private pensions. The total enrollment in private schemes was about 11 mil-

lion persons. The 1975 report of the government actuary left little
doubt that without these private funds, reform would be impossible. In 1975 the government was already contributing over a
billion pounds to the national insurance funds plus another billion
in supplementary benefits. In the midst of the oil crisis and with
double-digit inflation, Castle did well to bring her colleagues along
with her and was dependent on getting private sector cooperation.
The main compromise with the private insurance industry was that
inflation-proofing risks were subsidized by government. Even so,
after-retirement pensions are not inflation-proof under either the
state or private plans.

Providing welfare extends beyond pensions, of course, and
Castle had other objectives, too. She was particularly eager to get
equal treatment for women. One equalization provision was that,
under "home responsibility" exemptions in the new Act, women
would receive the same pensions as men even if not contributing
for up to twenty years. She wanted to provide more adequately for
one-parent families, who were treated less fairly in relation to the
unemployed and pensioners (Turner, 1978). Part of Labour's welfare program was to do more for families (also a common theme
of the Conservatives), and in 1975 a child benefits plan was enacted to replace child tax deductions and family allowances (Phillips, 1978). The flat-rate, and therefore more redistributive, benefit is paid directly to mothers of low-income families. The payments
are tax exempt and begin with the first child. By 1978–79 the cost
of child benefits doubled to £1.7 billion although it seems unlikely that increases would have been so rapidly forthcoming had
not a cabinet report leaked to the press showed the financial disadvantages of families under the British welfare program (*New Society*, June 17, 1976).

Every reform of national insurance made the elimination of supplementary benefits part of its aim and its justification. By this
criterion all the reforms since 1974 have failed. In 1977 over 3
million British were receiving special, means-tested benefits at a
cost of over £2 billion. More than half were retired persons with
inadequate incomes, but there were also 700,000 unemployed
(about half the total unemployed) who did not qualify for national insurance, over 300,000 single parents, and 240,000 sick
and disabled with no other support. Beveridge had, of course,
envisaged national assistance as a last resort, mainly designed to
help those with low pensions until his new scheme was fully ef-

fective. Neither of these things happened. No government has been able to find an alternative, and the most important change by Labour in the 1970s was to give the Supplementary Benefits Commission more autonomy in hopes that open discussion and further self-examination might improve the situation. Since 1975 the SBC has published its own reports, which are in themselves vivid testimony to the plight of the poor in the industrial state.

Britain is not alone among the industrial democracies in having such an intricate mix of cash welfare benefits that it becomes virtually impossible to devise a coherent strategy to alleviate poverty (see Reading 6-2). It becomes extremely difficult, first, simply to define what poverty is. Estimates for the British population range from under 4 to nearly 10 percent of the population (Atkinson, 1969, p. 37). Welfare clientele possess a striking common characteristic, need, but they are highly differentiated and each group tends to develop its own lobby. These problems are compounded as the proportion of national resources that can be devoted to social security is held constant. The chairman of the SBC, David Donnison, has noted that the "poverty lobby" may cause even more confusion by making excessive demands, sometimes increasing inequities among social security beneficiaries (1976, pp. 356–57). On the other hand, Frank Field, leader of the CPAG, has shown that the share of national income received by the poorest has remained roughly constant since 1886 (1975). The policy problem increasingly becomes how to weigh social benefits against taxes, and how to estimate what proportion of national resources can be devoted to welfare. In this respect, it appears that taxes plus social security contributions as a proportion of GNP actually declined from 1969 to 1975 (*Economic Trends*, 1977, p. 113). Questions of this kind are difficult to ask, much less answer, as the array of benefits becomes more intricate.

Perhaps the most pressing issue is that British reliance on means-tested benefits becomes more and more cumbersome. An inquiry by the DHSS (1978) produced few new ideas, but the alleged inefficiency of the SBC again came under scrutiny with the Thatcher government. The search for economies tends to displace concern for need. Constant or diminishing resources also seem to widen the "poverty gap" in several ways. In 1978 the difference between short-term (sickness and initial unemployment) payments and long-term (pension and industrial disability) payments increased so that the long-term dependent couple had more than a £7 weekly advantage (Dean, 1979). The 1979 Thatcher government had few new ideas, but they were determined to impose cuts on social services (see Reading 6-5). Their solution to the disparities in the system was simply to abolish the Supplementary Benefits Commission and, they hoped, to bring means-tested benefits into line with national insurance benefits.

A second major source of confusion is the complexity of the tax system. There are both direct effects, as tax thresholds are changed from government to government, and indirect effects depending on the tax status of various benefits. Some payments, such as child benefits, are tax free and are therefore a tax advantage for those qualifying. Most contributory benefits, such as pensions, are not. Thus, the overall effect on personal income, which many would argue is the important final effect of social security systems, may vary without benefits changing. The larger the tax burden becomes, the more the chances that this might happen. With numerous small benefits that are frequently adjusted, the income effect may be virtually impossible to calculate (Gough, 1975). On the other hand, when the Conservatives reduced income taxes in 1979, there was much less income tax relief for lower-income groups. The British tax structure, compared to most countries, reaches across a wide band of incomes and rises fairly steeply (Kay and King, 1978), which means that using tax changes to affect social bene-fits is difficult. In countries that depend more heavily on indirect taxes, transfers between tax revenues and social security are easier because one can avoid the tax inequities that manipulating income taxes may create. To alleviate these differences, Heath proposed that a tax credit scheme be devised (see Reading 6-4). However, the mechanical problems of building a social security system on the tax system are many, and it appears that it would be costly. Atkinson (1976) estimated that income taxes would increase about 10 percent.

Tax credits are, therefore, difficult for Conservatives to imple-ment because the decrease in social security contributions is less evident to upper-income groups than is the tax increase. For La-bour, there are no less difficult complications, because the unions see this as a threat to unemployment benefits and many working people prefer direct payments. However, tax effects on social se-curity cannot be entirely avoided and become more complex in periods of high inflation (Reading 6-1). The pressures to increase wages and benefits are both strong, but are not necessarily in balance. Benefits that are indexed tend to rise automatically with inflation. But the major parties differ over indexing pensions in relation to prices or earnings. The Conservatives favor indexing based on earnings, which rise more slowly than prices. One of their spending cuts proposed in 1979 would shift pensions back to earnings index, which would likely mean no pension increases until 1983 once one allows for the rises permitted under Labour's price-indexed pensions over recent years. Thus, the third major confusion is "uprating" itself (Reading 6-2). Smaller groups with more specialized needs tend to be neglected. Better-organized and more politically influential groups are able to protect themselves against inflationary erosion of social security benefits.

Thus, the policy choices presented by the scope and size of social security in most democratic countries raise a host of new problems, most of which evade easy calculation by voters and even by MPs. The paradoxical effect is that what we would regard as one of the major advances of the welfare state, protection against economic and social uncertainty, is less and less subject to simple political controls. Adversarial politics increases temptations to tamper with carefully designed financial arrangements and funds, and may give unfair advantage to more easily identified and more politically active groups. The British system, itself complex and wide-ranging, seems particularly vulnerable to this kind of manipulation. For example, a saving proposed by the Thatcher government in 1979 was to delay paying sickness benefits three additional days in order to save a mere £70 million. Originally meant to be a self-financing and self-regulating program of benefits, the British system, like that of most welfare states, is now an integral part of the public sector and public spending. But the diversity of the benefits, the organizational problems, and the inability of a stagnant economy to make marginal changes mean that a fully integrated income maintenance system has yet to emerge.

Readings

6-1. INFLATION AND THE TRADITIONAL CONCEPT OF WELFARE*

From the mid-1970s severe inflation radically affected the British social security system. Insurance and pension funds were thrown into disarray and the choice between future and present income became more difficult. Rudolf Klein points out how the traditional concept of welfare was breaking down under these pressures.

To compound the problems of social policy in this new era of perplexity and stringency, the costs of dealing *with* inflation have to be added to the costs imposed *by* inflation. Dealing with inflation means—at least within the framework of present assumptions about what is possible in terms of economic and political management—higher unemployment. In turn, higher unemployment has obvious social costs, some of which are met out of public expenditure and some of which are carried by the families directly hit.

The changed relationship between social and economic policies is evident in other ways as well. Inflation, as already noted, has increasingly persuaded successive governments to use social expenditure as an instrument of economic policy. In 1974–75, and to a lesser degree in 1975–76, many of the increases in public expenditure, including higher pensions, were specifically designed to provide a social dividend in return for wage restraint. Far from helping to restrain inflation, this expenditure may indeed perversely have contributed towards it: to the extent that it was financed out of taxes, and to the extent that it is the aim of trade unions to safeguard the post-tax income of their members, so it will have pushed up demands for higher wages.

All this would suggest that attaching the adjective "social" to a particular form of expenditure should not automatically confer on it the modern equivalent of clerical privilege: immunity from the axe. Any analysis of the options available for future expenditure (and other) policies must therefore start with the acceptance that new circumstances [force] new choices.

*Rudolf Klein, "Social Priorities in an Age of Inflation," *New Society*, July 3, 1975. This first appeared in *New Society*, London, the weekly review of the social sciences.

Take, for example, the much-debated question of how much scope there is for financing public services by consumer charges. The debate about this issue has tended to be seriously lopsided. The argument has concentrated on consumer *payments* (are they socially desirable? are they administratively possible?) to the neglect of the other side of the equation, consumer *costs*. It has been assumed that because a service is free, it is also necessarily cost-less to the consumer. This is nonsense. In the case of the national health service, for instance, there has been a great deal of fuss about prescription and other charges, but hardly any discussion about the costs imposed on the public by the present system of rationing through waiting lists and shortages.

There is another traditional concept of social policy which per-haps requires re-analysis in the light of changed circumstances: the concept of relative deprivation. This is essentially a dynamic con-cept born of the growth society, which usefully mobilised opinion in support of policies designed to share out the increased wealth in a way which would ensure that the standards of living of the poor rose in line with the rest of the population. Given a static economy, this concept is not particularly helpful. (Its double-edged nature can be seen when the possible consequences of apply-ing the relative deprivation doctrine to a condition of falling living standards are examined: logically it might mean maintaining rela-tivities—and thus cutting everyone's standards of living, including those of the poorest.) It may be that more traditional concepts—based on judgments as to what is considered to be a tolerable way of life, and what resources are required to sustain it—may be more appropriate in the second half of the seventies.

More critically still, should the traditional values which inform the present pattern of social priorities be applied unquestioningly in a new situation? For example, it could be argued that in condi-tions of economic crisis, overriding priority ought to be given to those aspects of social policy which sustain industrial activity: this might imply putting money into those health services which help to keep people at work, as distinct from those which merely pro-long life, into industrial retraining schemes rather than provision for the elderly. Again, much of social expenditure in the past has been designed—whether deliberately or not—to encourage con-sumers to raise their expectations and demands: for example, as in the case of housing, by cushioning them against rising costs. In the new circumstances, it could be argued that the emphasis of policy ought to be to discourage additional demands which the nation cannot afford to meet.

To ask questions about social priorities in the age of inflation is to ask questions also about the capacity of Britain's existing institutions of government to cope with them. It is to raise the issue of who should decide on the priorities. The rhetoric of national priorities is the language of centralisation: must greater stringency inevitably lead to greater control by Whitehall over local authorities? But if greater power is going to be assumed by Whitehall, has parliament the ability to make ministers and civil servants accountable for their use of it. In the past there has been a basic assymetry in the political control of public expenditure: MPs have tended to call for cuts in the total of spending, while demanding increases in specific items. Now the challenge is to adapt a political system which seems almost designed to generate demands for extra expenditure to a situation which calls for decisions about who should get less.

6-2. CONFLICTS OVER ADJUSTING BENEFITS TO INFLATION*

The struggle to preserve the benefits of small groups with special needs, and to add new kinds of beneficiaries becomes more severe once inflation begins to erode social security benefits. In Britain, this has most often taken the form of "uprating" controversies, especially in trying to keep pensions at a reasonable level.

This month social security benefits are due to be uprated, by law. Yet for a long time the amount of benefit was purely a matter of discretion for the government of the day. As a result, inflation, though less ferocious than at present, consistently eroded the real value of benefits in the period between upratings. These occurred sporadically—on average, every 2½ years—but hardly at random: in six of the seven general elections between 1950 and 1970 there was a pension increase during the election year, or the year immediately before. As inflation gathered pace, and rates of benefits, particularly of national insurance retirement pensions, became a live political issue, this haphazard approach was sharply reversed.

*Laurence Lustgarten, "Society at Work: The Uprating Scandal," *New Society*, Nov. 4, 1976. This first appeared in *New Society*, London, the weekly review of the social sciences.

Successive governments enacted legislation to require periodic reviews. The results are worthy of examination, for they determine the standard of living of over 10 million national insurance beneficiaries and their dependents. They also shed sombre light on the social values that increasingly dominate the social security system.

The Social Security Act, 1973, first required an "annual review of benefits for purpose of uprating." The Social Services Secretary was directed to determine whether current rates had "retained their value in relation to the general level of prices: as they had changed during the year, and to lay before parliament the draft of an order increasing benefits at least to the extent necessary to restore their real value.

But no uprating actually occurred under this legislation. The minority Labour government, savouring its somewhat unexpected and precarious presence in office and anticipating another election shortly, moved quickly to implement its campaign promises to help old age pensioners. In addition to instituting a large immediate increase in all benefits, the National Insurance Act, 1974, replaced the discretionary power with a requirement that the Secretary of State base the uprating on the level of earnings rather than prices if this would be to beneficiaries' advantage. Since earnings had risen faster than prices in every year since 1945, the idea was to enable beneficiaries to share in the rising prosperity of the country; adjustment of benefits with respect to prices alone would mean that they become poorer relative to the working population.

This reform was overdue. It represents a commitment to the idea of community and a rejection of the values of the market. But this commitment was only partial. While the Conservative legislation applied across the board, the Labour reform excluded certain beneficiaries: the unemployed, the sick, and women receiving maternity allowance, as well as the additions for their dependents.

The distinction is not between those who have contributed and those who have not—supposedly the basis of the national insurance scheme—but between those whom the authorities view with suspicion if they are unable to work, and those whose absence from work is regarded as acceptable. In official euphemism, the two groups are distinguished as "short-term" and "long-term" beneficiaries; in reality the notion of the deserving poor is alive, well, and increasingly influential in social security policy. Quite apart from other issues, the distinction produces absurd anomalies, such as the more generous treatment accorded to widows with dependents than to women who leave work to care for their new-born children.

The justification for excluding the unemployed, the sick, new mothers, and their dependents, from the new uprating provision was neither offered nor questioned when the 1974 act was debated in parliament. The Conservative opposition, indeed, were hardly in a position to be vehement. When in office the previous year, they had introduced a similar, but even more fundamental, change in the structure of benefits. Beveridge had insisted that identical provision be made for *all* involuntary interruptions of earnings: he defined social security as the (partial) replacement of earnings when interrupted, or rendered inadequate, by the "eight primary causes of need" his programme was designed to meet and overcome.

Earnings-related benefits, introduced in 1959 and 1966, created a differentiation in the amounts of benefit, but this was based on the recipient's income and contributions, not the cause of his need. From October 1973, however, old age and widows' pensions were paid at a higher rate than unemployment, sickness and maternity benefits. Labour's 1974 increase more than trebled the gap, and its differential uprating was superimposed upon this dual system of benefit. Because upratings are done in percentage terms rather than an absolute sum, the gap widens each time the rate is changed. The result is dramatic: in 1973, the long-term benefit rate for a single person exceeded the short-term rate by only 40p; for a married couple the difference was 60p. Now, after three Labour upratings, the gaps are respectively, £2.20 and £3.20; in the former case, this is a difference of 19.8 per cent.

One of the fundamental principles of social security has been quietly torn out by the roots, and it is difficult to find sensible justification for what has been done. The plight of the aged always commands sympathy, but it is far from clear that their need is always the greatest. The "short-term" beneficiary suffers the most drastic drop in standard of living when he is unable to work, yet it is he who receives the most niggardly treatment in return.

Nor can the distinction be justified by the fact that pensions, unlike short-term benefits, are taxable. The age allowance introduced last year gives a man or his wife who are over 65 at any time during the income tax year, a tax allowance—an amount of income on which no tax is payable—of £1,555, 50 per cent higher than that granted ordinary taxpayers. At current rates, they would receive a flat-rate pension of £21.20, or roughly £1,100 yearly. They would thus have to receive just under £9 per week in occupational pension or other incomes before they paid any income tax at all. For most former wage-earners, this means that pensions are effectively tax free. Similar calculations can be made for single pensioners and widows.

It should be noted that the favouritism shown to widows and pensioners is, for many individuals and their families, of no advantage whatever. Of eight million old age pensioners some two million receive supplementary benefit. Anyone whose sole income is a national insurance pension automatically qualifies for supplementary benefit. For this vast number of people, a pension rise merely reduces their supplementary benefit entitlement. Even if earnings consistently outpace prices, it is unlikely that those now in this group can ever escape dependence on supplementary benefit. Indeed until the mid-1980s, when the new scheme envisaged by the Social Security Pensions Act, 1975, begins to have substantial effect, they will be joined by scores of thousands more newly retired people. On the other hand, nearly 900,000 pensioners eligible for, but not claiming supplementary benefit . . . will find the new method of uprating particularly valuable.

6-3. UNCERTAINTIES OF PENSION REFORM*

The political weight of the elderly meant that they have regularly received more careful attention, and over the past two decades the most successful reform of the social welfare system has been to devise a unified pension scheme involving both public and private retirement plans. Margaret Stone assesses the change.

Today is an historic day. It is the first, albeit the least significant, of the several deadlines leading to the launch of the state earnings related pension scheme. Few outside the Government and pensions industry will mark the occasion—yet it is an event of great importance for everyone.

Since its tentative beginnings in 1908 with the Old Age Pensions Act, the state pension scheme has finally come of age. From April, 1978, the principle that everyone (at least those in employment)

*Margaret Stone, "Earnings Related Pensions: End of a Seventy-Year Journey," *The Times* (London), Dec. 7, 1977.

should be entitled to an earnings related pension at retirement will become a fact—thanks to Richard Crossman, Sir Keith Joseph and finally, and successfully, Barbara Castle.

In a mixed economy it is appropriate that there is no ideological insistence that it is the state, or alternatively, the employer, who must pay the benefits.

Each employer, after consultation with his employees, has had the right to determine whether to stay within the state scheme—in which case the state pays the guaranteed minimum earnings related pension (gmp)—or to contract out of it and pay the gmp through the mechanism of an occupational pension scheme.

Today is the final day when employers who have decided to stay within the state scheme should notify their employees of that choice. In practice, it is, in fact, a fairly meaningless requirement.

Even if employees, or more likely a union, took an employer to court over his failure to notify them, the worst that could follow seems to be a public wigging off.

Much more excitement centres on the next stage of the countdown, now December 23, which is the final day for deciding to contract out of the state scheme without incurring financial penalties (because of higher than necessary contributions), for both the employer and his employees.

This is because the last day for applying to the Occupational Pensions Board for a contracting out certificate is March 23, by which time the employer should have had a statutory three-month consultation with the unions, which theoretically must begin on December 23 at the latest. . . .

There is also little doubt that the administrators seriously underestimated the strain the new arrangements would impose upon the limited number of organizations, pension consultants, insurance companies, and law firms, the wholesalers who had to educate, advise and help their clients implement the final decision.

Then the Occupational Pensions Board was starting from scratch too and has not been able to act as quickly or as decisively is would-be contracting-out companies would have wished.

Over and above all this has been financial uncertainty. It is not so difficult to recall the impact the sagging pound, ever-rising interest rates, an equity market in the doldrums and question marks over a future pay policy had on everyone's confidence. Complicated and difficult-to-grasp company pension schemes were pushed to the bottom of many an in-tray. . . .

Although about 11,000 to 15,000 company schemes (out of some 65,000 in the country) are expected to be contracted out, only 500 have received their contracting-out certificate while another 2,300 applications to contract out are in the pipeline. Many more will be made within the next three months and even those which fail to make the deadline will not be barred from acquiring their contracting-out certificate later.

Most of the country's top companies have contracted out and the nationalized industries too, but among the rest there seems to have been a greater enthusiasm for staying within the state scheme and living on top of it (providing an extra occupational pension on top) than was envisaged. That way the state picks up the bill for the guaranteed minimum pension and the firm provides as much extra cream as it sees fit or the Inland Revenue allows.

After the excitement and the trumpeting that is bound to accompany the actual start of the scheme, interest in pensions will probably wane for a little. But not for long; the history of pensions in the last few years has proved conclusively that it is not a static subject. Even before the new state earnings related scheme gets officially under way the experts are already looking forward to the modifications that are bound to come, one day.

6-4. INTEGRATING TAXATION AND SOCIAL WELFARE*

The complexity of the social security system increases pressure to devise a simpler way of assessing how well it is achieving its objectives. The intricacies of the British system made this apparent even before the economic shocks of the seventies, and Heath explored using a tax credit scheme. As the Economist *argues, tax exemptions and tax deductions are in many ways also part of the social security system, and a fully developed tax credit system seems the desirable system.*

The painful fourth way is to broach the cardinal political principle governing change, which is that it should never make (or at least be seen to make) anybody (except the wicked rich) worse off. The simplest example of how all change is impeded by this rule of "don't hurt any large class of voters" is the extraordinary sex

*"How to Reform Social Security," *The Economist*, July 9, 1977.

discrimination in favour of women in their retirement age. On average, British women live five years longer than men, but they retire on a pension five years earlier. A reduction in the male retirement age to 60 would cost an indigestible £2 billion a year. But no British government is going to grasp the nettle of nil cost equalisation, because this would mean denying women the pension until they were 64½. In the same way, a campaign for universal benefits may enlist "the sharp elbows of the middle class"—if they can be persuaded that someone else will foot the bill. But it always means that the proportion of increased expenditure going to the poorest is tiny.

The dilemma between universal benefits (expensive, wasted on the rich, but not discriminatory) and means-tests (echoes of the poor law, discriminatory, inquisitorial, dependent on take-up, but cost-effective in concentrating benefit on the poor) is as old as social security itself. All governments, however much they may decry means tests in their political manifestoes, find it hard to abolish them in practice. Family income supplement (fis), a Labour-despised temporary expedient introduced by the Tories, is still running. It would cost £5 billion a year to raise universal child benefit to the level that would give the same amount of help as fis to the very poorest. Middle-class fathers' elbows are not going to flail for an increase of that order, which they know would have to be taxed back from them.

The childless, like the rich, are not a bottomless source of extra tax. Improvements in social security must, at Britain's nil growth rate, be made at someone's (taxpaying, ie means-tested) expense. Pretended, or encouraged, ignorance of this fact is only made possible by the practice of running tax and social security policy in two separate compartments. This becomes, year by year, more self contradictory. About 60% of those working parents whom social security policy now dictates are poor enough to need fis are simultaneously deemed rich enough to pay tax.

There are smaller, but similar, idiosyncrasies in maintaining the now-bogus distinction between national insurance and income tax; in running two distinct systems of income support for the unemployed, or two systems for the allocation of rent assistance; in the innumerable different means-tests systems for different benefits dependent on income; and in the distinctions between taxed and tax-free benefits, or between national insurance-based and other benefits.

Wanted: A Bipartisan Tax Credit Scheme

The first attempt to fuse taxes and (some) benefits came with the Heath government's green paper in 1972. All such schemes tend to be expensive, because of the difficulty of fixing high enough basic credits (ie, minimum income levels for those with no other income) without having to set the tax rate on the first tranche of income (ie, up to the point at which the credits are exhausted, or matched by tax due) discouragingly high. But this Tory scheme was exceedingly expensive, precisely because it sought to buy acceptance of the tax-credit idea by designing one which appeared to make everybody slightly better off.

What is now needed is bipartisan agreement that the tax and social security systems do need to be fused (Labour politicians should be encouraged to remember that their scheme for replacing tax allowances with child benefit is identical to the child credit slice of the tax-credit scheme) so that whoever wins the next general election will be able to make progress towards this fusion without having to buy electoral support by expensively sugaring the switchover.

The choice for that government will be between big decisions that make rather painful changes in the patterns of advantage and disadvantage, or small ones that give little real help to those most in need. Even during Britain's North Sea bubble in the 1980s, no British government is going to be able to double the real value of social security at a stroke, nor rebuild its structure without piling bricks on someone's toes.

6-5. COMPLEXITIES OF LIMITING SOCIAL WELFARE COSTS*

Social security benefits are the largest single transfer within the British budget: about £20 billion of £70 public spending. The Thatcher government searched hard for ways to reduce this transfer, but encountered many of the complications and dilemmas that every welfare state confronts. The DHSS even found it impossible to estimate the largest cuts of 20 percent. Malcolm Dean reviews the difficult options for any government hoping to reduce social welfare payments.

*Malcolm Dean, "The Poor's Biggest Blow since the Workhouse," *The Guardian*, Jan. 29, 1980 (selections).

"If this is Dunkirk, then we're going to insist that everybody has to share in the suffering—not just the poor."

The quote comes from one of Whitehall's embattled spending departments as the Conservative cabinet continued its review this week of the latest round of expenditure cuts.

But will everyone share in the suffering? No, the first Conservative Budget has seen to that. There probably will not be any further tax cuts this year—from the hints being dropped by the Treasury— but the £20,000-a-year man, who received a £2,000 tax free bonus for the tax cuts in last year's Budget will still be able to sit back and enjoy an extra £42 per week this year.

We know Mr. Carlisle (Secretary of State for Education) has instructed educational authorities to cut £240 million from their budgets through reductions in school meals, milk and transport plus increased charges. And we know social services, which have had an effective 9 per cent cut imposed on their planned expenditure from April, are already planning reductions to home help services, meals on wheels, old people's homes and day centres.

Yet, the most worrying development in Whitehall in the last six months has been the break up of the social policy coalition. The big spending departments' ministers are no longer fighting together. Labour ministers too had their differences, but they would never have exhibited the hostility towards social security which Conservative spending ministers have shown in recent weeks.

The reason why social security has been protected so far is mostly a mixture of law and bluff. The Government had to increase pensions, unemployment benefits and sick pay by Law. Legally, it did not have to increase supplementary benefits but by pointing to the established conventions, officials were able to hold the line.

Just what are the government's options? Ideally it would like to tax short-term benefits. In this approach it could claim the support of Beveridge, the Supplementary Benefit Commission and most social policy specialists. The principle which would be applied is that all income should be subject to tax. Once a government tries to distinguish between worthy and unworthy sources of income, it has started down the road to pitfalls.

The reason why we don't tax the benefits at the moment is because of the extra staff which would be needed. Labour tried to tax the benefit when it first started in 1949 but found it hopelessly complex. Today, it is even more complex. About 20 million bits of paper would need to pass between local social security and tax offices. More important still 10,000 extra staff would be needed to administer the scheme.

If the taxation of benefits is ruled out then breaking the index-link which protects benefits is the obvious alternative. But there are problems here too. If the protection of short-term benefits is abolished, several thousand additional claimants will be tipped into supplementary benefits. But SB is about three times as expensive to administer as unemployment benefit. And the Civil Service unions are in no mood to allow this increase in work without the equivalent increase in staff.

That leaves the government looking at supplementary benefit—a benefit which the supplementary benefit commission has already said is too low. True, the five million poor people who SB supports were given a small increase to their standard of living under Labour. The short-term benefits went up by 3.7 per cent in real terms and the long-term by 9.6 per cent. But this still leaves a family on welfare today with only 76p a day to meet all the needs of a child aged five to 10.

There is one final social security problem for the government which is also an embarrassment: child benefit.

This was their invention but how do they increase it when a mere £1-a-week increase costs an inhibiting £600 million? One way, of course, would be to discount the benefit from public expenditure. If, for example, child tax allowances were still in operation instead of being merged with child benefit, an increase in the allowance would not have been included in the public expenditure figures. In opposition, the Conservatives called for this reform but now that they are in government, they seem unready to apply it.

There is, at the moment, only one small glimmer of hope for social reformers. This is the swing in the opinion polls against the cuts. Even last year, when the arch-enemies of public expenditure, the Institute of Economic Affairs, asked people whether they would vote to "reduce taxation and accept fewer services," two out of every three said they would not. Now there are signs that the majority against the cuts is becoming even bigger. It is the one voice which Mrs. Thatcher may [be] forced to listen to.

7 Race and Immigration: A Consensual Non-decision

Of all the issues presented in this study, race relations raises the most profound doubts about the effectiveness of the two-party system and parliamentary politics. Race is an issue that cuts across party loyalties. Except for a brief period in the late 1950s when Hugh Gaitskell, the Labour leader of the Opposition during the Macmillan government, fought the early attempts to cut off the flow of Asian and African immigrants to Britain, consensus has prevented Britain from seeking new solutions to racial conflict; indeed, party leaders and other national figures have often exploited racial fears.

Although Britain has a smaller nonwhite population than France or Germany and only a fraction of the American black population, there are lengthy and futile controversies over how many non-whites are in Britain. The Department of Environment has no figures on race and housing and the Department of Education collects nothing on the progress of nonwhites in teacher colleges and other educational programs essential to achieving integration (Select Committee, 1974–75, p. xxi). The best aggregate information appears to be collected by a travel survey done for the Department of Industry (Select Committee, 1977–78, p. xvii). The inadequate statistics both reflect and encourage avoidance. Even worse, ignorance leaves the field open to more drastic and arbitrary proposals, such as that of the Parliamentary Group on the feasibility and usefulness of a Register for Dependents (1977), which proposed compulsory registration.

The use of immigration statistics has been no better. Even after complex immigration laws cut off the flow of immigrants from Asia and the West Indies, political leaders still used the threat of nonwhite immigration to avoid facing up to racism within their own country. In fact, the flow of black immigrants has been virtually stopped since 1962 and more recent laws limit Asian immigration primarily to dependents of Asians already in the country. Only about 35,000 immigrants a year now enter Britain, but in 1978 the Conservative leader and later prime minister, Margaret Thatcher, could talk of Britain being "swamped" by immigrants.

The census classification itself is not particularly useful in estimating the scale of Britain's racial problem (Lomas, 1973). The 1971 census showed slightly over a million "coloured" persons from the New Commonwealth, meaning the West Indies, Africa, Pakistan, India, and Bangladesh. But this does not identify all the Asian population, much of which came to Britain from East Africa under earlier immigration legislation. Perhaps the most useful figure is that there are about 750,000 "coloured" adults in Britain in a total black and Asian population of about 1.8 million. This means about one in thirty Britons is nonwhite. By the turn of the century the estimated nonwhite population will be 3.3 million or roughly one of seventeen Britons, though this figure may be too high given the declining birth rates of both Asians and West Indians. A more practical consideration is that the racial population is concentrated regionally, with about 80 percent in London and the Midlands (Smith, 1976, pp. 15–19). Nonwhites are concentrated in urban centers although there has been some dispersion of Asians over recent years. About three-fourths of the nonwhites live in cities, compared with 40 percent for the total British population. There are large concentrations in Midland industrial cities, such as Leicester, Birmingham, and Bradford, and in particular London boroughs, such as Islington, Brent, and Camden.

The pattern of location and housing makes race remote from the daily lives of most British citizens and handicaps political activity by nonwhites to defend their interests. The religious and ethnic differences among Indians, Pakistanis, and West Indians have also hindered the formation of a minority political movement similar to the Black Power Movement in the United States. Although New Commonwealth immigrants have legal and political rights under British law, social discrimination against minorities is often similar to that found on the continent. For over a decade there has been ample evidence of unfair housing policies, unequal access to job training and employment, and inadequate education (E. Rose, 1969). Like the continental European countries, Britain is a relatively homogeneous society confronted with the immense problem of becoming a multi-cultural society. In this respect, the migrant workers and their families, who number over 3 million in France and Germany, are no different from the Asians and West Indians in Britain.

Context

Numerous attitudinal studies have revealed the depth of racial feeling in Britain (Daniel, 1968). Britain is not distinguished as much because of its profound racist dispositions as because in most policy areas it has placed a high premium on equity and fairness in dealing with the disadvantaged. The surveys all point in one direction, summed up by Richard Rose (1974, p. 30), who noted that immigrants are considered "British blacks" rather than "black Britons." The effect is to perpetuate political and administrative ambiguities that would surprise many Americans and possibly many Europeans whose governments have taken even fewer steps than Britain to achieve integration. For example, a razor suitable for cutting blacks' beards was banned for importation into Britain on grounds that it could be sold to only one group ("Barberous," 1977). Racial hostility cuts across class, region, and party (Studlar, 1977). The curious effect has been to "depoliticize" race in the British system. Political leaders have no incentive to act because neither societal nor elite consensus presses for change.

The measures that have been taken show how confused and uncertain the political response has been. A number of factors contribute to this neglect. The colonial heritage weighs heavily on the British elite. Its importance is not so much that racism finds its origins in colonies; the vast majority of the British population had little or nothing to do with the British Empire. But the notion of "Little England" is deeply imbedded in British society and politics. The history of British relationships to nonwhites is not all that different from that of most European countries. The contemporary effect is a pervasive ambivalence between patronizing and fearing the once colonized who have taken refuge in Britain. Thus, we find the Labour government in 1968 (in the midst of passing new immigration restraints) announcing that providing help to the victims of political repression in Kenya is "a duty laid upon our shoulders as trustees" (from Thornton, 1968, p. 378). However much alarm race creates among Britons, they also came to the rescue of successive waves of Asians expelled from East African countries. The British did not seem aware that the refugees were welcomed to a country where eight or ten Asians or West Indians often sleep in shifts in one room.

Britain has also vacillated between passing more stringent laws to keep racial minorities out and hoping that timid measures to encourage racial harmony will suffice. The result has been that British immigration laws are "a jungle" (Bohning, 1972, p. 133) that can be manipulated by immigration officials in extraordinary ways to exclude those who are entitled to join families in Britain. An alarming study of overseas screening of dependents (Akram, 1974) shows how confusing questions and bureaucratic obfuscation deny and delay entrance. More recently, under pressure, the government admitted that Asian women joining their fiancés or husbands in Britain were subjected to humiliating virginity examinations, and dangerously inexpert x-rays were used to determine age on the chance that the results might justify rejection of their applications. Within the country race legislation is still only feebly reinforced with legal sanctions. The first official notice of racial discrimination in a public establishment (presumably outlawed under the 1968 Race Relations Act) was served in 1978 (*Times*, Nov. 24, 1978). By not deciding what policies should be pursued, government, in effect, lives from emergency to emergency, improvising legislation with no clear purpose and with little enforcement.

Another manifestation of indecision in racial matters is the ambiguity surrounding British nationality. The first attempt to restrict entry was the 1905 Aliens Act, designed to keep out Jews fleeing from Russia and Eastern Europe. This Act was replaced by the Aliens Restriction Act of 1914, which was annually renewed with no debate and was the major legislation on immigration until 1971. During this period it was claimed that all the members of the Commonwealth were British citizens. With Indian and Pakistani independence in 1947, however, nationality was subdivided between citizens of the United Kingdom and Colonies and those of the independent, or "New," Commonwealth. There is today a tangle of laws and rules governing British "citizens" outside Britain that substitute for clear legislation about what it means to be a citizen in Britain. Clarifying nationality, the simplest way to establish the rights of British citizens, has been avoided by both major parties even though Commonwealth citizenship has ceased to have any real meaning. The Labour government did produce a

Green Paper (weak White Paper) on nationality in 1977, partly to fulfill an election pledge made three years before and partly with an eye to the growing importance of Asian and African voters in several marginal constituencies. It was obvious that the proposal was launched so late in the life of the Labour government that no decision would be forthcoming.

Until 1958, British policy toward race continued to be a curious amalgam of colonial nostalgia and refusal to notice growing racial tensions within British society. But popular alarm was growing and was often fueled by an alarmist press. When five hundred West Indians set out for Britain in 1948, there was a full debate in the House of Commons. Both parties seemed to see the incident "not as a free movement of voluntary labour but as a sort of slave transportation engineered by evil agencies somewhere in the Caribbean" (Lewis, quoted in Hiro, 1973, p. 188). A fivefold increase in West Indian immigration from 2,000 in 1953 to 10,500 in 1954 spread alarm among Tories and in 1955 the Conservatives' Central Council voted to apply alien restrictions to Commonwealth immigrants. One Conservative MP warned, "A question which affects the future of our own race and breed is not one we should merely leave to chance" (Foot, 1965, p. 130). A Labour MP responded that the "coloured races" would soon outnumber the white races by five to one and become a threat to the white world. From such sentiments emerged a bipartisan consensus that Britain must be protected.

From these early years of the race debate to the present both parties have been internally divided. The Conservatives were under severe pressure from strongly reactionary backbenchers but the leadership remained loyal to the Commonwealth and was reluctant to abandon their symbol of world power. Nearer to the truth is the fact that very few leaders took much interest in race and immigration. Churchill complained in 1954 that immigration "is the most important subject facing this country, but I cannot get any of my ministers to take any notice" (Bradley, 1978). As often happens with neglected social issues, violent protest flared up with the Nottingham and Notting Hill riots of 1958. After severely punishing the offenders the Conservative leaders preached calm and indifference. But in one of the more remarkable and disastrous examples of backbench and grassroots pressure the 1958 and 1961 Conservative Party Conferences voted for strong restrictions on immigration.

By 1960 public opinion had clearly consolidated in favor of more controls. A survey of six urban constituencies showed over 80 percent of both Labour and Conservative voters favoring restrictions (Katznelson, 1973, p. 133). The Tory leadership was undecided but under great pressure from its reactionary right wing. The Queen's Speech of the fall of 1961 promised more control and the next day a bill was published that became the 1962 Commonwealth Immigration Act. The Act required that Commonwealth citizens have work permits from the Ministry of Labour. The rules and procedures, much as in France, were left to Ministry officials. The law established three categories of permits: Commonwealth citizens coming for specific jobs; those with special skills and qualifications; and those without immediate employment arrangements. Part of the emerging bipartisan agreement was that the last category of permits was abolished by the Labour government in 1965.

Since the Labour Party was in severe disarray in the late 1950s, too much can be made of the views it expressed then. Labour's position seems no more considered than was the imposition of controls by the Conservatives. If anything, Labour was influenced by its vague desire to help the underdog and sympathies among its more intellectual leaders to preserve Commonwealth ties. Gaitskell, the party leader, led a dramatic attack against the 1962 Tory immigration law that exhilarated its discouraged and rebellious left wing. But the overwhelming public disapproval of his liberal stand was made clear. The shadow foreign secretary, Patrick Gordon-Walker, also attacked the Tory bill but was subjected to such a torrential protest from his constituency that he did not take a position on the 1962 Act. The lesson was driven home more forcefully in the 1964 election, when Gordon-Walker lost the normally safe Labour seat of Smethwick (Deakin, 1968). When another safe seat was vacated for him in early 1965 so that he might join his colleagues in the House of Commons, he was again defeated. Left with a majority of three the Labour Party realized that, as Hiro noted (1973, p. 198), it had to be seen as tough on immigration whatever its ideological values might be.

A more pragmatic politician than Gaitskell, Wilson promised additional immigration restrictions in the 1964 Labour Party Manifesto. Prior to taking office he had also offered bipartisan support for the renewal of the 1962 Act. But the Labour Party had also been committed for a decade or more to a liberal race policy.

The contortions needed to reconcile these objectives or, more accurately, to continue to treat them as unrelated issues, tell us a great deal about the shortcomings of British policymaking. Because of Labour's small majority in 1964, they were fair game for the Conservatives, who launched a fierce attack on the proposed Race Relations bill. Labour support was lukewarm at best, and in the 1965 Race Relations Act the proposed criminal penalties for discrimination in public places were abandoned for pitifully small civil fines. In a process described as "haphazard, secret and inefficient" (Hindrell, 1965, p. 198), Parliament agreed there was no need to punish discrimination in housing or employment.

Conservative acceptance was purchased by the close consultation between the two parties in drafting the bill. The compromise was signaled with Labour's 1965 White Paper, which promised a tougher line on immigration and was enthusiastically acclaimed by both sides of the House of Commons. Labour promised voluntary repatriation at government expense, stiffer administrative controls on immigration, compulsory police registration for immigrants whose papers seemed doubtful, and discretionary powers for the home secretary to deport illegal entrants. The permissible age for the entrance of dependents would be reduced from eighteen to sixteen years of age. Most important, Labour promised to reduce entry permits from 20,000 to 8,500 a year and do away with work permits for immigrants without jobs. In effect, Conservatives and Labour joined forces on the immigration issue. A weak Race Relations Act was accepted by the Conservative Leader as "sensible and fair" (Katznelson, pp. 148–49) in return for a mutually advantageous promise to toughen immigration policy. In fact, the Conservatives had wanted even tougher controls, including a "grandfather clause" to limit entrance of dependents.

The 1965 Race Relations Act marks the formation of consensus between the two major parties to do little or nothing about growing racial problems within the country. The home secretary, Roy Jenkins, had made a courageous attempt to obtain stronger legislation, but was beaten back by his own party and by Conservatives. Both parties were eager to bury the issue as the 1966 elections approached, and both mistakenly thought that this could be done by reassuring the British public that immigration would be strictly regulated. That the origins of British racial problems might be within Britain seemed to elude the nation's leaders. A consensus had been formed but it was totally inappropriate to the problem.

Agenda

A consensus that is inappropriate to the problem is constantly vulnerable to crises. Two such events erupted to shatter the complacency that British leaders hoped to construct. The first was the deportation of thousands of Asian Kenyans in 1967. Oddly enough, few took notice of Britain's obligation to help both white and Asian settlers when the Conservatives conceded Kenyan independence in 1963. The cry of alarm came from Enoch Powell, the Conservatives' most vehement opponent of immigration, and the press proclaimed that a new "flood" of Asian immigrants would soon arrive. In fact, about 95,000 Kenyan Asians were eligible for British citizenship and of these only 66,000 arrived in Britain (Hiro, 1973, pp. 209–10). The second trigger was the increased politicization of race for immediate political advantage. Though Enoch Powell was no doubt sincere in his convictions, his Birmingham speech of April 1968 effectively destroyed the equilibrium of 1965. His prophecy of "the River Tiber foaming with much blood" created a new hysteria. Thousands of dockers demonstrated before Parliament and MPs were besieged with protests from frantic citizens.

Out of this panic emerged the Commonwealth Immigration Act of 1968, which the *New Statesman* (March 1, 1968) described as "the first incontestably racialist law to be placed on the statute books." Fed by reports of the black protest in America, Parliament resurrected the "grandfather" clause of earlier legislation in the United States in order to enable white settlers to reenter the United Kingdom before Asians. Asians were to be limited to 1,500 entry permits a year. The 1968 Act produced little debate. It was presented, debated, and passed through both Houses of Parliament in a week. Only sixty-two MPs voted against it, although it was unanimously opposed by the minority Liberal Party. Later polls showed that 39 percent of the public favored a ban on *all* immigration and three-fourths or more of *both* Labour and Conservative voters favored the Act (Hiro, 1973, p. 212).

The home secretary, James Callaghan, tried to reduce the racist tone of the Act by emphasizing Labour's plan for a new Race Relations Act. Under the 1965 legislation a weak Race Relations Board had been established and a powerless advisory group, the National Committee for Commonwealth Immigrants (NCCI), had been created to advise the government. The previous Labour home secretary, Roy Jenkins, had committed the government in 1967 to legislation forbidding discrimination in housing and employment. When a bill emerged nine months later it forbad discrimination in housing, business, and land sales and in hiring, training, promotion, and dismissal of workers. For a moment it appeared that Britain, which has never had clear legal definition of individual rights, might break with its tradition to protect racial minorities. With most Conservatives abstaining, only 182 of 360 Labour and Liberal votes could be rallied to pass the 1968 Race Relations Act.

The new Act recognized that change must occur at the community level. The Race Relations Board could hear and give opinions on individual complaints of discrimination but it had no legal powers to assist investigations, produce evidence, or impose penalties. The NCCI was converted into the Community Relations Commission (CRC). With its encouragement local community relations committees were organized, and in 1966 the government authorized local government subsidies of up to three-fourths of the cost of local projects to advance social integration. Progress was painfully slow. An investigation showed that one of the oldest and best-organized local committees, Nottingham, had placed only twenty nonwhite families in council (public) housing after more than a decade's effort (Burney, 1967, p. 200). A careful study of the Nottingham effort concluded that the local committees were no more than "buffering institutions" to protect national leaders and to defuse racial protest (Katznelson, 1973). Another author (Lawrence, 1974) found that minority representation was more effective. What is clear is that Parliament wanted no direct involvement in racial politics and refused to set legal standards to prevent discrimination.

Although race had been on the national agenda since the 1964 election, the 1968 Act was only a timid recognition that something must be done to protect minorities. Positive action against racial discrimination was difficult because responsibility for integration was widely dispersed throughout Whitehall (see Chapter 2). One could more easily attribute governmental lethargy to racial hostility in government were it not that other complex policies were similarly mired down in central bureaucracy. An indication of the low priority placed on race was that racial integration programs were assigned to a small bureau of civil servants in the Department of Economic Affairs, by this time a lame-duck ministry with no leverage over other departments. Oddly enough, fundamental social needs had been recognized. The 1965 White Paper noted the importance of dispersing nonwhite children into white schools and the 1966 Local Government Act provided additional funds to local authorities for bilingual instruction. The government began organizing Educational Priority Areas in 1967. Within a few days of Powell's "rivers of blood" speech, Wilson announced the Urban Programme (Holman and Hamilton, 1973) to provide additional assistance to racial minorities. Based in the Home Office, it had little or no authority to press other departments to cooperate. In 1969 the Urban Programme spawned the Community Development Projects, twelve intensive experiments in racial neighborhoods and modeled after the American Community Action Program (Batley and Edwards, 1978). But as we have seen (Chapter 5), the political subordination of British local government does not assure policy compliance, and the heavily burdened local governments were not eager to take on such controversial tasks with only ambiguous directions from the center.

The new programs deserve special mention for they are the first move toward "positive discrimination." Though similar in form to Affirmative Action in the United States, the rationale for special assistance to minorities was actually much closer to the Victorian notion of the deserving poor (Batley, 1978). The Urban Programme cloaked special assistance for racial minorities in conventional terms, thereby avoiding the issue of racial politics. The Home Office gave some consideration to creating a program similar to the American Office of Economic Opportunity, but this was soon abandoned in favor of voluntary efforts by local authorities. The first phase of the Urban Programme designated thirty-four municipalities as particularly needy because of overcrowded housing (more than 1.5 persons per room) or because there were more than 6 percent immigrant children in the schools. In later versions funds were made available for nurseries, family centers, and special education projects. In another manifestation of center-local problems in Britain (see Chapter 5), the local voluntary efforts may have created "the worst of all possible situations." The local committee "cannot use all the pressure group tactics of public exposure and criticism because it is a quasi-statutory body dependent on the support of the Government-created national agency. At the same time, it has no statutory powers of its own and cannot compel a local authority to co-operate or even, in some cases, acknowledge its existence" (Hill and Issacharoff, 1971, p. 286).

One might attribute this device to racist intentions to build "buffering institutions" between racial minorities and government, but very similar institutional structures have handicapped other British programs and policies.

Compared to other European countries in 1968, Britain was a leader. The great irony of British racial policy is that the issue was constantly reverting to citizenship and immigration in order to exploit partisan political advantages. Leaders wanted the internal question of race depoliticized, but were never willing to depoliticize the international dimensions of race. Well before the 1970 election both Labour and Conservative leaders were vying over who would appear to be firmer in excluding immigrants, apparently oblivious to the fact that many African and Asian Britons were listening. James Callaghan, the home secretary, took pride in announcing that any family unable to support itself could now have its way home paid by DHSS. His announcement was promptly belittled by Quintin Hogg (now Lord Hailsham), normally a moderate voice on racial matters, as a "mouse of a scheme . . . for dropouts" (Hiro, 1973, p. 303). The Tory election manifesto proclaimed new efforts to hasten voluntary repatriation. Although the leader of the Opposition, Heath, dismissed Powell from the shadow cabinet after his racist speech, the two men appeared together during the campaign and Heath announced that the new government might forbid *all* immigration including dependents of Asians and Africans. Not to be outdone, in early 1969 Labour rushed through an amendment to the Immigration Act that stiffened entry requirements on all Commonwealth immigrants including dependents.

Process

British racial policy might be characterized as regularly taking one step forward and two steps backward. Although race is thought to have been less important in the 1970 elections than previously (Deakin and Bourne, 1970), the reason is that both major parties were so insistent that they would control immigration that their stands on the issue could hardly be differentiated. Race was clearly a powerful latent issue. Both major parties reassured their voters that they would bend to the racist sentiments that appeared so strong in British society. There seems little doubt that race was on the minds of most voters. By now Powell was a popular hero and campaigning for massive repatriation. He was not repudiated by the party leader, Heath. If the outcome shows little influence of race on voting, it is because both major parties acknowledged that popular prejudice would guide their future decisions. The failure to confront the schizophrenic and improvised nature of racial policy is perhaps the most dramatic illustration of the weaknesses of unrestrained adversarial politics.

To understand the policymaking process that surrounds racial issues in Britain it is important to see not only that few wanted to take positive action, but that few had any idea of what might be done. Richard Rose has pointed out (1970, p. 183), "Legislation on race relations in Britain has been characterized by a series of *ad hoc* and hasty Government responses to specific immediate and political controversies." Race is one of these rare points where political leaders and political scientists agree on the frailty of parliamentary government. Commenting on the 1968 Act, Crossman (1977, p. 31) writes, "Parliament is the buffer which enable our leadership to avoid saying yes or no." Perhaps the truth is that in a world of immense complexity Parliament and probably most other legislatures of the world cannot substitute for political leaders who lack the will and initiative. The response of the new Heath government in 1971 demonstrates this problem.

The Immigration Act of 1971 is a confused and confusing piece of legislation that was obviously drawn up hastily to deliver on the Conservatives' promise to limit immigration more than Labour had done. The Conservatives were not clear whether their aim was to link immigration more directly to British manpower needs or make further concessions to racist feelings in the country. As the provisions of the bill were shown to be unworkable or undesirable, it was substantially rewritten. The Conservatives, for example, removed the provision making police registration of Commonwealth citizens compulsory when it was attacked by Labour, and the Labour left, for their part, increased alarm by constantly pressing the Conservative leaders on how they would deal with unrestrained labor migration in the European Community. The biggest blunder was the discovery during the debate that the tougher exclusions intended for Asians and Africans would apply equally to white Commonwealth citizens. The ensuing hasty revision revealed the bill's racist intent.

The Act did little more than reinforce Labour's 1968 immigration law. Though never clarified, the new law tried to make a distinction between "permanent" and nonpermanent Commonwealth citizens, the unspoken assumption being that the latter category could be shipped home at the government's will. The result was that Britain now has six varieties of immigrants and aliens (Humphrey, 1973). The law hoped to consolidate immigration laws into coherent form but the impression was that the numerous administrative hurdles to becoming a citizen only provided more opportunities to exclude Asians and Africans. The fact that the Labour Opposition had no clearer concept of the future of racial groups in Britain meant that they found reinforcing "patriality" compatible with their own 1968 legislation, as Callaghan pointed out during the debate (H. Rose, 1972, p. 72). In effect, Commonwealth citizens now have to "earn the right" to become British citizens over a five-year period. Even the Conservative spokesman, Lord Hailsham, was distressed by the ambiguities of the new law, which left immense scope for administrative discretion. In his words, "We established one of the less liberal and one of the most arbitrary systems of immigration laws in the world" (H. Rose, 1973, p. 187).

In effect, the 1971 law was another attempt by the major parties to outbid each other in their severity against entry to Britain. Although the Labour Party published an "Opposition Green Paper" during the debate, it appeared to be no more clear than the Conservatives on minority rights regarding deportation, the entry of dependents, and the appeal of citizenship hearings. Some vague references were made to linking immigration to manpower policies but, contrary to marxist interpretations of migration, the recommendations were not specific (and if they had been would very likely have offended the trade unions). The futility of the legislation as the basis for public policy was borne out within a year. When Ugandan Asians found themselves forced to leave in 1972, there were renewed rumors, often fed by the press, of a new "flood" of immigrants. The irony is that a party as sensitive to Britain's imperial splendor as the Conservatives could not say no. The government agreed to admit all 50,000 Ugandan Asians if necessary and about 28,000 actually came to Britain. It was during this crisis that the home secretary restored the "grandfather clause" to full force. Conservatives congratulated themselves for their humanity while reassuring the British public that it would never happen again.

On the home front the bipartisan effort to mollify minorities without firmly confronting discrimination continued. The Urban

Programme suffered a setback in 1972, when economy-minded Conservatives decided that its funds should be deducted from local authority grants rather than be treated as additional spending. The criteria for allocating the funds were no clearer than under Labour. The Conservatives tried to relate community programs to their notion of deprivation and the focus moved toward supporting voluntary efforts by the poor whether immigrant or not. But the funds remained pitifully small, seldom more than £4 million a year. As Holman and Hamilton (1973, p. 312) suggest, the budget was seldom enough to support the Manchester United football team for a year.

Responsibility for improving community relations ultimately depended on the good will and effort of the local authorities, who, as we have seen, were struggling with double-digit inflation in the mid-1970s. National government was doing no better (see Reading 7-1). Aside from the community relations projects in 1975 the Home Office seemed "inert" to the House Select Committee on Race Relations and Immigration. The Department of Employment had only a small unit concerned with race and ten regional officers. The Department of Education had just established a small unit to investigate educational disadvantage. In the giant ministries of Environment and Social Security there was no recognition. The advisory bodies concerned with race relations were not much better off. The Race Relations Board had a staff of 92, 32 of them working as conciliation officers in regional offices, where they received and investigated complaints. The Community Relations Commission had a staff of 130 that supervised the efforts of 85 community relations councils. As the Runnymede Trust testified to the House Committee, the "net effect may have been to promote cynicism" rather than express determination to combat racial discrimination. After a decade of near hysterical political agitation about immigration, often fueled by major political figures and the press, racial minorities within Britain still had no effective statutory protection.

Consequences

Deeply rooted social problems do not have simple solutions. The British approached racial issues reluctantly and their efforts always fell short of confronting the peculiarly difficult nature of racial politics. Race unavoidably raises fundamental questions about the nature of the society. The British political system seems especially ill suited to engage in such basic social change. That it

has difficulty doing so is further evidence of the highly institutionalized nature of parliamentary politics in Britain, possibly even evidence of the limited capacity of a highly stable system. There were
certainly progressive voices in the 1960s, such as Fenner Brock-
way and Sir Edward Boyle (now Lord Boyle), but they were
seldom listened to by politicians or the public. Race became a
"non-bargainable" issue among the parties. Party leaders did not
resist injecting racial issues into electoral politics in ways that exacerbated racial fears in the society. Perhaps the most costly
shortcoming of stability was that political procrastination made
extremist politics more attractive to both the left and the right.

The political debate under the Heath government made one
wonder if leaders even knew the new dimensions of race relations
in Britain. The succession of immigration acts had effectively cut
off the flow of Asians and Africans to the country except for family dependents, wives, and husbands of those who had arrived
under the old Commonwealth citizenship laws. There were less
than 7,000 "New Commonwealth" immigrants in 1973, though
the number increased to about 18,000 in the mid-1970s. Race had
become a question of providing jobs, housing, and services for
racial minorities. The realization that the racial problem was *in*
Britain rather than *outside* Britain was pressed by a growing battery of pressure groups and agencies.

Important among these was the House of Commons Select Committee on Race Relations and Immigration. Its influence was, no
doubt, enhanced by the failure of party leaders to take constructive action. From 1969 onward it issued a series of reports on
housing, education, and employment that officially recognized the
effects of discrimination. The Race Relations Board became increasingly militant. Its 1975–76 report, for example, indicted the
government for neglect and warned that the consequences of
avoidance could easily become disruptive and dangerous (see
Reading 7-2). Most important perhaps, the Board pointed to the
unwillingness of government to use its vast commercial and financial powers to alleviate racial discrimination. The activity of the
Community Relations Commission also spawned a more militant
pressure group, the National Association of Community Relations
Councils, which quite bluntly told Parliament that Britain's race
policies no longer made sense.

As we have seen in previous cases in this study, a key to exercising influence in the welfare state appears to be penetrating the
administrative apparatus. By the mid-1970s, what the British call

the "race relations industry" had a number of footholds in White-hall. Similar to the work of the Rowntree Trust on poverty, the Runnymede Trust took the lead in sponsoring studies of discriminatory policies and practices. Using the elitist structure of British government to advantage, a new group of advisors and consultants took shape (Evans, 1978). By 1975 the "race lobby" had direct access to the Foreign Office, the Home Office, and the Central Policy Review Staff, which did a special study of race policy for the cabinet. It was not published, but the message was gradually permeating higher levels of government. Awareness was also increased by the growing militancy of the women's lobby. In the Labour government of 1974 sex discrimination became a major issue for Barbara Castle, the secretary of state for social services, and a close friend of Wilson.

Although race did not become a major issue in the 1974 elections, there was growing uneasiness about sex and race discrimination in Britain. Though the needs of women and racial minorities are often in competition, the advance of sexual antidiscrimination legislation under Labour paved the way for stronger racial antidiscrimination laws. Both parties published proposals on equal pay and equal opportunity during the 1974 elections, Labour making the extravagant claim that its experience in "the use of law to promote equality of opportunity" (Plender, 1975) gave it special qualifications. Shortly after taking office, Labour passed the 1975 Sex Discrimination Act, which established an Equal Opportunities Commission (EOC). The Act was modeled on the 1968 Race Relations Act, but given teeth. The EOC does not have to wait for complaints to be brought to it; it has legal powers to issue orders to desist from a discriminatory practice, a public register is maintained of discrimination notices, and noncompliance following a discrimination notice can be pursued through a court injunction. Unlike the Race Relations Board, the EOC was not to be a conciliator and complainants were encouraged to pursue court action directly.

The stronger stand taken on sexual discrimination highlighted the weakness of Britain's race policies. There are, of course, reasons why sexual discrimination is easier to define and why legal sanctions are more readily enforceable (White, 1977). In the major social service ministries there were immense demands and the giant departments of government were still reluctant to change their practices or upset their local government clients (Jones, 1977).

The House Select Committee report on housing made in 1971 only elicited a noncommittal reply from the Department of the Environment in 1975. The important departure was Labour's White Paper (1975) on racial discrimination. Like the Conservatives, Labour related the plight of racial minorities to deprivation in British society, but went further to claim, "It is the Government's duty to prevent these morally unacceptable and socially divisive inequalities from hardening into entrenched patterns" (p. 3). From this paper emerged the 1976 Race Relations Act.

Considerable ambiguity remained about the aims of race policy, but the immediate objective appeared to be to bring racial policy in line with the stiffer sex-discrimination laws. As we have seen in other policy areas, confusion within government persisted over where responsibility rested. The Community Relations Commission under the Home Office still depended on the voluntary cooperation of local authorities to initiate local projects, while the Race Relations Board had no legal powers. The new policy brought these two activities under a single body, the Commission on Racial Equality (CRE) and, as in the case of sexual discrimination, looked to the courts to enforce the law. There remained considerable ambiguity about how the CRE chairman would relate to the Home Office and through it bring pressure on other ministers. Like most legislation affecting the core of British government, cabinet prerogatives and ministerial status were insulated against overzealous external pressures. It took nearly two years to get the new unified body in place and staffed (*Economist*, June 18, 1977).

As Legum argues (see Reading 7-3), it may be a mistake to confuse racial and sexual discrimination. Leaving racial policy centered in the Home Office rejected the advice of nearly all the race pressure groups, who feel that a more serious effort must be made by the social service departments. There were no moves in this direction until the Urban Aid Programme (Batley and Edwards, 1978) was moved to the Department of Environment in mid-1978, but this change was meant more to bolster Labour's effort to reorganize local government (see Chapter 5) than as an attack on local reluctance to help racial minorities. By 1978 most of the community development projects were being terminated though in some cases they had built new local machinery to deal with race. The main source of funds to alleviate racial disadvantage directly still came from the Local Government Act of 1966, which provided subsidies for local education projects. But the response to this effort was varied and often did not correspond to areas of greatest need (*New Society*, Aug. 3, 1978). Nonetheless, it should be noted that even such modest efforts at direct community action were in advance of France and Germany, which had large permanent migrant labor populations by the 1970s.

Although the migrants fill many less desirable jobs, it is difficult to argue that economic incentives, which figured heavily in French and German migration policies, played an important role (see Freeman, 1979). Indeed, as we have seen (Chapter 3), British economic policy is not built on market and manpower policies that would permit systematic exploitation of cheaper labor. Though racism can be found in continental policies, these countries also have more workers from European Community members and therefore must be more responsive to European labor market requirements. The more purely racist character of Britain's problem became unmistakable in the summer of 1977, when the National Front, a neo-fascist organization, began to exploit racism. In ugly demonstrations in Notting Hill and Lewisham over two hundred persons were injured. The Front fielded nine hundred candidates in the 1978 local government elections, and the six hundred candidates in the London local election received over 100,000 votes. Although the Front made little electoral impact overall, Britain was reaping the bitter fruit of racial neglect.

The curious dualism of the British response remained visible despite new race relations legislation. In order to arrest Africans and Asians on suspicion, the police resurrected vagrancy legislation from 1824, which ironically had been passed to permit forced repatriation of paupers to their home towns. If the victims have immigrant status they can be held indefinitely and have no legal recourse (Runnymede Trust, 1978b). Of the 22,000 police in London in 1978, less than a hundred were black. Perhaps a more ominous change was the merger of the criminal and immigration responsibilities of the Home Office, a change that the home secretary did not voluntarily announce to Parliament and the public (*Times*, June 26, 1978). Thus, "positive discrimination" was accompanied by stricter law enforcement and more stringent, sometimes humiliating, overseas screening of Asian and African dependents joining their families in Britain. Many obvious devices are still not used. For example, racial and sexual discrimination is forbidden in all government contracts, but compliance is not even monitored by the Department of Employment (Runnymede Trust, 1978a).

Evidence of discrimination in employment continued to appear, but awareness was spreading to business and labor organizations. For example, the respected Institute of Personnel Management published a report (Carby and Thakur, 1977) on the extent of job discrimination in private firms. The TUC had also been ambivalent toward recruiting and assisting minorities (see Runnymede Trust, 1974), but was alarmed by the National Front and realized that the exploitation of minority workers threatened TUC influence. In 1978 the first intensive recruitment drive of Asian workers took place in London's East End.

Although the national government has not given forceful direction to local efforts to reduce racial tensions and to combat discrimination, there has been a significant shift in local racial policies. In 1978, Birmingham, for example, was spending over a million pounds on special school programs for minorities and had 124 bilingual teachers (*Times*, Nov. 11, 1978). Leicester, which had been the scene of racial violence, had built new organizations to make contact with and to assist racial minorities. Though a diverse and sometimes confused effort, there were eighty-six community relations councils in 1975 and the National Association of Community Relations Councils had become an outspoken and influential critic of governmental lethargy. Perhaps the most dramatic change was the decision of the Camden borough of London to exercise "positive discrimination" in filling local government jobs. Other London boroughs had also begun to take race seriously although the response varied a great deal. But these programs remained voluntary and Whitehall was noticeably reticent to use its financial controls over local government to hasten progress. The readiness to use similar controls over local housing, education, and social services for other reasons contrasts sharply with the refusal of ministers and cabinet to use them to combat racial discrimination. The problem again suggests how territorial politics is avoided in the British political system (see Chapter 5).

The evidence that British political leaders are willing to confront racial prejudice at home remains mixed. Despite the early reports from the House Select Committee on Race and Immigration that exposed discrimination, the 1977–78 report advocated compulsory local registration of nonwhites and reducing the age of admissable dependent children from eighteen to sixteen years. (Conservative party reactionaries later suggested twelve years.) Although the Labour government quickly rejected these recommendations (*Observations*, 1978), Callaghan had also removed from the Home Office the minister, Alex Lyon, who was known to have strong integrationist views. It was a mixed record at best and only further confused by the 1979 national elections.

Adversarial politics provides few incentives to exclude issues that might provide a few extra votes, particularly when they may be concentrated in marginal seats. Once Thatcher made her "swamping of Britain" speech in early 1978, Labour could easily reap the benefit of watching the disarray within the Conservative ranks. Heath repudiated Thatcher's views and Powell, now more comfortable as an Ulster Unionist MP, came out in favor of forced repatriation. Although the backbench resistance forced the Thatcher government to abandon its election pledge for an immigration register, the new government managed to produce a bill that many thought both racist and sexist. No woman will be allowed to bring a husband or fiancé into the country if it appears the marriage is intended to obtain British citizenship. The collection of evidence, procedures, and evaluation remains at the discretion of the Home Office.

The outcome of British efforts to combat racial discrimination is not encouraging. The highly consensual structure of British politics and society is poorly suited to problems of the assimilation and adaptation needed to achieve racial equality and justice. Every country has its quotient of deep-seated social prejudice, but few have national political institutions that so effectively concentrate legitimacy and power. For this reason, the ambiguity and vacillation of Britain's response to racism at home is a more serious reflection on the system than similar behavior might be in weaker, less stable political systems. Social and economic differences that trigger racial prejudice require complex policy decisions and close coordination at many levels of government. The remarkable consensus of British society about its institutions made the political response to racism uncertain. The most serious flaw of a highly consensual system may be its inability to devise ways to differentiate national policy if underlying political values are threatened. Protecting consensual values paradoxically becomes the greatest barrier to effectively fighting racial discrimination.

Readings

7-1. GOVERNMENTAL INDECISION AND SOCIAL DISCRIMINATION*

Although the race relations debate remained split between immigration and racial policies, by the mid-1970s there were outspoken critiques of official neglect of underlying social and economic inequities. The Race Relations Board points out how governmental indecision tends to compound social inequity.

103. So far as the Commission for Racial Equality is concerned, there will be a difficult problem of priorities, especially because of the meagre resources being made available to it. We recognise that other forms of disadvantage may currently press more heavily on minorities than discrimination. This exists quite independently of other forms of social and economic disadvantage and constitutes a serious threat to the welfare of minorities and to the cohesion of our society as a whole.

104. It is here that the new Commission will have considerable advantages over the Board in promoting affirmative action to secure equal opportunity. Whereas the Board for this purpose has been obliged to rely exclusively upon a process of education and persuasion, the Commission will be able to combine this with the stronger law enforcement powers available to them. On the basis of our experience, education and exhortation by themselves yield poor results. They may create an awareness of the problems, but this counts for little in the provision of equal opportunity if the awareness is not translated into action. The central problem is the lack of motivation and of the will to take positive action; this we have found to be true in practically every sphere, public and private. The regrettable, but not surprising, fact is that action is not likely to be forthcoming unless the consequences of inaction are clearly seen to be more troublesome. Progress towards equal opportunity is more likely to be found where problems have already been experienced. While the powers of the new Commission to counteract the lack of motivation cannot be decisive, we hope

---

*Race Relations Board, *Report (1975–76)* (London: HMSO, Nov. 29, 1976).

that, where necessary, they will not hesitate to make the most of them and so impress upon everybody the reality and determination of public intervention in this field.

105. The climate in which the Commission will be operating is not entirely unpropitious. Whatever the extent of racial prejudice or the majority view on 'coloured' immigration, it is clear that racial discrimination is regarded as wrong by the vast majority of people. Independent surveys have shown that over 80 per cent considered it wrong in employment and services and around 70 per cent in housing. The holding of right principles is, of course, no guarantee of right behaviour, but the advantage that this gives should not be underestimated by the Commission in deciding how to use its powers and exercise its leadership. This applies also to politicians, trade unions and others with an influence on situations in which discrimination can occur, who probably have exaggerated fears of the consequences of taking positive steps to end it.

106. Indeed, it is now a commonplace that the paramount responsibility for leadership and action rests with the Government. They themselves recognise this in theory. As the White Paper so rightly says, "Legislation . . . is not, and never can be, a sufficient condition for effective progress towards equal opportunity. A wide range of administrative and voluntary measures are needed to give practical effect to the objectives of the law." We wish that the Government and local authorities had acted on this message with greater alacrity and determination in the past when neither we nor the Select Committee, to judge by its reports, could detect any signs that these principles had had much effect on the policies pursued by Government departments in this field.

107. It is unfortunate that the ability of the Government to exercise the full weight of its moral authority remains compromised by our immigration laws. We appreciate the difficulty of resolving the nationality question, but we hope that the Government will soon be in a position to introduce an immigration law free of racial elements. It is unlikely that the damage done to minority group confidence can be swiftly repaired, but significant improvement might be achieved when it can truthfully be proclaimed that immigration control is genuinely non-racial.

108. There are three main areas in which vigorous leadership by the Government is urgently called for. First, a counter-attack on the racist elements in society who will not be appeased by what are regarded as the right noises on the coloured immigration issue

and the marginal steps that, with humanity, may still be possible to tighten immigration control. The doctrine of repatriation should not merely be condemned but also shown to be a cruel deception upon the people about whom its advocates profess to be concerned. The deception is increased by the opposition of racists to measures which would help both black and white in the areas in which minorities have settled. Obviously many people regret, resent and fear changes in the character of their neighbourhoods which are inevitable when people of different cultures and customs enter, but hostility towards the minorities will increase and strengthen their propensity to remain apart and different. Measures to provide equal opportunity and to facilitate adaptation will have the opposite effect.

7-2. CONFUSION IN WHITEHALL OVER RACE RELATIONS POLICY*

Many problems of the welfare state cut across departmental and functional lines, especially race relations. The House of Commons Race Relations Committee points out how poorly organized Whitehall is to combat racial hostility and to implement local programs to reduce racial discrimination, although new programs had been in existence for nearly a decade.

12. In the Home Office, race relations is the direct concern of a Division in the Community Programmes Department, which also deals with other matters. The total complement of this Division is nine (including two personal secretaries). With such a meagre establishment, it was not surprising that Home Office witnesses, when asked about concerted Government policies replied that they were "a little sanguine in implying that there are common principles at present", when asked about race relations administration replied that "the Home Office does not know a great deal of what is going on", and that under present arrangements it has not the capacity to do so and told the Committee that the number of reports and recommendations at present before them total 300. The plain truth is that the Home Office is not at present equipped to give a lead or to deal effectively with race relations matters.

*Select Committee on Race Relations and Immigration, *The Organisation of Race Relations Administration* (H.C. 448-I; London: HMSO, 1974–75), pp. viii–xi.

13. The Department of Employment has a small advisory unit on race relations and ten specialist race relations employment officers attached to regional offices. In response to the Committee's Report on Employment the Department is considering the expansion of this advisory service. The Department has been reorganised by the creation of the Manpower Services Commission with its two Agencies, the Training Services Agency and the Employment Service Agency and the Committee's Report asked the Secretary of State to consider how the race relations employment officers can be connected more directly to the staff of the Agencies. This is being done but the major difficulty is a shortage of staff. As the witnesses from the Department informed the Committee "the position at the moment is that the staff are few and thinly spread by almost any standard."

14. The Department of Education and Science has an Educational Disadvantaged Unit for focusing attention *inter alia* on problems of race relations and an Assessment of Performance Unit and an Educational Disadvantage Advice and Information Centre is also being established. These are being set up, if somewhat belatedly, in response to the Committee's Report on Education and we welcome these developments. Nevertheless the Department remains singularly uninformed. Admittedly the Department has faced real difficulties regarding race relations' statistics but, as long as the Department has no essential information, it cannot claim to exercise any effective monitoring.

15. The Department of the Environment has no special unit or division concerned with race relations, although the Department apparently is now considering "a specialised unit of an advisory kind". At present there is not even one official specifically concerned with race relations matters. We were told that there is a principal "who devotes a considerable part of his time to race relations": but he himself told us that he had two other main preoccupations. The Department has regional officers but no information regarding their activities concerning ethnic communities. The Department's disregard of the race relations aspect of its activities is demonstrated by its continued failure to reply to the Committee's Report on Housing published four years ago.

The Department of Health and Social Security is responsible for the National Health Service and finances schemes for language training for immigrant groups at work but has neither a unit nor any establishment concerned specifically with race relations.

17. The Civil Service Department has issued "an unequivocal statement of the Government's equal opportunity policy" and is discussing a regular system of monitoring in the Civil Service. However, at present it still has neither a special unit nor any staff concerned with race relations.

18. If the Government must be committed against, and active in endeavouring to restrain racial discrimination, this Departmental indifference can no longer be accepted. The Committee therefore recommend:—

(1) The Home Office should have a much improved establishment, concerned with race relations and sex discrimination.

(2) The other Departments mainly affected, Employment, Education and Science, and Environment—especially Environment—should strengthen their staffs dealing with race relations and review their efficacy in developing more positive Departmental policies.

(3) The Department of Employment in their review should pay particular regard both to the recent reorganisation of the Department and to the transfer of responsibility to industrial tribunals which we have assumed will take place.

(4) The Department of Health and Social Security should have some staff solely engaged upon the race relations aspect of its work.

(5) The Civil Service Department should create a special Equal Opportunity of Employment Unit.

These recommendations would result in very modest expenditure but unless and until they are implemented, it is unrealistic to expect the Home Office to give an effective lead and deceptive for the Government to claim any meaningful commitment. Moreover, this is not merely a question of numbers, a change of Departmental policies and attitudes is essential.

7-3. COMPLICATIONS OF RACE AND SEX DISCRIMINATION*

By the mid-1970s there were stronger statutory controls against sexual discrimination than against racial discrimination. Margaret Legum writes on how confusing the legislation is becoming, and

*Margaret Legum, "On the Interdependence of Racial Discrimination Policy and Other Anti-Discrimination Efforts in Britain," *The Times* (London), Aug. 17, 1977.

how in some instances its objectives are poorly understood. She points out the differences between the Equal Opportunities Commisson to combat sexual discrimination, and the new Commission for Racial Equality.

The new Commission for Racial Equality, which began operations this month, is likely to join three other legislative reorganizations put through Parliament with a minimum of public interest and now generally regarded as monumental mistakes. Local government reorganization, the "Seebohm" changes in social services, administration, and the restructuring of the hospital services are now seen as vastly expensive exercises in theoretical blue-printing. I predict that this will also be the general judgement on the new race relations legislation two years on.

Such benefits as each of these has brought could have been achieved more cheaply, with less upheaval and allowing more flexibly for alteration with experience. What they have lost cannot be regained without another vast reorganization. What the new Race Relations Act has lost is an effective legal means for ordinary people to redress a personal grievance; it is easy to imagine what might fill that vacuum. What it has gained is considerable. But its gains could have been achieved without the sacrifices, and may be dissipated by the losses. The consequences for race relations in Britain could be very serious, yet very few people know what this reorganization was all about—just as they knew very little about the others.

The alternative was a reorganization, taking as its starting point that individuals aggrieved by discrimination would go to law themselves. New government agencies with subpoena powers would be set up in addition to make large-scale investigations and enforcement orders on sex and race discrimination respectively. They would have no duty to help individuals with their cases, but the right to do so—in practice where a case had strategic or widespread implications. This was the model chosen to outlaw sex discrimination; and the Equal Opportunities Commission (EOC) was set up. The question was should race legislation follow the same pattern with the Commission for Racial Equality (CRE) as equivalent of the EOC?

The established system of consultation was set up. A committee in the Home Office invited interested parties to give evidence in the usual way. Almost all of it came from within the race relations "industry" itself. For example, those who run the industrial tribunals system—which under the proposed new law would handle all employment complaints formerly taken by the board—gave no evidence during the consultation period. Apparently no one thought to examine the effect of the new proposals on the already overloaded tribunals system until the second reading of the Bill in the Commons. Yet the ability of the industrial tribunals—in terms of time and expertise—to establish the facts about race discrimination in the vital field of employment is central to the new law. Those concerned alternate, now that the law has been passed, between appalled anticipation of the clogging effect of their new responsibilities, and a relieved recognition that there will in fact be very few complaints. (In the first year of its operation, the sex discrimination machinery produced only about half a dozen complaints a week to the tribunals throughout England and Wales—a small proportion of the employment complaints the Board was receiving weekly.)

The most substantial evidence came from the Race Relations Board and the Community Relations Commission (CRC) together with their offshoots. The CRC was a grassroots bridge-building organization, without enforcement functions; and its job was to be incorporated into the work of the new commission. Representing as it did the victims of the weaknesses in the old system, and having no experience of operating the conciliation machinery, it welcomed the proposals to strengthen the law and had no particular objection to the passing of the board.

But the board itself, its officers and members of the conciliation committees—everyone, in other words, who had been associated with law enforcement on race—opposed the change. They pointed out that by making the simple changes they had long advocated, all the advantages of the proposed CRE could be gained without losing the advantages of the conciliation machinery and access by individual complainants to the services of trained officers in establishing evidence.

The new law, the board feared, would drastically reduce the number of complainants—not because race discrimination would cease, but because of the huge difficulty of proving it in court, and the intimidatory effect of open proceeding. One side is stamped *right*, the other *wrong*. Face saving for both sides would be a thing of the past. Lawyers would need to be paid, few would have any experience of investigating a subtle charge like race discrimination.

Industrial tribunals and county courts had equally little specialist experience; and such as they had proved the board's fears that discrimination would hardly ever be found. Indeed the mind boggles at the almost lunatic kind of courage an ordinary black citizen would need to go into court on his own against lawyers employed by a large institution on which his future may depend.

Both in its origins and in its consequences race discrimination is very different from sex discrimination. The need for a community bridge-building operation for race (Community Relations Councils), and the absurdity of any such for sex, speaks volumes. Race involves minorities, sex does not. The consequences of deterioration in race relations can be dangerous public violence deepening from generation to generation, whereas time and the facts of modern life are on the side of women.

But from the start it seemed the Home Office preferred race and sex discrimination legislation to follow the same pattern—for obvious administrative reasons. Roy Jenkins concluded that the proposed new law's advantages would outweigh the disadvantages of ending the conciliation and complaints-based procedure. He never met the point that you could have both. Jenkins's deputy, Alex Lyon, was influenced by an emotional point: the old procedure, he said, was "patronizing", blacks were now ready to stand up and fight for themselves in open court. I do not know about blacks, I told him, but timid old me would never risk it with the cards stacked as they are.

All the evidence of the board was rejected; some of its drafting amendments during committee stage found favour, but the principles had been lost.

In all this there was not one ounce of illwill. Everyone was genuinely striving for better race relations and an effective law enforcement procedure. We failed because the process of consultation and research was inadequate, so that the final judgment was half baked.

May one quote boring old Sweden once again? In that country a major change in the law is preceded by a process of detailed research and consultation, which is both highly educative and genuinely responsive. Proposals, together with the results of research, are sent to every public and private body which might be affected, with a request for detailed comments. This may be done several times, with proposals amended in the light of new evidence. By the time legislation is drafted, everyone is better informed, and the government has a consensus based on knowledge. Under that system, the evidence of those with the longest and deepest experience in the field could not possibly be overruled without detailed public explanation.

Consultation machinery apart, one illusion is responsible, I believe, for the mistake which has been made. It is that legislation to prevent overt acts of discrimination can prevent race prejudice. The fact that race relations were deteriorating under the old law was seen as a function of the inadequacy of the law. To a minor extent it was, but this was easily remedied. More fundamentally responsible were the problems of multiple deprivation among black families, cut-throat competition for housing and jobs, the poverty of homes and education, the clash of cultures, the historic scarring of black self-esteem, deep-rooted white myths about blacks. The solution to these ills involves social programmes which go far beyond legislation to outlaw overt discrimination.

This is not to decry the need for such laws. On the contrary, if there is no effective legal remedy against the grievance of race discrimination, public violence will fill the vacuum. The new law will certainly help to remove discrimination over large areas of the economy. But it will almost certainly prove less effective than the old in respect of individual response to personal grievance. There is already plenty of dry tinder about. Poor preparation for the 1976 Race Relations Act may well have left us with this dangerous legacy.

8 The Limits of Consensus: One-Party Government in a Complex State

The basic theme of this book is by no means new. The British have been intensely occupied with the shortcomings and inadequacies of their political system for the past twenty years. The policy analyses, it is hoped, add a more specific and more concrete dimension to this continuing debate. There are some obvious policy failures in Britain as in every society: the continuing drain of the conflict in Northern Ireland, the uncertainty about relations with the European Community, and in the past few years economic stagnation, possibly economic decline. The aim has not been to underscore failure, but to elicit how basic principles of British politics appear in the formulation, implementation, and evaluation of public policy. In more analytical terms, the concern has been with how a changing policy environment relates to politics.

There is little doubt that the advanced form of the welfare state has greatly changed the relation of politics to policymaking in every society. Hailsham (1976) points out how Gladstone, perhaps the most energetic prime minister of Victorian Britain, could still spend about five months a year working in his garden in a North Wales retreat. In 1911, by no means a quiet year in Parliament, 450 pages of statutes were produced; today the annual volume of legislation approaches 15,000 pages. Between 1850 and 1900 national public expenditure doubled, but it was still heavily concentrated on defense and posed few intricate policy choices. Between 1900 and 1955 national public expenditure multiplied by a factor of twenty-five. The magnitude of change is unmistakable. The more interesting question is, *how* has the political system changed in response to these enormously increased responsibilities? On the whole, the political framework for policymaking in contemporary Britain would be easily understood by Gladstone or

Disraeli; even the Duke of Wellington or Lord Melbourne could probably sit in for most modern actors at the pinnacle of the British system. (They would not like it, but they could do it.)

The policymaking constraints of British politics are derived from the requirements of consensual politics as enshrined in the British constitution, institutions, and parties. There are two ways of examining this problem. The first is to see how new policies might challenge these political traditions, and how British policymakers avoid issues that imply fundamental political change. Nondecisions and procrastination are part of such a demonstration. The point is not that such evasions are not to be found in other European countries and Japan. In some ways, other democracies have been even more timid. The point is rather that policymaking requirements present substantial constitutional, institutional, and party challenges as the complexity of the welfare state increases. We can then observe in what ways and how much established political habits and procedures change.

Aversion to political change is deeply rooted in British political history. As noted in Chapter 1, most historic changes such as mass parties, competitive elections, administrative modernization itself, were grafted onto a set of principles that were clearly recognized, if not fully elaborated, by the nineteenth century. In the late nineteenth century, Britain's advantage over other democracies was that it had a working political system that met the basic requirements of democratic politics. Republican France was engulfed in a bitter struggle against the last remnants of nineteenth-century aristocratic rule. German democracy flickered late in the century only to be manipulated by Bismarck, and eventually extinguished by the Kaiser. Japan was emerging from the humiliation of its feudal past. The United States was trying to blend the excesses of popularism with presidential rule. As new problems arose, most countries also engaged in major institutional experiments. Some were failures and some successes, but all were attempts at making political adjustments to the changing problems of policymaking.

Some might argue that the constitutional crisis of 1911 belies this argument. While it is true that the Parliament Act of 1911 removed the veto power of the House of Lords, even this change is notable for the way in which it avoided a constitutional crisis by making an informal agreement among a small elite (namely that, should the Lords veto major bills, the monarch would create large numbers of peers for the ruling party). In relation to policy-making the Lords are of more interest as a display of how easily partisan controversies can dominate British politics. Much time has been spent trying to abolish what is little more than a symbolic element in British lawmaking. To pacify the Labour left wing in the late 1960s there were prolonged and unproductive negotiations on the future of the Lords; again, in 1978, Callaghan's refusal to include abolition of the upper house in Labour's 1979 election manifesto contributed to internal party strife. The example is instructive because it shows how parties can focus on constitutional reforms of marginal significance at the expense of more urgent and perplexing policy problems. The general explanation offered by this study is that the solidity of both elite and societal consensus, as well as the long-standing harmony of these two sets of beliefs, has enabled adversarial politics to prevail, possibly at the cost of failing to examine how well policy is defined, implemented, and evaluated in the British political system. The opportunity costs of relatively unrestrained adversarial politics may be very high, and some of these costs have been specified in the policy analyses. Of course, to some extent, competitive party politics and democratic politics generally depend on adversarial behavior. But, compared with most democracies, British adversarial politics is heavily geared toward generating and maintaining support for the system, and rather less toward the criticism and formation of policy. The critical distinction is whether those aspects of policies singled out for adversarial treatment contribute to finding better solutions, to relieving long-standing pressures and conflicts of major issues, and to learning from past errors and oversights. One would expect adversarial behavior in any political system, but there are few, if any, systems where the concentration of power in a relatively small elite at the center can so effectively control the terms and substance of adversarial struggle regardless of policy consequences. The point is not that immediate partisan advantage should be disregarded, but that it should be related to the formulation and implementation of policies.

The policy analyses have also tried to underscore how the terms of the policy debates, the formulation of alternatives, and the specification of desired outcomes is controlled by the governing elites and, in turn, by the way that the civil service supports those elites. The extraordinary influence that central policymakers exercise is perhaps most dramatically illustrated by the ease with which they can reverse their ground. In our six cases there have been many examples: the dilution of administrative reform; the economic "U-turns" of 1968, 1972, and 1976; the disastrous fluctuations of trade union legislation; the reversal of local and regional government reform. Though the electorate ultimately passed judgment on these changes, the policy process itself was marked by remarkably arbitrary and sometimes erratic change. More important, British policymaking provides few ways that an Opposition, a competing elite, or even a pressure group can contribute to defining new objectives. Cabinet and ministerial power make this unlikely, and are reflected in the weak policymaking role of the Opposition, the weakness of parliamentary committees, and the insulation of national political leaders from local political leaders and party activists.

The politics of policymaking seems to have changed little over the past two decades. This seems more surprising because there is evidence that the two-party system is weakening, that electorates are less strongly committed to the two major parties, and that referenda provide an increasingly attractive way to avoid political risks. Even the leadership struggles within parties appear remote from the underlying assumptions about the policymaking process. Even when the general direction of party policy is at stake, specific issues are left to the party leader. In brief, only by scrambling to the pinnacle of the British political structure does one begin to have policymaking influence. Aversion to change is most visible whenever any critically important assumption of the existing framework is called into question.

Both elite and societal consensus seem to place limits on policy change. But the more distinct roles of societal and elite consensus in other democracies are not necessarily a function of diminished support for government, and even less of determined political opposition by minority parties. Differences among elites and divisions within society compel leaders of most other democracies to concentrate more on the consequences of their decisions. A central argument of the policy analyses has been that the growth of government, and its concomitant increase in responsibilities, has made such emphasis on performance more important. When governments were small, political actors could more readily relate policies to society and, in turn, to electoral demands. With the emergence of the welfare state, politicians have been inadvertently left more and more to devise their own interpretations of consensus. In this respect, Britain is no different from other welfare states, but the problem is more acute because reconciling demands and performance takes place within a more restricted arena. Oddly enough, it is the informality of the political system, a major advantage in accommodating political change in the nineteenth century, that now appears to extend executive powers in unforeseen ways, and to insulate policymaking from its environment.

Possibly the most important effect of renewed interest in policy analysis in political science has been to underscore how seriously eroded the liberal assumption of harmonious societal and elite consensus has become. An early work raising this problem in the American political system was Schattschneider's study (1961) of the "semi-sovereign state." It is not coincidental that awareness of the weakened relationship between demands and performance would appear very early in a political system where politicians are more deeply immersed in policymaking than in most European countries. The policy analyses have tried to show how the growth of governmental policymaking, essential to the development of the welfare state, has strained the relationship between elite and societal consensus in the British political system.

In other democracies territorial politics and clearer definition of executive powers help identify the problem of integrating societal and elite consensus as policymaking responsibilities increase. Territorial politics compensates for the distance between national decisions and localized results, and defined powers help place responsibility for performance. Modern democracies can be roughly described by the model shown below. Societal consensus affects

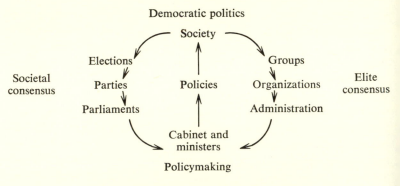

The Political System of the Welfare State

policies through the traditional democratic linkages of elections, parties, and parliaments. Elite consensus operates more freely in an elaborate structure of voluntary associations, pressure groups, and intergovernmental agencies. There is a great deal of discussion about the erosion of societal consensus, often subsumed under very abstract discussions of "legitimacy crises." In fact, these crises have not been as severe as many predicted (and a few hoped), and the relative ease with which elite consensus could openly or surreptitiously build new policymaking links probably accounts for preservation of democratic government. Conversely, it seems unlikely that societal support unaided by the intricate organizational network generated by elites could have constructed the welfare state.

As the growth of the welfare state has required more complex and more specialized policies, the links between society and government have been put under strain. More than most political systems, the British system has two rather distinct sets of inputs affecting policymaking: those of groups, officials, and social leaders who directly communicate with the political elite as part of the pattern of elite consensus; and a second, more familiar pattern of conventional political inputs from elections, parties, and Parliament that reflects societal consensus. So long as the values represented in the two patterns are compatible, there are not likely to be major breakdowns of government, and adversarial politics can continue to fulfill the expectations of both structures. The concentration of power in the cabinet and ministers, essentially a result of an historical compromise in the development of British democracy, provides the political elite with enormous powers over administration, pressure groups, and intergovernmental organizations, but these powers must also be exercised within the confines of societal consensus. One can marvel at the tolerance and ingenuity of successive generations of British political leaders, but one must also ask whether the delicate balance they maintain serves Britain well in an era of extremely complex and demanding policymaking.

In summarizing the policy analyses of this study, we shall examine, first, how policies have shifted and changed to meet the needs of adversarial politics, a situation made possible only because of Britain's remarkably strong elite consensus. Then we shall look at some of the changing circumstances and problems in the policymaking environment that might have had a greater impact on British leaders had not adversarial politics prevailed and so successfully kept elite and societal consensus in harmony.

Elite Consensus and Adversarial Politics: Guarding Fences While Losing Territory

The preservation of elitist policymaking privileges might be considered the most costly and most distinctive aspect of British politics. As we argued in Chapter 1, this is most apparent in the workings of cabinet government and ministerial powers. Within Britain this issue is most often discussed as the centralization problem, which many recognize but few want to unravel. In a forthright critique, Johnson (1977, p. 88) writes, "It is unreasonable to expect that ministers and their agents should be capable of discharging effectively *both* the tasks of conception and design of policy and powers *and* the supervision of executive action by such an enormously diverse range of subordinate authorities" (his italics).

Among the policymaking restraints of adversarial politics, administrative reform (Chapter 2) is perhaps the most striking illustration of how easily efforts to reorganize have been repulsed, even though both major parties are unhappy about administrative performance and influence. Heath quite possibly said more than he intended when he described Whitehall as existing "roughly between Watford and Haywards Heath," two comfortable and very middle-class London suburbs (Committee on Expenditure, 1977, p. 773). As with so many British reforms, Heath's plan gave no more power to Parliament. Unlike top civil servants in most countries, British elite civil servants need no well-cultivated political allies. Nonetheless, Heath's reforms were in many ways a more devastating threat to the civil service than anything proposed by Labour. His plan recognized, for one thing, that if administrators are to be accountable, then ministers must also change their behavior. Moreover, superimposing effective manpower planning on departments by strengthening the Civil Service Department would have required fundamental constitutional changes. Heath's proposals were defeated in a curious alliance of departmental ministers and their top civil servants with the Treasury, whose public expenditure role would have been reduced.

Labour's attitude toward the civil service is more ambiguous, which may explain why their attack on it has been less effective.

They wanted a more "efficient" civil service, but they also wanted a more responsive and socially representative civil service. As with many socialist ideas that government can somehow be simultaneously attractive and forceful, at the end of the day efficiency (sometimes cloaking political aims) usually wins out, producing even more arbitrary decisions. The political truth is possibly encapsulated in the experience of a prominent Wilson advisor, John Hunt (now Lord Crowther-Hunt), who became minister for higher education in 1976. He worked very hard to create a planning agency within his office that would produce cost-benefit studies of higher education. When he left government, bitterly disappointed that civil servants seemed to resist his well-intentioned efforts to combine democracy and efficiency in British higher education, his embryonic unit was quickly dissolved by his superior, the Labour secretary of state for education (Crowther-Hunt, 1976 and 1977). The moral is that administration is not likely to be reformed from within, not just because civil servants are unwilling to participate in their own demise, but also because ministers have no incentive to diminish the power of their departments or to create problems where none exist.

The politics of making economic policy (Chapter 3) is in some ways simpler than that of administrative reform, but more complex in relation to the diverse effects and outcomes that economic policies encompass. As we have seen, Parliament has virtually no effective power over public expenditure. The Finance Act is more carefully debated because it directly touches people's pockets, but MPs tend to concentrate on those elements that relate to their constituencies and, of course, seldom make important changes. Sir Geoffrey Howe, chancellor of the exchequer in 1979, commented that "before the bill is published they [MPs] have little or no chance of being heard; and after the bill is published, there is scarcely time to heed their advice" (1977). In numerous ways, the complexity of a mixed economy, now further compounded by economic stagnation, has confirmed whatever doubt there may have been about Parliament's ancient right to control spending and taxation: budgets are amended three or four times a year and are regularly adjusted in other legislation; public spending accounts are necessarily intricate and often difficult to reconcile with each other; and private and public sector interests have little need for MPs to represent their interests because they have direct access to ministers and civil servants when crucial decisions are made.

Unlike most mixed economies, the political calculations of public spending decisions are guarded by a very small number of leaders in the cabinet, and their decisions, except for major industrial deals, are kept secret. At the root is the power of the Treasury. Ministers much prefer the confidential discussions of cabinet meetings and interdepartmental conspiracies to extract their money from an unwilling Treasury, to the frantic political bargaining and intricate administrative compromises found in most modern welfare states. But it is precisely the secrecy of bargaining over economic policy that makes control and accountability such intractable problems. The Conservatives have been most comfortable with this exclusionary process because it helps accomplish their general goal of reducing public spending, and if control fails they hope for more cooperation from the private sector.

As in the case of administrative reform, Labour's approach involves an important contradiction: they want to increase public spending and they also want more equality, which means that the benefits of a larger public sector must be delivered as planned. They want to be more generous and more demanding. Both aims make Labour suspicious of the Treasury, which does not have and does not want responsibility for implementation and evaluation. Thus, the various experiments to devise strong economic planning agencies: the Department of Economic Affairs (1964–68), the Ministry of Technology (1968–70), and the strengthened Department of Industry (1974–76). Oddly enough, these experiments failed because political objectives and economic policymaking are so tightly controlled. The political checks on spending can only be fully exercised by compromising cabinet rule. Everyone can agree on spending more, but ministers and departments still fight about their shares. Once the economy was in deep trouble from 1975 onward, Treasury power was easily recovered by means of cash limit budgeting.

Conservative economic policies have regularly encountered industrial reluctance to invest at higher rates, banking preferences for higher interest rates, and commercial tendencies to meet increased demand with increased imports. The full irony of adversarial industrial policy appeared in 1979, when Sir Keith Joseph, the Conservative secretary of state for industry, found that his efforts to liberate nationalized firms and to sell publicly owned industrial assets were often rejected by industrial leaders. Determined to dismantle the NEB, his only solution was for government to oversee firms directly where it had large holdings, a reversal of nearly a decade of development to give publicly owned firms more autonomy.

The effect has been that every reform effort has eventually been defeated by political forces *within* the government despite the relatively bipartisan interest (for different reasons) that Conservatives and Labour have in improving economic policymaking. Too much has been made of public-private sector conflicts. Bailing out a declining industry injures Conservatives by making them appear too collectivist, as they did during Heath's government; and for Labour it diminishes the resources available for public benefits and services. Strange as it may seem, Heath's ruthless demands for industrial efficiency were a greater threat to private industry than was Labour's moderate socialism.

Countries that have followed growth policies have a long history of overlapping business and government interests. The most curious aspect of Britain's poor growth record is that *neither* major party has been able to develop more intricate machinery that might align public and private sector decisions. Both parties, for example, envied French indicative planning, but neither government nor industry wanted the elaborate network of consultation or the relatively flexible system of government incentives needed to make business listen more closely to economic objectives. One might call this a case of bipartisan failure. But at the root of this question is the exclusionary nature of top-level policymaking itself. Neither ministers nor civil servants are expected to participate in the log-rolling and bargaining that is found in France, Germany, and the United States. Nor are there the extraordinary powers used to organize the close collaboration of government and business in Japan or the administrative permeation of the private sector provided by the Swedish civil service. To do so would be to make fundamental changes in both constitutional and institutional prerogatives of top policymakers.

In industrial relations (Chapter 4) the realities, and in more recent years the illusion, of two-party politics reproduces a similar dilemma, especially for Labour. As we saw, there was a large measure of bipartisan agreement about the need to harness trade union power. Adversarial politics makes it awkward for Labour to restrict trade unions, just as it made it difficult for Conservatives (until Heath) to talk openly about restructuring industry and banking. The unproductive result, as we have seen, was that frustration with incomes policy drove Labour to propose severe restraints in 1969; and frustration in developing a new industrial strategy drove the Conservatives to legislate severe union restrictions in 1971. Viewed in the perspective of cabinet and ministerial power, it is perhaps the most striking demonstration of the extraordinary detachment of policymaking from the realities of power in British society. Labour's primary strategy, elaborated in the Donovan Report, was that if unions could put their own house in order then the complications of incomes policy would disappear as enlightened union leadership led workers into a natural alliance with government. This course of action vastly underestimated the variations within the Labour movement and industrial organization itself. In an odd way, Labour's failure made the Conservatives' confrontation of 1971 even more outrageous.

The fatal error was to think that unions could be either cajoled or bludgeoned into taking a more enlightened view of society. The great loss has been that this narrowly conceived and poorly executed strategy perpetuates the historic hostility between the working class and government itself. Preserving the concentration of lawmaking and policymaking power at the top helps perpetuate a pitifully inadequate view of labor-management relations. Adversarial politics not only ignores the great variation of labor relations among industries and among unions, but it encourages hopeless confrontations. The Labour Party receives roughly nine-tenths of its income from the unions and, in any event, is dependent on worker votes. The Conservative Party struggles to prevent its right wing from creating new labor strife, while Conservative moderates hope to add worker votes to the roughly 30 percent of the workers now supporting the party (about 40 percent in 1979).

Possibly no other area of policymaking has been more damaging to British society and the economy. Adversarial struggle under Wilson and Heath gave way to the virtual capitulation of the 1974 Wilson government to union demands. In 1979 the Thatcher government continued to be divided over moderate proposals to curb the most excessive powers of unions (secondary pickets and checks on union officer elections), and more reactionary pressures to renew the punitive measures of 1971. The result is that there are no serious political choices for unions because they can benefit from either party. There are few reasons why labor should take more social or economic responsibility when unions are, in effect, sheltered by the political system itself. In the detached setting of

Whitehall, unions will always win and parties have little choice but to support simplifications that no longer correspond to the realities of society.

The alternatives appear in other countries where even more ideologically inclined labor leaders have taken more responsible policymaking roles. Socialists and Communists predominate in the French labor movement, but this does not keep labor leaders from plant-level and industrial wage bargaining. The odd result is that the TUC is represented on endless numbers of boards, public corporations, and advisory councils without having to make policy commitments. Perhaps the best demonstration of the costs of preserving concentrated power is the gradual deterioration and collapse of incomes policy under Labour (1974–78). It is easy to say that unions are irresponsible; it is much more difficult to point to ways that the political system could create situations where durable compromises on wage policy, working conditions, and industrial development might actually be made. The negative response to labor participation from both the TUC and CBI in 1976 suggests that neither welcome more politicization. Why enter the political arena when one does not need to? The more difficult question is why ministers prefer this stalemate.

The impasse that we observe in making sectoral policies is reproduced in dealing with territorial politics and policies (Chapter 5). Because local government systems necessarily embody more political actors, it is perhaps, more than industrial relations, the most dramatic illustration of the insulation of cabinet government from political bargaining and from diverse political pressures. It would be difficult to construct a local government system that more effectively protects ministers and the Cabinet from their own errors, contradictions, and neglect. For most of this century leading politicians have recognized the inequities and inadequacies of the 1888 Local Government Act. When legislation finally appeared, it was neutralized, if not sabotaged, by Conservatives, who preferred to keep the useful "town versus country" distinction alive and well. The laborious ways of adjusting center-local relationships in France or the United States must be weighed against the ease with which major legislation can be simply reversed in British policymaking. The realities of a highly urban society do not easily accommodate the needs of adversarial politics.

There is considerable evidence that neither Labour nor Conservatives are prepared to see policymaking decentralized. It suits national parties and simplifies central policymaking to see party majorities at the local level fight the same battles that the center does rather than formulate their own political strategy. The complex organization of the local government system itself means that local coalitions against the center are difficult to build. The huge transfer to counties and cities makes local politics more threatening, while at the same time providing the basis for strong ministerial control over local policies. As in the case of labor relations, the result has been that a decade or more of tinkering leaves local councils with the same problems they had initially. The system is inordinately complex, invites administrative manipulation, and so severely burdens local political leaders that they have little time or energy left to question national priorities. Every suggestion that territorial politics might be restructured in a way that might challenge Westminister encounters remarkably bipartisan resistance. Devolution was only seriously considered when regional sentiments endangered a government majority, and once this threat diminished it was quickly forgotten.

The unhappy result is that local government has been in almost constant turmoil since 1969. The Labour secretary of state of the DOE, Peter Shore, worked hard to devise a plan that would rescue the Labour-controlled districts within Conservative-controlled counties. His scheme for "organic change" would have returned powers to the second-tier authorities, districts, and left the organization of local government in even more confusion than it is under the new Act (Stewart, 1978). The new proposals would have forced one local authority, Cleveland, through four reorganizations in fifteen years. Labour stealth was replaced by Conservative domination in 1979. The new secretary of state of the DOE, Michael Heseltine, imposed cuts that disrupted local social services, tried to use the Rate Support Grant to force local authorities to make local pay agreements of no more than 14 percent (inflation was 19 percent), and restructured the grant to favor the Conservative-run counties. Like industry, local government found itself in the middle of an adversarial tug of war that took little notice of the actual difficulties existing at the local level.

The provision of social security (Chapter 6) takes us a step closer to the complexity of the welfare state, and the difficulties of deciding who will benefit and how benefits will be delivered. The history of social welfare policy is essential to understanding how social security policy is made because from its earliest stages it was associated with class differences and cultural values in ways that made political consideration of welfare difficult and controversial. The most altruistic of early Victorian reformers insisted that treatment should be identical throughout the country and that accountability should reach standards that became an obstacle rather than a help in improving the welfare system. Nineteenth-century Tories and Liberals were essentially in agreement on these principles, and (for different reasons) Conservatives and Labour still agree that nationally administered welfare is superior. Out of this agreement grew the unwieldy SBC.

The odd political result is that bipartisan agreement about the structure of the social security system has tended to give the Conservatives more political rewards than the more equalitarian-minded Labour politicians. In part this is simply a demographic reality because the elderly need pensions, vote regularly, and tend to be more conservative. More important perhaps, the Conservatives are less encumbered with equalitarian principles and therefore can identify neglected groups and redirect existing benefits without hurting their own support. Labour has a monumental obligation to preserving unemployment benefits, which has left children's benefits and new family needs to Conservative initiatives.

This said, the acceptance of increased benefits and services in the welfare state has made them less politically controversial. For example, despite the eagerness of the Thatcher government to make public spending cuts, some social benefits had to be increased. Adversarial politics must live off fairly minor scraps such as school milk, heating subsidies for the poor, and construction of ramps for public buildings. Despite the pushing and hauling of successive Labour and Conservative governments, the task of pension reorganization, as we have seen, was essentially an extended exercise in bipartisan politics. The actuarial and financial mysteries of this complex process are not suited for party or electoral politics.

More than most areas of policymaking, social security is dominated by professional and client groups that both make and judge detailed policies. No matter what party is in power, such groups as the British Association of Social Workers, the National Association of Pension Funds, and the Child Poverty Action Group are looking over the minister's shoulder. More difficult to calculate is the damage done by what little partisan intervention is now possible. For example, soon after the Conservatives took office in 1979 they announced that pensions would again be indexed to average earnings rather than to average prices. Whether ministers, much less Parliament, have any idea of the ultimate costs of such reversals we are never told.

If the politics of social welfare tend to become mired in marginal changes and adjustments, the politics of racial policy (Chapter 7) reveal the stalemate that can occur when a major decision creates cross-pressures in both major parties. In a two-party system the ways to reshape coalitions for specific legislation are limited. What does not fit within the adversarial system is easily, almost necessarily, excluded. For many years race was seen as an extension of old Commonwealth obligations and bipartisan colonial policy delayed recognition of the internal proportions of Britain's race problem. While Katznelson (1973) is correct in arguing that the initial steps to help racial minorities represent "institutional buffering" of the center against local controversy, this has also been the same political strategy followed by cabinet government during nearly every major social crisis since the Poor Laws of 1832. There is nothing distinctly "racial" in Westminster's strategy of using locally administered social services and locally organized groups to resolve serious problems. More realistically, Whitehall does not have the capacity to intervene effectively in complex social issues (as opposed to easily standardized issues like school construction and housing standards).

Although there are now more influential local racial groups, they are isolated from national policymaking in the same way that the entire local government system is held at arm's length. The result is that national politicians can inflame racial hostility at very low cost to themselves, while the national administration has great difficulty penetrating the specialized local services in order to focus assistance on racial inequities. At the root of the impasse is the way in which individuals are disarmed before an adversarial electoral and party system. If individual rights were defined, then the carefully guarded fictions that protect cabinet and ministerial power would be threatened. Consequently the Home Office can continue to manipulate immigration procedures without fearing parliamentary intervention, much less individual redress. Under the Conservative government of 1979 new orders appeared to screen immigrants for sexual deviance as another way of denying entry. An even greater challenge looms in the future because European Community membership entailed endorsement of the European Commission of Human Rights, and ultimately responsibility before the European Court of Human Rights. Feminist organizations have already appealed to the Court and there is every reason to think that racial minorities will begin to do the same.

As we have pointed out in Chapter 1, there is little reason to believe that the normal workings of democratic and electoral politics can alter the immense concentration of policymaking power in British cabinet government. A close look at political participation in British politics reveals substantial obstacles to dispersing power. It is doubtful, for example, if a two-party system can provide the variety of options that occur in multiparty systems. Nor does it appear likely that democratic processes will check the concentration of executive power. Thus, the most surprising aspect of cabinet and ministerial power is that it is sustained with such apparent ease. Some may consider this an unfair criticism because British electoral and party politics are not organized to check executive power. There are few ways to introduce the cross-pressures and alternatives at the top levels of decisionmaking. Adversarial confrontation within Parliament is not meant to improve policymaking but to bait the ruling party and if possible to embarrass ministers.

The argument is not that politics alone explains the failures and successes of British policymaking, but that the political elite constrains policymaking in peculiar ways. Adversarial politics in cabinet and parliamentary government leaves little room for long-term assessment, redefining policy objectives, resolving policy conflicts, and testing policy proposals against the changing environment of policymaking. Indeed, to do so would be evidence of political indecision and cast a shadow over a ruling party's governing capacity. Within government, consensual politics means accepting cabinet rule and acquiescing before the majority in Parliament. As Shonfield wrote, "The rules of the game allow the government to be endlessly teased but not seriously incommoded in the conduct of its ordinary work." The policymaking arena is limited to relatively few actors, who, in turn, guard their territory very carefully. Outside the charmed circle of ministers, politicians are not supposed to enter into the policymaking process. Regardless of how well or poorly policies work, government tends to be deprived of the benefit of its own experience. New departures are formulated with more secrecy and more detachment from lesser politicians than in most modern democracies.

The full irony of the politics of policymaking in Britain is that many of the most intractable problems of the welfare state presuppose continued effort through several governments and over long periods of time. There has been sustained agreement, for example, over the reorganization of nationalized industries and pensions. As policymaking becomes more complex, demarcating the areas of agreement among competing political forces becomes essential. Adversarial politics makes admission of such broad agreement on policy objectives more difficult, perhaps even risky. In addition to the six cases described, there are other complex problems confronting Britain where fundamental objectives are confused: public housing, the National Health Service, and relations with Europe. In comparing the formation of British and American foreign policy, Waltz noted similar disadvantages because "the quick indentification of problems, the pragmatic quest for solutions, the ready confrontation of dangers, the willing expenditure of energies, and the open criticism of policies" is hard to reconcile with the traditions of British policymaking (1967, pp. 311–12). Were British leaders to change the behavior associated with these policymaking habits, it would be considered a sign of political weakness. A curious by-product is that special interests, pressure groups, and corporate bodies can operate with more confidence and more confidentiality than they enjoy in most modern democracies.

In outlining the cases in this volume, we have seen that the most important feature in policymaking has been how forging new solutions and approaching new problems have been consistently limited by the prerogatives to the top policymakers. When consensual politics is translated into agreement about how to make policy, it appears intransigent and defensive. Of course, there is no reason why national leaders should complicate their lives if they do not need to. If adversarial forays suffice to sustain the democratic necessities of parliamentary politics and popular control, there is no reason to reexamine the underlying assumptions of British politics. In analyzing administrative reform, economic policymaking, local government, labor relations, social security, and immigration and racial policies, one sees how policymaking has consistently been shaped by the rules of the game whenever changes threaten ministerial powers. Ministers in other welfare states would welcome comparable insulation against external and competing political forces.

The Changing Environment of Policymaking: Can Politics Be Put to Work?

In Chapter 1 we discussed some ways that the policy environment has become more complex and more uncertain because of the development of the welfare state. The extent to which top officials have been able to defend underlying agreement about their prerogatives and procedures appears more surprising when one begins to consider how the social and economic setting of government has changed in the welfare state. Not only is government being asked to do more in an absolute sense, but the interdependencies of decisions proliferate, hierarchical authority is blurred, and the environment itself produces new needs and new complications as policy objectives are translated into benefits and services. A second major argument contained in the policy analyses has been that the acceptable formulation of policy aims often fails to deal with closely related and acknowledged problems in the same policy area. In democracies where policymaking powers are more dispersed and elite consensus is not as strong, social, economic, and localized preferences more easily penetrate the upper levels of decisionmaking. The argument is not that societal consensus can itself fashion policies, but that where social and political differences can more easily challenge and qualify the policy process, environmental changes are less easily ignored by policymakers. The intensity of adversarial politics itself may mean that British leaders are less disposed to follow clues and to adjust decisions as society changes.

In many respects, the most threatened and yet the most secure component of the British policymaking process is the administration itself (Chapter 2). The threat is that, were the political neutrality and anonymity of British civil servants removed, their usefulness to ministers would decline. However, the paradox of administrative power is found in all welfare states; it is only more pronounced in Britain. As civil servants are asked to do more, they are also likely to make more errors, to create unforeseen inequities, and to misuse discretionary powers. The effect is that civil servants begin to mount their own defense. But as this is done in the British system, political self-interest creates severe strains. Because their special status is a crucial link in maintaining cabinet and ministerial power, the dilemmas of reform are more severe for Britain than for countries where administrators more openly pursue their political interests and are more openly involved in exchanges with elected officials.

There is, for example, the occasional disobedient civil servant, such as Leslie Chapman (1978), who simply cannot bear to ignore serious inefficiency. There have been an increasing number of scandals over misuse of administrative power such as the 1977 Crown Agents affair. (The government only agreed to a public inquiry after its plans for a confidential inquiry were defeated in the House of Commons.) More interesting indications of the inexorable pressures of the welfare state are the signs that the civil service no longer relies on ministerial protection, thereby breaking this long-standing alliance. Among the more interesting leaks in recent years was a cabinet minute of 1978 explaining how a cabinet committee would protect the civil service against public attacks. By no means purely anecdotal evidence of the recognized power of top civil servants is the wide press coverage of competition for top jobs. When Sir Robert Armstrong became the new secretary to the cabinet in 1979, there were long analyses of his views and experience in the leading newspapers. The same happened when Sir Ian Bancroft became head of the civil service in 1977.

The welfare state may change British administration in ways that politics cannot. The power of the administration is exposed as it takes an increasingly defensive stance. For example, when it was revealed in 1979 that Department of Energy officials had released some £100 million in industrial grants for North Sea oil development without complete compliance with directives (oddly enough revealed by a Labour-chaired Public Accounts Committee in the House), the chief official broke with precedent and defended himself in public. Civil service unions actively resisted Labour plans for further dispersal of officials and commissioned their own study. When Mrs. Thatcher brought an efficiency expert into the government to examine government departments, a warning was promptly issued by the civil service unions. As the borderlines between the public and private sectors fade, there is also more demand for top civil servants from business. Between 1972 and 1975, forty-one top officials asked to leave, and like retired American generals increasing numbers of retired top civil servants become well-paid company directors. Few have ever been under the illusion that top civil servants lacked influence, but as administrative machinery grows the civil servants become a pressure group rather than privileged members of an elite. When we consider other welfare states, however, the surprising thing is not that the political interests of civil servants are now more openly expressed, but that it has taken so long for this to happen.

The power of the civil service unions also erodes the privileges of civil servants. Government employees are more highly organized than private sector workers (80 percent of public sector workers are in unions) and several important public sector unions are extremely militant. Public employee pay claims tend to become the focus of incomes policy because government finds public wages are more easily restrained and hopes public sector controls will guide private sector wage claims. Oddly enough, the reverse tends to be the case, and public sector pay awards have sometimes exceeded industrial pay awards. The complexity and size of the administration makes it difficult, even if acceptable to unions, to work out comparability with private employment and to calculate productivity. At times what appear to be inadvertent blunders put the civil service in a bad public light. For example, top civil servants make a much smaller pension contribution (2.6 percent of wages) than teachers and workers in nationalized industries (6 to 8 percent). The overall effect is to make the administration both a more visible target of popular skepticism and, more importantly, a politically controversial body of employees in working out income, welfare, and industrial relations policies. Their importance in the welfare state makes them vulnerable.

As we have seen in the analysis of administrative reform, the interdependencies of public sector wages with incomes, employment, and labor relations policies were not anticipated nor has it been easy to introduce these considerations. Administrative reform once meant internal reorganization of the civil service, not the more complex issue of how public manpower is best allocated in the welfare state. Most of these reforms failed, but the important issues confronting a government that is increasingly dependent on public sector workers have not been resolved. The most dramatic illustration was the British "winter of discontent" (1978–79) when a walkout by sanitation, hospital, and social workers paralyzed the country. (The work loss reached the level of the 1926 general strike.) The development of the welfare state has produced an entirely new set of problems that the administrative reform effort of the past two decades barely touches.

The vicissitudes of British economic policy over the past two decades go far beyond the scope of this study, but we have seen (Chapter 3) how difficult it has been to redirect the focus and procedures of economic management at the national level. The task of prime ministers and chancellors has not been an easy one, for they have repeatedly been caught between the imposed dislocations of adverse world economic conditions and internal economic dilemmas. The two arenas cannot be separated, but the international blows to the economy made it more difficult and more urgent for leaders to concentrate on internal weaknesses of economic policymaking. All this granted, the first Wilson government (1964–70) had few developed proposals to relate public spending to industrial growth. The Wilson approach was in many ways an extremely mechanical and rational view, assuming that long-term plans could be effectively translated into policy instruments and programs. The effort to build a Department of Economic Affairs degenerated into an interdepartmental fight with the Treasury. The cost, as Clarke points out (1978), was that the beginnings of firmer public expenditure controls, which the country needed a decade later, were discontinued or delayed.

In some ways adversarial politics make economic planning inconsequential. Heath brought a more sophisticated view of economic policymaking to government, but he too ran into Treasury and Civil Service Department opposition. As we have seen, his approach was further complicated because the Civil Service Department was divorced from the Treasury. A decade of "stop and go" ended when the oil crisis of 1973 and the financial crisis of 1975 forced Britain to curb the rate of growth of public spending. Opinions vary as to how much public spending planning and controls improved up to this time, but Britain was unprepared for new public spending problems. Until the early 1970s the Public Expenditure White Papers left out large amounts of expenditure (local government and nationalized industries), and once these were included there remained several ways of "fiddling." For example, the 1977 PESC White Paper showed less spending by removing nationalized industries' capital expenditure in preference for net borrowing (*Economist*, Jan. 14, 1978). Indicative of the weaknesses of devising better machinery, problems that are more easily compartmentalized within government, such as the nationalized industries, have been clarified as long-term objectives had to be defined. For different reasons, the parties followed a common strategy to make nationalized corporations more self-reliant.

All the mixed economies separate general economic policy from government spending and taxation. Britain differs only in degree. But until 1972 little was done to breach the barriers between public and private sector decisions. A retired chief economic adviser to the Treasury, Sir Bryan Hopkin, wrote in 1977, "One of our deep troubles is that we are absolutely schizophrenic about private enterprise. We have never made up our minds whether to go for socialism or to have an efficient capitalism. As a result we have messed up capitalism" (quoted in Keegan and Pennant-Rea, 1979, p. 108). The odd result has been that the government made repeated attempts to bail out private firms without ever extracting clear obligations from these firms and industries. There are numerous reasons why France, Germany, Japan, or even a strongly socialist Sweden would find this a doubtful bargain. Labour was hesitant because its aim (in theory if not in practice) was public ownership of production while the Conservatives were torn between their increasing dismay over poor industrial performance and their respect for private enterprise.

The public expenditure controversies made it easier to overlook deeper weakness in economic policymaking. Conservative political needs were met by outcries that Labour was not cutting enough, and Labour's political aims were met by outrage over social service cuts. The initial Thatcher "cuts" in 1979 did little more than eliminate modest increases in public expenditure that Labour had promised in its closing (and pre-electoral) years. Conversely, because controls were too crude, Labour was blamed in 1978 for "underspending" by about £2 billion. The Conservative drive to scale down public spending by £5 billion was reduced to £4 billion as ministers fought to preserve their departmental fiefdoms. Public spending plans did not seem to help government or the economy, and Britain was poorly prepared for the economic strains of the 1980s.

As we have seen in Chapter 4, the strength of the trade union movement has had the inadvertent effect of reducing, rather than increasing, worker involvement in economic policy. In the 1960s, the general secretary, George Woodcock, actively pursued a policy of moving "out of Trafalgar Square and into Whitehall." Little did the unions realize that eventually both Labour and Conservative governments would sponsor legislation striking at the heart of collective bargaining as traditionally conceived in British industrial relations. Government proved to be a more treacherous partner than the businessman. Moreover, as public sector unions played an increasingly important role in the TUC, union vulnerability was compounded. Not only were public sector wages more readily singled out for control, but wage controls could even be extended well beyond the public sector by placing conditions on government contractors to hold to wage policies. But the biggest cost was that public policy and union preferences worked together to reinforce distrust of industry and business.

But the most important sacrifice of the concentration on collective bargaining was that changes in the workforce, in industry, and in Britain's economic position were simply neglected. Wage bargaining tended to overshadow new needs such as child care, wage differentials, training, and equal rights that are beginning to be important in labor relations. The unions were under few pressures to develop a more comprehensive view of Britain's social and economic problems, nor were there many incentives for government to complicate bargaining intentionally. In fact, the composition of the workforce was changing, and, as we have seen, in 1976 pressures from more privileged union members (white-collar employees) made pay guidelines without recognition of pay differentials unworkable. By 1971, nearly 3 million nonmanual workers belonged to the TUC, nearly 30 percent of TUC membership (Minkin, 1978). Similar repercussions were felt from the rise of female employment. Between 1973 and 1977, employed females, mostly married, increased from about 400,000 to nearly 3 million persons. The total workforce increased by about 800,000 in this period, making a huge net change in the social composition and needs of workers. In early 1979 the average wage of men was £99 a week, but for women it was £63 (Department of Employment *Gazette*, 1979, p. 965).

Similarly, neither unions nor management have been quick to devise ways of relieving the effects of unemployment, whatever its causes. The TUC has endorsed the thirty-five-hour week, but neither unions nor management want to accept the risks of making available jobs employ more people. Next to workers in Luxembourg, British workers put in more overtime than those in any European country. In 1977 overtime represented about 400,000 full-time jobs (*New Statesman*, July 21, 1978). Nor have the major victims of unemployment shown much interest in integrating the dispersed, though considerable, employment policies of Whitehall. In addition to the relief given by national insurance, which in itself does little to find new solutions, in 1978 £500 million was spent by the Manpower Services Commission (training and placement), £200 million by the National Enterprise Board (job creation), and £100 million by the Department of Employment (youth employment). Though there are exceptions, neither unions nor industry feel a responsibility for the design and implementation of these programs that compares to the more active roles taken by French and German unions and firms.

The dilemma of labor-management relations becomes twofold. First, adversarial politics discourages unions from taking responsibility. Political affinities make unions heavily dependent on Labour and uncertain about the Conservatives. Second, the unions may have actually lost influence over their members and, in turn, in bargaining with government because of the more complex environment. A good case has been made that since 1975 unions have in fact regularly lost in their encounters with government. Many would agree with Taylor (1978, p. 19) that "for too long the unions have concentrated their limited resources in pushing for higher pay. They need to widen their range for bargaining over all fringe benefits as well as manpower policy, investment decisions and the other issues [such as] industrial democracy and manual/ non-manual inequalities." Concentration on collective bargaining fits well with British political realities, but provides few initiatives. Even wage demands are more complex because they affect not only the employed but also "the low paid, the old, the unemployed and those who do not belong to a union" (p. 18). The societal effects of wage policy cannot be evaded, but government has not been able to encourage unions to recognize these complexities. In fact, the growth of public sector unions means that "there will always be a pay policy in the public sector. Cash limits and public sector borrowing requirements ensure this" (p. 19). Thus, as Taylor concludes, "a punk rock philosophy based on sectionalist self-interest and muscle power" no longer works and may even be rejected by union members.

Although dealing with territorial rather than sectoral problems, the efforts to reorganize local government (Chapter 5) duplicate many of the same difficulties. Though not politically stalemated by national politics in the same way as those of unions, local authorities' political interests at the national level are diffused, and most nationally sensitive issues are quite easily superimposed from above. The local governments are condemned to an organization (town vs. country) that sets them against each other, and that make coalitions against national policies or even in pursuit of local interests difficult.

From a policymaking perspective, the combination of political subordination and administrative supervision from the center produces strong functional controls. So long as the grant could increase, the financial impact of increased national demands was less apparent, and few localities resented dependence so long as the Treasury paid the bills. The forced public spending cuts in 1975 and 1976 exposed this dilemma, but except for broad consultative arrangements within Whitehall the local governments still do not question their dependence. The Layfield Report asked for new revenues at a time when it was easy to say no, but there have been few new ideas on sharing policymaking responsibilities with the center. As in the case of the unions, one has the impression of a vast pool of talent and experience that is not tapped or, worse, is intentionally structured so that it cannot readily check national policymaking.

The effect is similar to conflict between employers and unions. Adjustment goes on with very little warning to those ultimately bearing the cost of change, and political opportunism is encouraged. For example, when the Labour secretary of state for the environment, Peter Shore, proposed "organic change," he was responding to demands of about twenty disgruntled districts that were demoted in the reorganization. In his speech defending the changes (restoring powers over education, planning, and social services to the districts), he refers to how "the Tories brutally imposed a rigid uniformity throughout this kingdom" (1979, p. 46), though it was Labour who initially wanted larger unitary authorities and itself made the first compromise to fit large metropolitan areas into their plans. Adversarial politics avoids the enormous problems of the complex local government system. Carried to its logical conclusions, which many Labour backbenchers wanted, the counties would be depleted of their functions and the disruptive parliamentary fight over local organization further fueled.

Under the Thatcher government, a whole new set of policies was imposed in no less an arbitrary way than earlier changes. The White Paper on reorganization (1979, cmnd. 7457) promised to remove some detailed controls (1979, cmnd. 7634), but the thrust of change only stimulated the historic controversy between town and country. There were large spending cuts (£300 million for 1978–79; and £600 million for 1979–80) and central pressures to limit rate increases, both designed to favor more rural areas, and hence Conservative local authorities. Another indication of the concentration of power in Westminster was that the protests of the local government associations, although under Con-

servative control, were easily put aside. Conservatives also promised to abolish the cumbersome method of calculating grants,
which tends to favor cities, and replace it wtih a single block grant.
But disappointing as the results of the 1972 Act may be, the Conservatives were making sure that bitter, adversarial conflict would
be perpetuated.

Local politicians are so heavily burdened and so thoroughly
socialized into the national political system that it is difficult to
imagine how more complex political relationships between localities and the center might be developed. Most local councils are
now dominated by caucus politics that assure the reproduction of
nationally defined party issues at the local level. Contact between
councils and Whitehall by the local government associations is far
removed from the daily problems of local government, and the
associations themselves tread a narrow path between being coopted and trying to resist the most arbitrary of government
measures. MPs convey the most serious grievances to ministers,
but are not considered national-level representatives of local governments, nor would such a role fit easily into the pattern of ministerial rule. From this perspective, adversarial advantage at the
national level becomes the most serious obstacle to devising a
more adaptable system of local government (Ashford, 1981).

The transformation of the British social security system over
the past two decades (Chapter 6) would probably be considered
more successful than the local government reform. To some extent
this is because one major social change, namely the growing numbers of elderly, made redefining priorities easier. In general, social
policies have more clearly defined objectives because their aims
and beneficiaries are more readily delimited. Because both parties
found it electorally advantageous to increase pensions, the integration of pension schemes elicited forebearance.

The question remains whether the present scheme can withstand the political temptation to dip into the massive pension
funds in a period of economic stagnation. In 1978 the private pensions funds accounted for investments equaling roughly 5 percent
of the national budget (£3.2 billion) and private insurance companies another 5 percent (£3.4 billion) (Dumbleton and Shutt,
1979). The economic importance of these huge funds means that
protecting savings for old age is only part of the pension problem.
There are some signs that modifications have already begun to
create a new "pension jungle" (*Economist*, May 6, 1978).

The fact that many of the large pension funds belong to unions is one of the more interesting ways in which class lines are fudged in the welfare state and, in turn, complicate policymaking. The coalminers own whisky stocks and part of the Watergate Hotel, the postmen have shares in a large French department store, and the railwaymen have gone in for Picassos and Wagner manuscripts as a hedge against inflation. Most agree that the standard national insurance benefits should be "uprated" to allow for inflationary price increases, but supplementary benefits tend to lag behind inflation. Political forces create disparities in welfare treatment, which, in turn, are rooted in the structural problems of Britain's social policy in the 1920s. With rising unemployment and increasing differentials among wages, stronger unions begin to defend particular benefits, sometimes at the expense of invalids, children, and mothers. Because the amount spent on benefits of all kinds must simultaneously accommodate inflation, increased costs, public spending controls, conflicts within the welfare system multiply. In deciding simply to abolish the SBC, the Thatcher government only increased ministerial control over these intricate choices.

Holding the total social security budget almost constant creates more political conflict than did distributing the gradual increments in the past. As Klein points out (1977), the aims of most social policies presuppose centralization, equalization, and paternal control, but these tendencies are particularly strong in the British social welfare system. There have been forces within the social and welfare agencies, particularly at the grassroots, that oppose these tendencies, but adversarial politics places choices more squarely on national leaders, the welfare bureaucracy, and experts as resources diminish. As large cuts were considered in 1979, it appeared that even Conservatives were appalled at the implications of the proposed reductions (*Guardian*, Oct. 9, 1979). The interdependence of welfare policy with incomes policy (by adjusting the social wage), tax policy (by affecting what benefits can be taxed), and employment policy (by making long-term benefits initially less accessible to the unemployed), as well as its crucial importance in public spending and budgetary policies, became obvious.

Although the intensity of the political debate about racial policies diminished somewhat after two decades of legislation (Chapter 7), the interdependencies of antidiscrimination, industrial relations, and social policies also emerged more sharply with economic decline. Like the United States, Britain found that unemployment struck minority racial groups more severely (up to 50 percent in parts of London) and that crime among black school leavers was rising. Cuts in spending for education, housing, and social services tend to have greater impact on minority racial groups than on the white population. By 1978, Britain had better machinery to resolve these problems, but political ambivalence still ruled out stronger antidiscrimination laws, and grievance procedures remain weak and dispersed. Complaints about racial discrimination over jobs, for example, are investigated by labor tribunals. An assessment of the 1976 Race Relations Act (Runnymede Trust, 1979) found only 33 successful appeals among 524 cases heard in 1977–78. Although many communities had developed stronger community programs, the Thatcher government could still concentrate on limiting immigration (now virtually stopped except for dependents) and had little to say about racial discrimination.

Adversarial politics provides a disastrous setting for forging racial policy. Labour was more forthright because racial minorities became critical to winning certain constituencies, but neither party was eager to untangle the conflicting demands of nationality, antidiscrimination, and immigration policies. In 1979, electoral advantage took priority, and Conservative liberals reluctantly gave way to more discriminatory demands for compulsory registration of immigrants and a quota system for future entry. The beleaguered Commission for Racial Equality quickly had its budget cut by a million pounds, and was ordered not to investigate complaints about Home Office immigration officials. After several confused efforts to bar immigration of husbands and fiancés of immigrant women, the Tories aimed their White Paper (1979, cmnd. 7750) at restricting entry after arranged marriages of Asians (a mere 3,264 men in 1978) and was blatantly sexist in circumscribing women's rights to be joined by their husbands. Adversarial politics only seemed to create new injustices to replace old ones.

In general, British policymakers have had problems in detecting important changes in the environment and, in turn, have been slow to adapt to new needs and to redefine objectives. Certainly there are no ideal, rational solutions to Britain's problems, but Britain may have been too successful in excluding politics from the formulation, implementation, and evaluation of policies. Substantial social changes have gone unexplored, and sometimes have been simply ignored. Persistent social and economic weaknesses have been papered over with adversarial politics, which at times has only aggravated policy problems. There are two causes: on the one hand, adversarial politics does not thrive on admitting common ground between adversaries; and, on the other hand, the high levels of elite and societal consensus underlying British politics provide few reasons for policymakers to reconsider and reexamine their decisions. As Beer (1965) has shown, Britain fashioned a remarkable compromise between conflicting ideologies and party government in the nineteenth century, but the compromise may have been achieved by dangerously isolating the policy process from social forces and the changing environment of policymaking.

As the welfare state expands its activities, these weaknesses become more damaging to policymaking. There are perfectly good reasons why many policy instruments and procedures of the past do not work well now: inflation, increased labor militancy, large increases in unemployment and possibly a larger permanently poor population, new problems of inner cities, industrial obsolescence, and so forth. To some extent all the modern democracies have experienced these changes in the environment of policymaking. What seems to differentiate Britain are the difficulties experienced in fashioning new policy machinery and new alternatives that respond to social and economic changes. The policy analyses provide an analog to Hayward's argument about the inertia of British political institutions (1976). The environment of policymaking becomes more complex because the state provides more services, and intervenes in choices that were once left to market forces or individual choice, but political adjustments are slow to appear. British policymaking seems easily overtaken by social and economic change, the top-level policymakers appear swamped by new demands and new problems, and political institutions seem inadequate, not because of inefficiency or unresponsiveness, but because they refuse to alter the policymaking process itself.

Consensual Governing and the British Welfare State

In Chapter 1 we saw how the concentration of powers in ministerial offices and cabinet government has grown with the evolution of the welfare state. Although there have been institutional experiments within some parts of government, the political constraints on policymaking that are provided by elite and mass consensus have remained essentially unchanged. Compared to most modern democracies, Britain has not developed more intricate links between private and public sector decisionmaking, more vulnerable administration, and more open dependence between national and local government that serve to mobilize political forces at lower levels of the system and, in turn, to sensitize the elite to new needs and to the effects of existing policies. Adversarial politics takes place in a very limited arena and reforms that might mobilize more political resources and qualify the concentration of power in Westminster and Whitehall have regularly been resisted. Elite and societal consensus combine to provide a very stable political system, but they do not provide the wide-ranging criticism and diverse intervention in the policymaking process that exist in some form in nearly every advanced industrial state.

The interaction of these conditions—the assumptions of the elite, dislocating changes in the environment, and the adversarial effects —is summarized in the list on the following pages.

These observations are not intended to suggest that all the policies of any country can be measured by the same standards, even less that there are uniformly applicable standards of success and failure when we compare policies across several countries. Just as the strengths and weaknesses of policymaking vary with the problems encountered, so also the political strengths and weaknesses that a country brings to the policy process may vary in relation to other aspects of the political system. Obvious failures may make political inadequacies more visible, but not all failures are attributable to politics. Under some circumstances, such as extraordinarily adverse external conditions, even the most adept and responsive political system may fail to find appropriate solutions to policy problems. At the same time, it is important to remember that the political system, especially in democracies, serves other purposes than policymaking. If the constraints of elite and societal consensus have enabled adversarial politics to thrive in Britain at the expense of more effective policymaking, the answer may be no more complicated than the concern of the British people to keep democratic participation vigorous and effective even if the policy process appears less effective than in other advanced industrial states.

The analysis of politics and policymaking raises issues that economic and sociological policy analyses do not. As we noted in Chapter 1, political science is about the relationship of diverse values to institutions and collective authority more generally. Economists and sociologists can construct more rigorous models by

	Elite consensus	Environmental changes	Adversarial reactions
Administrative reform	Civil service anonymity; ministerial secrecy and cabinet coordination; few politicians in departments and strong permanent secretary; Whitehall clearly demarcated from other bureaucracies	Growing complexity of policy implementation and evaluation; increased coordinating role of Cabinet Office; more tribunals and more discretionary powers; more reliance on local government; growth of public sector unions	Less ministerial accountability to Parliament and public; confused demands on local government; complex procedures for administrative review and justice; reinforced secrecy; oversimplification of organizational complexity and obscuring of responsibilities through hiving off
Economic policymaking	Privileged status of Treasury; spending decisions divorced from taxation; partisan manipulation of public expenditure forecast; weak links to private sector; nationalized industry at arm's length but without initiative and autonomy	Growing manufactured imports and declining exports; severe inflation and weak incomes policy; energy crisis; increase in public spending and public employment; decline of heavy industry and relocation in south of England; EEC	Poor coordination budget and public spending forecasts; erratic pressures on nationalized industry; erosion of long-term expenditure controls; tax and spending options separated; indiscriminate budget controls; partisan use of incomes policy; poor coordination of industrial policy and assistance
Industrial relations	Unions polarized by two-party system; private and public sector unions kept distinct; uncertain and confusing wage policies; aversion to legal restraint of unions but worker needs and demands dispersed in Whitehall; TUC and CBI easily subsumed by adversarial politics	Rise of white-collar unions and female employment; diversity of internal union organization; increased militancy of public sector unions; social and unemployment benefits divorced from wage policies; slow response to industrial democracy; need to link productivity to wages	Return to legal battles over union restraint; abrupt shifts from incomes policies to inflationary wage constraints; increased reliance on public sector wage guidelines; industrial and labor consultation poorly aligned with economic policy; legal complexity of labor legislation underestimated

Local government reform	Local politicians as secondary actors and isolated from party; local service guidelines left to ministerial decisions; aversion to territorial politics; limit local authority direct revenues to property tax; distrust of community forces and antipathy toward regional government	Inner city decline and rural depopulation problems; increased fiscal dependence on center; industrial, social, and economic policies remote from local decisions; increased racial conflict; functional regional bodies remote from localities; adversarial treatment of devolution	Town vs. country debate continued; complex structure and confusing division of responsibilities re-created; increase of local resources declined; unproductive devolution debate; increased manipulation of grant; contradictory demands on local authorities and abrupt changes in local government law
Social security	Continued divorce between deserving and undeserving poor; intricate machinery for means testing; tax benefits separated from social benefits; self-financing insurance plans undermined; adversarial response to poverty gap; priority for children and women secondary to universal social benefits	Growth of number of single-parent families, homeless, and elderly; increased concern with sex discrimination; conflicting effects of tax and social benefits; increased need for unemployment relief; increased dependence on local authorities; problems of coordinating child, family, and health organizations; erosion by inflation	Adversarial response to poverty gap continued; adversarial manipulation of inflation-proofing procedures; pensioners given favored treatment; difficulty of conveying new social needs through complex organizations; tax policy still divorced from social policy; complications of relating housing and unemployment policies to social policy resisted
Race and immigration	Early ambivalence between colonial and national problems; reluctance to use nationality law; ease of electoral exploitation; preference for no national racial policies and weak enforcement tolerated; racial policies compartmentalized in ministries and effective coordination resisted	Inability to respond to concentration of racial minorities in inner cities and high unemployment areas; immigration virtually stopped but confusion of separated families; shift to social, housing and job needs; growing second-generation problems and crime	Cross-pressures within parties leading to procrastination without reducing electoral exploitation; arbitrary and inhumane immigrant review procedures; many social and housing needs left to localities; ambiguous role of race relations machinery and complex procedures to redress racial grievances

assuming that a single value should be applied to a particular problem or even to a number of different problems. The economic dislocations of the past few years have made such models more attractive to both the extreme right and the extreme left, but in each case it is usually clear that the analyst is projecting a single value as an ideal standard. There are reasons to think that political systems, especially democratically regulated systems, cannot fulfill the conditions imposed by such "objective functions." They are difficult to formulate without presuming what people should do, sometimes even what people should think, which removes one of the essential assumptions of democratic politics. Indeed, one of the most difficult dilemmas of the welfare state is that, as policymaking becomes more complex, it becomes difficult for citizens to follow the intricacies of the policy process (Klein, 1974).

Comparative policy analysis, either across policies within one country or of similar policies across several countries, presupposes that we can single out the particular requirements that democracy imposes on policymaking as well as the changing environment that alters the conditions and aims of policymaking. The strength of elite and societal consensus in Britain may mean that the political system is acquiring stability in the "inputs" of politics at the cost of neglecting the "outputs" of politics. The most obvious evidence is found in the materials assembled in the policy analyses that show how fairly dramatic changes in the policy environment have not led to reassessment and reexamination of many public policies. The existing rules, procedures, and organizations surrounding the policy process have remained remarkably stable. Efforts to make major structural changes often seem poorly planned, and in most instances are short lived. It is not surprising that politicians are not motivated to make major changes for the system serves their interests well and on the whole both societal and elite consensus confirms their view. The difficulties of changing the policy process may be lamented by those who feel that they have grasped the essentials of a perfect political system, and even more by those who think they have a totally reliable "objective function" to superimpose on policy problems, but it would also be misleading to think that the British people are not aware that they have preserved a rare combination of consensual talents even if the policy process appears deficient or inadequate.

In democratic systems, elite consensus is the institutionalized result of societal consensus, and is revealed in legislation, administrative behavior, party organization, and the roles of minor political actors. Societal consensus is *about* the political system; elite consensus operates *within* the institutions of the political system. Compared to most European democracies and Japan, Britain has carefully tuned these consensual structures to the formal institutions of government, and even more narrowly to the institutions governing the peak of the political hierarchy. Both West Germany and Japan, for example, have conceded more influence to the elites of the private sector and have devised fairly elaborate institutions linking them to government. Many would argue that this has been done by making the political system less important to the society as a whole. In France and Sweden pervasive and elaborate bureaucracies are much more important in guiding the political system and forming policies. Britain has never been comfortable with this solution to the complexity of policymaking, even though the civil service exercises enormous influence under the supervision of ministers. The tangled web of interest group politics in the United States means that national institutions and legislation more often seem the product of pluralist compromise than the purposive activity of national government. In none of these countries does adversarial politics so readily prevail in establishing policy objectives and assessing the problems of the future.

The paradox of highly adversarial policymaking combined with strong elite and societal consensus is resolved if one understands the interaction of these three forces in the British political system. On the one hand, were other democracies to indulge in such unrestrained and sometimes erratic policymaking, it seems very likely that their less united peoples and less entrenched consensual traditions would not withstand the strain and conflict. In countries with weaker political parties, less decisive cabinets and parliaments, and more intricate bureaucratic structures, rapidly made and ill-conceived proposals would not be tolerated. On the other hand, it would also be a mistake to think that adversarial politics is permitted to assume its full force in the British political system. As we saw in Chapter 1, the power of the cabinet and Parliament to make laws is virtually unrestricted. Were the British elite to misuse their enormous consensual trust, British democracy would not survive.

The greatest risk to the British political system, however, is not that adversarial politics will exceed the limits of democratic politics, but that it will be unable to deal with the complexities of policymaking in a much more intricate and rapidly changing world than in the past. The constitutional fictions and customs that produced parliamentary government may not be appropriate to a less stable world. The policymaking handicaps of the British system are relatively specific and concrete when viewed through the policy analyses. First, there is a remarkably small number of leaders concerned with very intricate problems and decisions. The institutionalized relationships between national leaders and MPs, parties and Parliament, national and local politicians, and even group leaders and their clients are structured in ways that tend to minimize threats to the upper levels of decisionmaking. Second, policies are usually thrashed out behind closed doors, with much of the critical evidence hidden from both Parliament and the people, and with very little exposure of the options facing government. Third, the stratified administrative system and anonymity of civil servants mean that many crucial steps in the policy process are unknown to ministers as well as to the public and groups interested in specific policies. Where special clients and groups are privileged to enter into earlier stages of policymaking, they are bound by the same secrecy that surrounds the policy process.

From a policy perspective, the conclusion is that British political leaders may perform their adversarial roles too well. Their dilemma is not an easy one to resolve, for were they to accept that elite consensus about government was mainly concerned with perform- ance, the underpinnings of British democracy might be shaken. As we have seen, even in policy areas such as pension reform and re- structuring nationalized industries, where there has been consider- able agreement on objectives, there is a constant temptation to relapse into unrestrained adversarial behavior that might undo the long-term solutions that have appeared. But in all the policy areas there are severe costs in practicing adversarial politics: for administrative reform Labour proposes internal democratization while Conservatives press for ruthless efficiency; for the economy Labour wants more public spending (and hopefully more equality) while Conservative battle (often without results) to dismantle the public sector; in local government Labour fights for the cities (and its voters), Conservatives for the suburbs and countryside (and their voters); in dealing with social security Labour seeks to extend benefits while Conservatives try to curb them; and in racial mat- ters both parties are confused by cross-pressures within their parties and the potentially high electoral costs of taking a firm stand against discrimination.

The politics of British policymaking, therefore, are about combining the adversarial requirements of British democracy with the necessity to acknowledge shared objectives and long-term problems in the policy process. The point is not that Britain has failed according to some arbitrary and presumably "objective" function of policymaking or that some mysterious *malaise* overshadows British leaders. On the contrary, if anything seems readily apparent about the politics of British policymaking, it is that the elite seems to behave much as it did a century ago. This is no mean accomplishment if one remembers that over the past century an enormous bureaucracy has been added to British government; that the party system has undergone a major transformation; and that the electorate has been steadily expanded. Britain has accomplished a great deal in perfecting the institutions of modern democracy, but rather less in terms of innovation and experimentation in policymaking. As we have seen, this may be because it is relatively easy to fulfill the needs of adversarial politics without confronting the full complexity of policy problems, including the complexities of the welfare state and, in recent years, the severe economic dislocations that confront all the advanced industrial states.

Given the close integration of elite and societal consensus, and the consequent ease with which adversarial intervention can influence policymaking, the question remains how this carefully structured balance might be changed. The first and most serious dislocation would be to the breakdown of societal consensus so that more demanding and more specific requirements would be placed on British policymakers. There are more than a few indications that the long-standing societal consensus about British government may be in jeopardy. As noted in Chapter 1, Britain has come close to one-party dominance over the past century, and only the rise of the Labour Party has restored party politics as a viable alternative to Conservative rule. Multiparty systems and to some extent even democracies with dominant party coalitions with internal factions such as France or Japan may provide a stronger stimulus for articulating policy options and for more careful definition of national objectives.

There are more than a few reasons to think that the democratic process in Britain is under severe strain. As Butt notes (1969,

p. 314), only the Liberals can indulge in the "luxury of opinion formation" because they have little hope of taking power. Were electoral seats distributed in proportion to votes for the October 1974 election, for example, Labour would have lost 69 seats and Conservatives 50 seats, while the Liberals would have gained an additional 103 seats (*Economist*, Nov. 5, 1977). The "winner-take-all" electoral system means that well over half the votes are in "safe" constituencies. The high proportion of safe seats may dull MPs' policy concerns and lull party politicians into thinking that performance is of secondary concern. The unruly party organizations of France and the United States may impose other policy constraints on democratic politics, but they also ensure that policies and alternatives must respond to local preferences and new social needs.

A second possibility would be that elite consensus over the form and procedures of government might be shaken. Intent as the parliamentary reformers of the 1960s were on restoring power to the MPs, the solution does not appear to rest in simply strengthening committees and debate in the House of Commons. Weaker parties and smaller majorities have been the effective means of compelling cabinet government to take Parliament more seriously. The fundamental views of both the extreme right and the extreme left suggest that MPs should be more responsible and independent, but both traditions have been eroded in order to meet the requirements of office. The 1970s have found the Conservatives divided between "hardliners" and "wets," who favor a more socially responsive form of conservatism; while Labour is even more severely divided between the more orthodox parliamentary wing under Callaghan and the more radical demands of the Labour left wing to make MPs directly accountable to their constituencies. The deterioration of both the Conservative and the Labour Party organizations is another indicator that the links between elite views and grassroots opinion are weakening. Should these ties become sufficiently weak and the parties internally divided, it would be difficult to sustain the strength of elite consensus. Whether better-designed policies would emerge remains to be seen, but at least the ease of adversarial manipulation of policies would be reduced.

Third, privileged groups and interests that now have virtually unrestricted entry to the policy process, while being protected against the consequences of their own influence, might be driven to compete more openly for power. Some tendencies are now visible because government and its departments must live with constant and sometimes diminishing resources. Because the process of bargaining and compromise has gone on largely within departments and has been sheltered by administrative confidentiality we know relatively little about how carefully alternatives are weighed and how consequences are mapped out. For example, local government associations have been severely strained to support government in the face of the radical changes planned by Heseltine even when they are controlled by local Conservative politicians. The decision to reduce the financial flexibility and resources of new towns also provoked a stiff protest from the Town Planning Institute, for many years a favored client of government. As national administration is "neutralized," to use Johnson's term (1977), its ability to manipulate government clients and to stand guard over ministerial proposals is diminished.

There are also important short-term forces that may lead to restructuring elite and societal consensus. The European Community, its controls on British life, and the net contribution of about a billion pounds required from Britain have divided both major parties. Labour eventually gave MPs a "free vote" on entry, and party leadership remains deeply split over EEC membership. Similarly, although savings from EEC contributions are vital to Mrs. Thatcher's severe monetarist policies, Heath and other "wets" (progressive Tories) still openly disassociate themselves from her severe criticisms of EEC. Thus, the elite may appear as openly and hopelessly divided as are the French political elite, for example, over numerous issues, which, in turn, erodes party strength and discipline and could eventually undermine societal consensus.

Another divisive issue that may plague British politics for a decade is economic decline. Even the slow rates of economic growth in the 1960s and early 1970s permitted marginal increases in social benefits, sheltered the private sector from the full blame for rising unemployment, and enabled ministers to make sufficient increases in public spending to forestall open conflict among departments. Both the ruthless monetarism of the Thatcher government and the protectionism advocated by the radical left put immense strains on elite consensus and in various ways fuel popular disillusionment with British government and even ignite more acute social conflicts. The response of government and administration under both Callaghan and Thatcher has not been encouraging. Essentially, government has turned to more arbitrary and indiscriminate controls, such as cash limit budgeting, which serve to exacerbate conflicts within government while making it less able to govern through the usual operation of adversarial politics.

The most serious challenge to adversarial politics is when it does not work within government and administration. One indication is the numerous leaks to the press from the cabinet, the departments, and high civil servants. Another is the widely publicized refusal of ministers dealing with key social services to consider the large public spending reductions demanded by Mrs. Thatcher. If leaders and the public become disillusioned with a political process that seems unable to grapple directly with the complex issues confronting British society, both elite and societal consensus may be strained. To the extent that British democracy has enjoyed stability and support in the past by practicing a form of adversarial politics that tended to paper over deeper weaknesses and profoundly complex issues, such tactics may not suffice for the future. On the other hand, if Britain embarks on the more deeply divisive forms of class politics and begins to rely on nationalistic appeals, the restraint and moderation that made adversarial politics possible will be sacrificed.

Axiomatic or empirical models will probably never explain how each country weighs consensus within government against consensus about government, but both are essential to democratic political systems. Until the recent past, the deep roots of societal consensus and the time-honored traditions of elite consensus permitted Britain to engage in a particular form of policymaking and supported restrained, but potentially immensely powerful, adversarial politics. A carefully constructed historical compromise enabled the British to fashion the first working democracy, but the assumptions of British democracy do not appear to be easily translated into new policymaking machinery and do not seem to focus easily on the performance of government. Creating less improvised policy procedures and reducing uncertainty in policymaking are major problems for adversarial politics. If solutions cannot be found, then Britain may be faced with the more painful process of rebuilding societal consensus or radically restructuring the nature of elite consensus. Despite the criticisms of the extreme left and extreme right, three centuries of steadily building democratic participation leave hope that British political inventiveness and ingenuity can also handle the complexities of policymaking in the welfare state.

References

General

Ashford, Douglas E. 1978. "The Structural Analysis of Policy or Institutions Really Do Matter." In Ashford, ed., *Comparing Public Policies,* pp. 81–98. Beverly Hills: Sage Publications.

————. 1981. *British Dogmatism and French Pragmatism: Central-Local Politics in the Welfare State.* London and Boston: George Allen and Unwin.

Beattie, A. J. 1974. "The Two-Party Legend." *Political Quarterly* 45:288–99.

————. 1975. "The Two-Party System: Room for Scepticism?" In S. E. Finer, ed., *Adversary Politics and Electoral Reform,* pp. 293–316. London: Anthony Wigram.

Beer, Samuel H. 1965. *British Politics in the Collectivist Age.* New York: Alfred A. Knopf.

Briggs, Asa. 1961. "The Welfare State in Historical Perspective." *Archives Européene de Sociologie* 2:221–58.

Brown, R. G. S., and D. R. Steel. 1979. *The Administrative Process in Britain.* 2nd ed. London: Methuen.

Bruce, Maurice. 1968. *The Coming of the Welfare State.* 4th ed. London: Batsford.

Butler, David, and Anne Sloman. 1975. *British Political Facts, 1900–1975.* 4th ed. London: Macmillan.

Butt, Ronald. 1969. *The Power of Parliament.* 2nd ed. London: Constable.

Castle, Barbara. 1973. "Mandarin Power." *Sunday Times,* June 10.

Chapman, Brian. 1963. *British Government Observed.* London: George Allen and Unwin.

Chapman, Leslie. 1978. *Your Disobedient Servant.* London: Chatto and Windus.

Clarke, Sir Richard. 1978. *Public Expenditure Management and Control.* London: Macmillan.

Crick, Bernard. 1964. *The Reform of Parliament*. London: Weidenfeld and Nicolson.

Crossman, Richard. 1976. *The Diaries of a Cabinet Minister*, vol. 2. London: Hamish Hamilton and Jonathan Cape.

Crowther-Hunt, Lord. 1976. "Whitehall—Just Passing Through." *Listener*, Dec. 16.

———. 1977. "Whitehall—The Balance of Power." *Listener*, Jan. 6.

de Smith, S. A. 1973. *Judicial Review of Administrative Action*. London: Stevens.

Drewry, Gavin. "Legislation." In S. A. Walkland and M. Ryle, eds., *The Commons in the Seventies*, pp. 70–94. London: Study of Parliament Group (Fontana Books).

Dumbleton, Bob, and John Shutt. 1979. "Pensions: The Capitalist Trap." *New Statesman*, Sept. 7.

Eckstein, Harry. 1961. *A Theory of Stable Democracy*. Princeton, N.J.: Center of International Studies.

Edelman, Maurice. 1975. "The Patronage Explosion." *New Statesman*, July 11.

Finer, S. E. 1975. "Manifesto Moonshine." *New Society*, Nov. 13.

———. 1977. "The Triumph of Entropy." *New Society*, Nov. 17.

Fraser, Derek. 1973. *The Evolution of the British Welfare State*. London: Macmillan.

Great Britain, Expenditure Committee. 1976. *Planning and Control of Public Expenditure* (Thirteenth Report). HC 718, Nov. 11. London: HMSO.

———. 1977. *The Civil Service* (Eleventh Report). HC 535-I, -II, and -III, July 25. London: HMSO.

Great Britain, Secretary of State for the Environment. 1979. *Organic Change in Local Government*. Cmnd. 7457. London: HMSO.

———. 1979. *Central Government Controls over Local Authorities*. Cmnd. 7635. London: HMSO.

Great Britain, Select Committee on Procedure. 1978. *Report* (First Report). HC 588-I, July 17. London: HMSO.

Great Britain, White Paper. 1979. *Proposals for Revision of the Immigration Rules*. Cmnd. 7750. London: HMSO.

Hailsham, Lord. 1976. "Elective Dictatorship." *Listener*, Oct. 21.

Harris, Nigel. 1972. *Competition and the Corporate Society*. London: Methuen.

Hayward, Jack. 1976. "Institutional Inertia and Political Impetus in France and Britain." *European Journal of Political Research* 4:341–59.

Heady, Bruce. 1974. *British Cabinet Ministers: The Roles of Politicians in Executive Office*. London: George Allen and Unwin.

Herman, Valentine. 1974. "What Governments Say and What Governments Do: An Analysis of Post-War Queen's Speeches." *Parliamentary Affairs* 28:22–30.

————. 1975. "Comparative Perspectives on Ministerial Stability in Britain." In James Alt, ed., *Cabinet Studies: A Reader*, pp. 56–76. London: Macmillan.

Hewitt, Christopher. 1974. "Elites and the Distribution of Power in British Society." In Philip Stansworth and Anthony Giddens, eds., *Elites and Power in British Society*, pp. 45–64. London: Cambridge University Press.

Holland, Philip, and Michael Fallon. 1978. *The Quango Explosion*. London: Conservative Political Centre.

Hood, Christopher. 1978. "Keeping the Centre Small: Explanations of Agency Type." *Political Studies* 26:30–46.

Howe, Sir Geoffrey. 1977. "Reform of British Tax Machinery." *British Tax Review*.

Jenkins, Roy. 1971. "The Realities of Power." *Sunday Times*, Jan. 17.

Johnson, Nevil. 1977. *In Search of the Constitution: Reflections on State and Society in Britain*. London: Pergamon Press.

————. 1978. "Politics and Administration as the Art of the Possible." *Political Studies* 26:267–83.

Johnston, R. J. 1979. *Political, Electoral and Spatial Systems*. London: Oxford University Press.

Jones, G. W. 1965. "The Prime Minister's Power." *Parliamentary Affairs* 18:167–85.

Jordan, Grant. 1977. "Grey Papers." *Political Quarterly* 48:30–43.

———— and Jeremy Richardson. 1979. "Pantouflage: A Civil Service Perk." *New Society*, Feb. 22.

Katznelson, Ira. 1973. *Black Men, White Cities*. Oxford: Oxford University Press.

Kavanagh, Dennis. 1971. "The Deferential English." *Government and Opposition* 6:333–60.

Keegan, William, and Rupert Pennant-Rea. 1979. *Who Runs the Economy? Control and Influence in British Economic Policy*. London: Maurice Temple Smith.

Klein, Rudolf. 1974. "The Case for Elitism: Public Opinion and Public Policy." *Political Quarterly* 45:406–17.

———— and Janet Lewis. 1977. "Advice and Dissent in British Government: The Case of the Special Advisers." *Policy and Politics* 6:1–25.

Lansley, Stewart. 1979. *Housing and Housing Public Policy*. London: Croom Helm.

Laski, Harrold. 1938. *Parliamentary Government in England.* London: George Allen and Unwin.

Letwin, S. R. 1965. *The Pursuit of Certainty.* Cambridge: Cambridge University Press.

Low, Sir Sidney. 1927. *The Government of England.* Rev. ed. London: T. Fisher Unwin.

Lowell, A. Lawrence. 1908. *The Government of England.* New York: Macmillan.

Mackintosh, John P. 1962. *The British Cabinet.* London: Stevens.

Minkin, Lewis. 1978. "The Party Connection: Divergence and Convergence in the British Labour Movement." *Government and Opposition* 13:548–84.

Mitchell, J. D. B. 1967. "Administrative Law and Parliamentary Control." *Political Quarterly* 38:360–74.

Neustadt, Richard. 1966. "White House and Whitehall." *Public Interest* 2:55–69.

Outer Circle Policy Unit. 1979. *What's Wrong with Quangos?* London: Outer Circle Policy Unit.

Page, Bruce. 1978. "The Secret Constitution." *New Statesman,* July 21.

Pulzer, Peter G. J. 1975. *Political Representation and Elections in Britain.* 3rd ed. London: George Allen and Unwin.

Punnett, R. M. 1975. "Her Majesty's Shadow Government: Its Evolution and Modern Role." In Valentine Herman and James Alt, eds., *Cabinet Studies,* pp. 140–56. London: Macmillan.

Putnam, Robert D. 1973. *The Beliefs of Politicians.* New Haven: Yale University Press.

Rose, Richard. 1974. *The Problem of Party Government.* London: Macmillan.

———— and Guy Peters. 1978. *Can States Go Bankrupt?* New York: Basic Books.

Rothschild, Lord. 1977. "Heads Reports from the Think Tank: They Could Irritate Sometimes." *The Times,* Sept. 5.

Runnymede Trust. 1979. *A Review of the Race Relations Act, 1976.* London: The Trust.

Ryle, M. T. 1975. "Developments in the Parliamentary System." In William Thornhill, ed., *The Modernization of British Government,* pp. 7–30. London: Pitman.

Sainsbury, Keith. 1965. "Patronage, Honours and Parliament." *Parliamentary Affairs* 19:346–50.

Schattschneider, Elmer E. 1961. *The Semisovereign People.* New York: Holt, Rinehart and Winston.

Shanks, Michael. 1961. *The Stagnant Society.* Harmondsworth: Penguin Books.

Shonfield, Andrew. 1958. *British Economic Policy since the War.* Harmondsworth: Penguin Books.

———. 1965. *Modern Capitalism: The Changing Balance of Public and Private Power.* Oxford: Oxford University Press.

Shore, Peter. 1979. "Organic Change." *County Councils Gazette* 72:46–48.

Smith, Brian. 1976. *Policy-Making in British Government.* London: Martin Robertson.

Smith, Trevor. 1979. *The Politics of the Corporate Economy.* London: Martin Robertson.

Stewart, J. D., et al. 1978. *Organic Change: A Report on Constitutional, Management and Financial Problems.* Birmingham: Institute of Local Government Studies.

Taylor, Robert. 1978. *Labour and the Social Contract.* Fabian Society Tract No. 458. London: The Society.

Wade, H. W. R. 1977. *Administrative Law.* 4th ed. Oxford: Clarendon Press.

Walkland, S. A. 1968. *The Legislative Process in Great Britain.* London: George Allen and Unwin.

———. 1976. "'Adversary Politics and Electoral Reform': A Review." *Political Quarterly* 47:52–58.

Waltz, Kenneth. 1967. *Foreign Policy and Democratic Politics.* Boston: Little, Brown.

Wilby, Peter. 1975. "The Think Groups." *New Society,* Oct. 2.

Willson, F. M. G. 1978. "Coping with Administrative Growth: Super-Departments and the Ministerial Cadre, 1957–77." In David Butler and A. H. Halsey, eds., *Policy and Politics,* pp. 35–50. London: Macmillan.

Wiseman, H. V. 1966. *Parliament and the Executive.* London: Routledge and Kegan Paul.

Wootton, Graham. 1978. *Pressure Politics in Contemporary Britain.* Lexington: Lexington Books.

Wright, Maurice. 1977. "Ministers and Civil Servants: Relations and Responsibilities." *Parliamentary Affairs* 30:293–313.

Administrative Reform

Abramovitz, Moses, and Vera F. Eliasberg. 1957. *The Growth of Public Employment in Great Britain.* Princeton: Princeton University Press.

Bacon, Robert, and Walter Eltis. 1978. *Britain's Economic Problem: Too Few Producers.* 2nd ed. London: Macmillan.

Balogh, Thomas. 1959. "The Apotheosis of the Dilettante." In Hugh Thomas, ed., *The Establishment,* pp. 83–128. London: Anthony Blond.

Bourn, J. B. 1968. "The Main Reports on the British Civil Service since the Northcote-Trevelyan Report." Memorandum No. 10. In *The Civil Service* (Fulton Report), vol. 3(2), pp. 423–65. London: HMSO.

Boyle, Sir Edward. 1965. "Who Are the Policy Makers? Minister or Civil Servant? I. Minister." *Public Administration* (U.K.) 43:251–59.

Brown, R. G. S., and D. R. Steel. 1979. *The Administrative Process in Britain.* London: Methuen.

Chapman, Richard A. 1973. "The Fulton Committee." In Chapman, ed., *The Role of Commission in Policy Making,* pp. 11–41. London: George Allen and Unwin.

Chester, D. N. 1963. "The Plowden Report: I. Nature and Significance." *Public Administration* (U.K.) 41:3–16.

———. 1968. "The Report of the Fulton Committee on the Civil Service." *Public Administration* (Aust.) 27:295–310.

Clarke, R. W. B. 1963. "The Plowden Report: II. The Formulation of Economic Policy." *Public Administration* (U.K.) 41:17–25.

Clarke, Sir Richard. 1972. "The Number and Size of Government Departments." *Political Quarterly* 43:169–86.

———. 1978. *Public Expenditure Management and Control.* London: Macmillan.

Fabian Society. 1964. *The Administrators: The Reform of the Civil Service.* Fabian Society Tract No. 355. London: The Society.

Great Britain. 1968–69. *The Civil Service: Report of the Committee* (Fulton Report), 5 vols. Cmnd. 3638. London: HMSO.

Great Britain, Chancellor of the Exchequer. 1976. *Cash Limits.* Cmnd. 6440. London: HMSO.

Great Britain, Civil Service Department. 1969. *Developments on Fulton.* London: HMSO.

———. 1970. *Fulton: A Framework for the Future.* London: HMSO.

———. 1971. *Civil Service Statistics, 1971–* (annual report since 1970). London: HMSO.

———. 1971. *The Reshaping of the Civil Service: Developments during 1970.* London: HMSO.

———. 1972. *The Shape of the Post-Fulton Civil Service.* London: HMSO.

———. 1975. *Civil Servants and Change.* London: HMSO.

Great Britain, Committee on Policy Optimisation. 1978. *Report* (Ball Report). Cmnd. 7148, March. London: HMSO.

Great Britain, Expenditure Committee. 1977. *The Civil Service* (Eleventh Report). HC 535-I (Report), 535-II (Evidence), and 535-III (Testimony), July 25. London: HMSO.

Great Britain, Prime Minister. 1978. *The Civil Service.* Cmnd. 7117. London: HMSO.

Heclo, Hugh, and Aaron Wildavsky. 1974. *The Private Government of Public Money.* Berkeley: University of California Press.

Howell, David. 1970. *A New Style of Government.* London: Conservative Political Centre.

Johnson, Nevil. 1971. "Editorial: The Reorganization of Central Government." *Public Administration* (U.K.) 47:1–12.

Klein, Rudolf. 1972. "The Politics of PPB." *Political Quarterly* 43:270–81.

Lee, J. M. 1978. *Reviewing the Machinery of Government, 1942–52: An Essay on the Anderson Committee and Its Successors.* London: Birkbeck College.

Maynard, Alan, and Arthur Walker. 1975. "Cutting Public Spending." *New Society,* Dec. 4, pp. 528–29.

Morton, W. W. 1963. "The Plowden Report: III. The Management Functions of the Treasury." *Public Administration* (U.K.) 41:25–35.

Nairne, P. D. 1964. "Management and the Administrative Class." *Public Administration* (U.K.) 42:113–22.

Painter, C. 1975. "The Civil Service: Post Fulton Malaise." *Public Administration* (U.K.) 53:427–41.

Parris, Henry. 1969. *Constitutional Bureaucracy: The Development of British Central Administration since the Eighteenth Century.* London: George Allen and Unwin.

Parry, Richard. 1979. "The Distribution of Public Employment in the United Kingdom." Unpub. ms.

Playfair, Sir Edward. 1965. "Who Are the Policy Makers? Minister or Civil Servant? II. Civil Servant." *Public Administration* (U.K.) 43:260–68.

Robson, W. A. 1968. "The Fulton Report on the Civil Service." *Political Quarterly* 39:397–414.

Smith, Brian. 1971. "Reform and Change in British Central Administration." *Political Studies* 19:213–26.

Wallas, Graham. 1948. *Human Nature in Politics.* 4th ed. London: Constable.

Wright, Maurice. 1977. "Ministers and Civil Servants: Relations and Responsibilities." *Parliamentary Affairs* 30:293–313.

Economic Policymaking

Bacon, Roger, and Walter Eltis. 1978. *Britain's Economic Problem: Too Few Producers.* 2nd ed. London: Macmillan.

Beckerman, Wilfred, ed. 1972. *The Labour Government's Economic Record, 1964–70.* London: Duckworth.

Blackaby, F. T., ed. 1978. *British Economic Policy, 1960–74.* Cambridge: Cambridge University Press.

Brittan, Samuel. 1971. *Steering the Economy: The Role of the Treasury.* Rev. ed. Harmondsworth: Penguin Books.

————. 1977. *The Economic Consequences of Democracy.* London: Temple Smith.

Brown, Lord George. 1971. *In My Way.* London: Gollancz.

Chester, D. N. 1963. "The Plowden Report." *Public Administration* (U.K.) 41:1–15.

Clarke, Sir Richard. 1978. *Public Expenditure and Management Control.* London: Macmillan.

Dow, J. C. R. 1964. *The Management of the British Economy, 1945–60.* Cambridge: Cambridge University Press.

Godley, W. A. H. 1975. "Public Expenditure, 1970–1 to 1974–5." In *The Financing of Public Expenditure* (1st Report of the Expenditure Committee). HC 69-I, Dec. 11. London: HMSO.

Grant, Wyn, and David Marsh. 1977. *The CBI.* London: Hodder and Stoughton.

Great Britain. 1961. *Control of Public Expenditure* (Plowden Report). Cmnd. 1432. London: HMSO.

Great Britain. 1961. *The Economic and Financial Objectives of Nationalised Industries.* Cmnd. 1337. London: HMSO.

Great Britain, Expenditure Committee. 1978. *Financial Accountability to Parliament* (14th Report). HC 661, Session 1977–78, July. London: HMSO.

Hatfield, Michael. 1978. *The House the Left Built: Inside Labour Party Policy-making.* New York: Verry.

Heclo, Hugh, and Aaron Wildavsky. 1974. *The Private Government of Public Money.* Berkeley: University of California Press.

Holland, Stuart. 1976. "Socialist Alternatives." *Economist*, April 3.

Jones, Aubrey. 1973. *The New Inflation: The Politics of Prices and Incomes.* London: Deutsch.

Keegan, William, and Rupert Pennant-Rea. 1979. *Who Runs the Economy? Control and Influence in British Economic Policy.* London: Maurice Temple Smith.

Klein, Rudolf. 1976. "The Politics of Public Expenditure: American Theory and British Practice." *British Journal of Political Science* 6:401–33.

Mackenzie, William J. M. 1963. "The Plowden Report: A Translation." *Guardian*, May 25. Reprinted in Richard Rose, *Policymaking in Britain* (London: Macmillan, 1969).

Maynard, Alan, and Arthur Walker. 1975. "Cutting Public Spending." *New Society* Dec. 4, pp. 528–29.

National Economic Development Office (NEDO). 1976. *A Study of U.K. Nationalised Industries.* London: NEDO.

Organisation for Economic Cooperation and Development (OECD). 1976. *Revenue Statistics of Member Countries.* Paris: OECD.

———. 1978. *Public Expenditure Trends.* Paris: OECD, June.

Peacock, Alan, and Jack Wiseman. 1961. *The Growth of Public Expenditure in the United Kingdom.* Princeton: Princeton University Press.

Posner, Michael, and Richard Pryke. 1966. *New Public Enterprises.* London: Fabian Society.

Roseveare, Henry. 1969. *The Treasury.* New York: Columbia University Press.

Shonfield, Andrew. 1958. *British Economic Policy since the War.* Harmondsworth: Penguin Books.

Stewart, Michael. 1977. *The Jekyll and Hyde Years: Politics and Economic Policy since 1964.* London: Dent.

Stout, D. K. 1975. "Incomes Policy and the Cost of the Adversary System." In S. E. Finer, ed., *Adversary Politics and Electoral Reform*, pp. 117–42. London: Anthony Wigram.

Ward, T. S., and R. R. Neild. 1978. *The Measurement and Reform of Budgetary Policy.* London: Institute of Fiscal Studies.

Worswick, G. D. N., and F. T. Blackaby, eds. 1974. *The Medium Term: Models of the British Economy.* London: Heinemann.

Wright, Maurice. 1977. "Public Expenditure in Britain: The Crisis of Control." *Public Administration* (U.K.) 55:143–70.

Industrial Relations

Bauman, Zygmunt. 1972. *Between Class and Elite*, trans. Sheila Patterson. Manchester: Manchester University Press.

Butler, David, and Dennis Kavanagh. 1964. *The British General Election of February 1974.* London: Macmillan.

Clegg, Hugh. 1976. *The System of Industrial Relations in Great Britain.* 3rd ed. Oxford: Blackwell.

Confederation of British Industry (CBI). 1977. *Communication with People at Work.* London: CBI.

Conservative Party. 1968. *Fair Deal at Work.* London: Conservative Central Office.

Crossley, J. R. 1968. "The Donovan Report: A Case Study in the Poverty of Historicism." *British Journal of Industrial Relations* (issue on Donovan Report) 6:296–302.

Crouch, Colin. 1977. *Class Conflict and the Industrial Relations Crisis.* London: Heinemann.

Elliott, John. 1978. *Conflict or Cooperation? The Growth of Industrial Democracy.* London: Kogan Page.

Flanders, Allan, and Alan Fox. 1969. "Collective Bargaining: From Donovan to Durkheim." *British Journal of Industrial Relations* 7:151–80.

Forester, Tom. 1976. "How Democratic Are the Unions?" *New Society*, May 13, pp. 343–45.

Fox, Alan. 1979. "Labour in a New Era of Law." *New Society*, March 1, pp. 480–83.

Goldthorpe, John H., et al. 1969. *The Affluent Worker*. Cambridge: Cambridge University Press.

Great Britain. 1956. *The Economic Implications of Full Employment*. Cmnd. 9725. London: HMSO.

———. 1964. *Joint Statement of Intent*. London: HMSO.

———. 1969. *In Place of Strife*. Cmnd. 3888. London: HMSO.

———. 1978. *Industrial Democracy*. Cmnd. 7231. London: HMSO.

Great Britain, Committee of Inquiry on Industrial Democracy (Bullock Committee). 1977. *Report*. Cmnd. 6706. London: HMSO.

Great Britain, Department of Employment. 1977. "Industrial Disputes: International Comparisons." *Gazette*, Dec., pp. 1342–43.

Great Britain, Royal Commission on Trades Unions and Employers' Associations. 1968. *Report*. Cmnd. 3623. London: HMSO.

Hinton, James. 1973. *The First Shop Stewards' Movement*. London: George Allen and Unwin.

Inns of Court Conservative and Unionist Society. 1958. *A Giant's Strength*. London: The Society.

Jenkins, Peter. 1970. *The Battle of Downing Street*. London: Knight.

Jones, Aubrey. 1973. *The New Inflation*. London: Deutsch.

Kilroy-Silk, Robert. 1973. "The Donovan Royal Commission on Trade Unions." In R. A. Chapman, ed., *The Role of Commissions in Policy-Making*, pp. 42–80. London: George Allen and Unwin.

Kynaston, David. 1976. *King Labour: The British Working Class, 1850–1914*. London: George Allen and Unwin.

McCarthy, W. E. J. 1966. *The Role of Shop Stewards in British Industrial Relations*. Royal Commission on Trade Unions, Research Paper No. 1. London: HMSO.

———. 1970. "The Nature of Britain's Strike Problem." *British Journal of Industrial Relations* 8:224–36.

——— and N. D. Ellis. 1973. *Management by Agreement*. London: Hutchinson.

Milligan, Stephen. 1976. *The New Barons: Union Power in the 1970s*. London: Temple Smith.

Minkin, Lewis. 1974. "The British Labour Party and the Trade Unions." *Industrial and Labour Relations Review* 28:7–37.

Moran, Michael. 1977. *The Politics of Industrial Relations.* London: Macmillan.

Panitch, Leo. 1976. *Social Democracy and Industrial Militancy.* London: Cambridge University Press.

Pelling, Henry. 1968. "The Concept of the Labour Aristocracy." In Pelling, *Popular Politics and Society in Late Victorian Britain,* pp. 37–61. London: Macmillan.

———. 1976. *A History of British Trade Unionism.* 3rd ed. London: Macmillan.

Phelps Brown, E. H. 1959. *The Growth of British Industrial Relations.* London: Macmillan.

Price, Robert, and George Sayers Bain. 1976. "Union Growth Revisited: 1948–1974 in Perspective." *British Journal of Industrial Relations* 14:339–55.

Rogaly, Joe. 1977. *Grunwick.* Harmondsworth: Penguin Books.

Shonfield, Andrew. 1965. *Modern Capitalism.* London: Oxford University Press.

Taylor, Robert. 1978. *The Fifth Estate: Britain's Unions in the Seventies.* London: Routledge Kegan Paul.

———. 1979. "Unions above the Law?" *New Society,* Jan. 18, pp. 131–32.

Tholfsen, Trygve R. 1977. *Working Class Radicalism in Mid-Victorian England.* New York: Columbia University Press.

Trades Union Congress (TUC). 1969. *Programme for Action.* London: TUC, June.

———. 1971. *Special Report on the Industrial Relations Bill.* London: TUC, March.

———. 1974. *Industrial Democracy: Report by the TUC General Council to the 1974 Trades Union Congress.* London: TUC.

Turner, H. A. 1969. *Is Britain Really Strike Prone?* Department of Applied Economics, Paper No. 20. Cambridge: Cambridge University Press.

———. 1969. "The Donovan Report." *Economic Journal* 79:1–10.

Wigham, Eric. 1968. "The Arduous Path to Consensus." *The Times,* June 14.

———. 1969. *Trade Unions.* 2nd ed. Oxford: Oxford University Press.

———. 1974. *Strikes and Governments, 1893–1974.* London: Macmillan.

Local and Regional Policies

Ashford, Douglas E. 1976. "Reorganizing British Local Government: A Policy Problem." *Local Government Studies* (NS) 2:1–18.

———. 1981. *British Dogmatism and French Pragmatism: Central-Local Politics in the Welfare State*. London and Boston: George Allen and Unwin.

Batley, Richard, and John Edwards. 1978. *The Politics of Positive Discrimination: An Evaluation of the Urban Programme*. Cambridge: Cambridge University Press.

Crossman, Richard. 1965. *Municipal Review* 36:655–60.

———. 1975. *The Diaries of a Cabinet Minister*, vol. 1 (1964–66). London: Holt, Rinehart and Winston.

Fraser, Derek. 1976. *Urban Politics in Victorian England*. Leicester: Leicester University Press.

Great Britain. 1967. *Local Government in Wales*. Cmnd. 3340. London: HMSO.

———. 1972. *The New Local Authorities: Management and Structure* (Bains Report). London: HMSO.

———. 1977. *Policy for the Inner Cities*. Cmnd. 6845. London: HMSO.

Great Britain, Central Policy Review Staff. 1977. *Relations between Central Government and Local Authorities*. London: HMSO.

Great Britain, Committee of Inquiry into Local Finance (Layfield Committee). 1976. *Local Government Finance*. Cmnd. 6453. London: HMSO.

Great Britain, Committee of Inquiry into the System of Remuneration of Members of Local Authorities (Robinson Committee). 1977. *Remuneration of Councillors*. London: HMSO.

Great Britain, Department of the Environment. 1971. *Local Government in England: Government Proposals for Reorganisation*. Cmnd. 4584. London: HMSO.

Great Britain, Ministry of Housing and Local Government. 1970. *Reform of Local Government in England*. Cmnd. 4276. London: HMSO.

Great Britain, Royal Commission on Local Government in England. 1969. *Community Attitudes Survey: England*. Research Study No. 9. London: HMSO.

———. 1969. *Memorandum of Dissent*. Cmnd. 4040-I. London: HMSO.

———. 1969. *Report* (Redcliffe-Maud Report), 3 vols. Cmnd. 4040. London: HMSO.

Great Britain, Royal Commission on the Constitution. 1973. *Report.*
Cmnd. 5460. London: HMSO.

Great Britain, Secretary of State for the Environment. 1979. *Central
Government Controls over Local Authorities.* Cmnd. 7634. London: HMSO.

————. 1979. *Organic Change in Local Government.* Cmnd.
7457. London: HMSO.

Gyford, Jack. 1976. *Local Politics in Britain.* London: Croom
Helm.

Hambleton, Robin. 1977. "Policies for Areas." *Local Government
Studies* (NS) 3:13–29.

Hepworth, N. P. 1978. *The Finance of Local Government.* London: George Allen and Unwin.

Jackson, P. W. 1976. *Local Government.* London: Butterworth's.

Jones, George. 1966. "Mr. Crossman and the Reform of Local Government." *Parliamentary Affairs* 19:770–89.

Keith-Lucas, Brian, and Peter Richards. 1978. *A History of Local
Government in the Twentieth Century.* London: George Allen
and Unwin.

Labour Party Consultation Document. 1977. *Regional Authorities
and Local Government Reform.* London: The Labour Party, July.

Labour Party National Executive Committee. 1977. *Local Government Reform in England.* London: The Labour Party, Oct.

Minogue, Martin, ed. 1977. *Documents on Contemporary British
Government,* vol. 2: *Local Government in Britain.* Cambridge:
Cambridge University Press.

McKay, David, and Andrew Cox. 1978. "Confusion and Reality in
Public Policy: The Case of the British Urban Programme." *Political Studies* 26:491–506.

Pesheck, David. 1976. "The Reorganization Story: The Reform
that Never Was." *Municipal Review,* June, p. 74.

Plumb, J. H. 1969. *The Growth of Political Stability in England,
1675–1725.* Harmondsworth: Penguin Books.

Rhodes, R. A. W. 1974. "Local Government Reform—Three Questions—What Is Reorganisation? What Are the Effects of Reorganisation? Why Reorganisation?" *Social and Economic Administration*
8 (Spring): 6–21.

Richards, Peter. 1973. *The "Reformed" Local Government System.*
London: George Allen and Unwin.

Stanyer, Jeffrey. 1973. "The Redcliffe-Maud Royal Commission on
Local Government." In R. A. Chapman, ed., *The Role of Commissions in Policy-Making,* pp. 105–42. London: George Allen
and Unwin.

Wiseman, H. Victor, ed.   1970.   *Local Government in England 1958–69*.   London: Routledge and Kegan Paul.

Wood, Bruce.   1976.   *The Process of Local Government Reform, 1966–1974*.   London: George Allen and Unwin.

Social Security

Abel-Smith, Brian.   1963.   "Beveridge II: Another Viewpoint."   *New Society*, Feb. 28, pp. 9–11.

———   and Peter Townsend.   1965.   *The Poor and the Poorest*.   Occasional Papers on Social Administration No. 17.   London: Bell.

Atkinson, A. B.   1969.   *Poverty in Britain and the Reform of Social Security*.   Cambridge: Cambridge University Press.

———.   1974.   "Poverty and Income Inequality in Britain."   In Dorothy Wedderburn, ed., *Poverty, Inequality and Class Structure*, pp. 43–70.   Cambridge: Cambridge University Press.

———.   1976.   "Social Security: The Future."   *New Society*, Aug. 5.

Bruce, Maurice.   1968.   *The Coming of the Welfare State*.   4th ed.   London: Batsford.

Crossman, Richard.   1977.   *The Diaries of a Cabinet Minister*, vol. 3.   London: Hamish Hamilton and Jonathan Cape.

Donnison, David.   1976.   "Supplementary Benefits: Dilemmas and Priorities."   *Journal of Social Policy* 5:337–58.

Fieghen, Guy.   1978.   "The Need for a New Measure of Poverty."   In Muriel Brown and Sally Baldwin, eds., *Yearbook in Social Policy in Britain, 1977*, pp. 107–16.   London: Routledge and Kegan Paul.

Field, Frank.   1975.   "What Is Poverty?"   *New Society*, Sept. 25, pp. 688–91.

Fraser, Derek.   1973.   *The Evolution of the British Welfare State*.   London: Macmillan.

Gilbert, Bentley B.   1970.   *British Social Policy, 1914–1939*.   Ithaca, N.Y.: Cornell University Press.

Glennerster, Howard.   1977.   "The Year of the Cuts."   In Katherine Jones et al., eds., *Yearbook of Social Policy in Britain, 1976*, pp. 3–20.   London: Routledge and Kegan Paul.

Gough, Ian.   1975.   "Inflation and Social Policy."   In Katherine Jones, ed., *Yearbook in Social Policy in Britain, 1974*, pp. 14–31.   London: Routledge and Kegan Paul.

Great Britain.   1942.   *Social Insurance and Allied Services* (Beveridge Report).   Cmd. 6404.   London: HMSO.

———.   1969.   *National Superannuation and Social Insurance*.   Cmnd. 3883.   London: HMSO.

———.   1971.   *Strategy for Pensions*.   Cmnd. 4755.   London: HMSO.

315   **References**

————. 1972. *Proposals for a Tax-Credit System.* Cmnd. 5116. London: HMSO.

————. 1974. *Better Pensions.* Cmnd. 5713. London: HMSO.

————. 1979. *Social Trends, 1979* (annual series). London: HMSO.

Great Britain, Department of Health and Social Security. 1978. *Social Assistance: A Review of the Supplementary Benefits Scheme in Great Britain.* July. London: HMSO.

Great Britain, Government Statistical Service. 1977. "International Comparisons of Taxes and Social Security Contributions, 1969–1975." In *Economic Trends,* pp. 107–19. London: HMSO.

Hall, Phoebe, et al. 1975. *Change, Choice and Conflict in Social Policy.* London: Heinemann.

Harris, Jose. 1979a. "From the Cradle to the Grave: The Rise of the Welfare State." *New Society,* Jan. 18, pp. 127–30.

————. 1979b. "What Happened after Beveridge?" *New Society,* Jan. 27, pp. 190–93.

Heclo, Hugh. 1974. *Modern Social Politics in Britain and Sweden.* New Haven: Yale University Press.

Kay, J. A., and M. A. King. 1978. *The British Tax System.* London: Oxford University Press.

Organization for Economic Cooperation and Development (OECD). 1976. *Public Expenditure on Income Maintenance Programmes.* Paris: OECD, July.

Phillips, Melanie. 1978. "Family Policy: The Long Years of Neglect." *New Society,* June 8, pp. 531–34.

Rathbone, Eleanor. 1924. *The Disinherited Family.* London: Edward Arnold.

Reddin, Mike. 1977. "National Insurance and Private Pensions." In Katherine Jones, ed., *Yearbook of Social Policy in Britain, 1976,* pp. 70–95. London: Routledge and Kegan Paul.

Seldon, Arthur. 1963. "Beveridge: 20 Years After," *New Society,* Feb. 14, pp. 9–12.

Titmuss, Richard. 1962. *Income Distribution and Social Change.* London: George Allen and Unwin.

————. 1969. "Superannuation for All: A Broader View." *New Society,* Feb. 27, pp. 315–17.

Townsend, Peter, and Dorothy Wedderburn. 1965. *The Aged in the Welfare State.* Occasional Papers in Social Administration No. 14. London: Bell.

Turner, Jill. 1978. "One-Parent Families: The Undeserving Poor?" *New Society,* July 6, pp. 11–12.

Walley, Sir John. 1972. *Social Security: Another British Failure?* London: Knight.

316   References

Race and Immigration

Akram, Mohammed. 1974. *Where Do You Keep Your String Beds?* London: Runnymede Trust.

"Barberous." 1977. *The Economist,* Dec. 17.

Batley, Richard, and John Edwards. 1978. *The Politics of Positive Discrimination: An Evaluation of the Urban Programme.* Cambridge: Cambridge University Press.

Bohning, W. R. 1972. *The Migration of Workers in the United Kingdom and the European Community.* London: Oxford University Press.

Bradley, Ian. 1978. "Why Churchill's Plan to Limit Immigration Was Shelved." *Times,* March 20.

Burney, Elizabeth. 1967. *Housing on Trial: A Study of Immigrants and Local Government.* London: Oxford University Press.

Carby, Keith, and Manat Thakur. 1977. *No Problem Here?* London: Institute of Personnel Management.

Crossman, Richard. 1977. *Dairies of a Cabinet Minister,* vol. 3. London: Hamish Hamilton and Jonathan Cape.

Daniel, W. W. 1968. *Racial Discrimination in Britain.* Harmondsworth: Penguin Books.

Deakin, Nicholas. 1968. "The Politics of the Commonwealth Immigrants Bill." *Political Quarterly* 39:25–45.

——— and Jenny Bourne. 1970. "Powell, the Minorities, and the 1970 Election." *Political Quarterly* 41:399–415.

Evans, Peter. 1978. "The Lobby That Just Grew and Grew." *Times,* Nov. 21.

Foot, Paul. 1965. *Immigration and Race in British Politics.* Harmondsworth: Penguin Books.

Freeman, Gary. 1979. *Immigrant Labor and Racial Conflict in Industrial Societies: The French and British Experience, 1945–1975.* Princeton: Princeton University Press.

Great Britain, Home Office. 1978. *Observations on the Report of the Select Committee on Race Relations and Immigration.* Cmnd. 7287. London: HMSO.

Great Britain, Prime Minister. 1965. *Immigration from the Commonwealth.* Cmnd. 2739. London: HMSO.

———. 1974. *Equality for Women: A Policy for Equal Opportunity.* Cmnd. 5724. London: HMSO.

———. 1975. *Race Relations.* Cmnd. 6234. London: HMSO.

Great Britain, Select Committee on Race Relations and Immigration. 1974–75. *Report: The Organisation of Race Relations Administration,* vol. 1. HC 448-I, July. London: HMSO.

———. 1977–78. *First Report: Immigration,* vol. 1. HC 303-I, July. London: HMSO.

Hill, Michael, and Ruth M. Issacharoff. 1971. *Community Action on Race Relations: A Study of Community Relations Committees in Britain.* London: Oxford University Press for the Institute of Race Relations.

Hindrell, Keith. 1965. "The Genesis of the Race Relations Bill." *Political Quarterly* 36:390–405.

Hiro, Dilip. 1973. *Black British, White British.* Rev. ed. London: Monthly Review Press.

Holman, Robert, and Lynda Hamilton. 1973. "The British Urban Programme." *Policy and Politics* 2:97–112.

Humphrey, Derek. 1973. "Now We Have *Six* Varieties of Foreigners." *Sunday Times*, Jan. 28.

Jones, Catherine. 1977. *Immigration and Social Policy in Britain.* London: Tavistock Publications.

Katznelson, Ira. 1973. *Black Men, White Cities.* London: Oxford University Press.

Lawrence, Daniel. 1974. *Black Migrants, White Natives.* Cambridge: Cambridge University Press.

Lomas, Gillian B. 1973. *Census, 1971: The Coloured Population of Great Britain, Preliminary Report.* London: Runnymede Trust.

Plender, Richard. 1975. "The Sex Discrimination Bill." *New Community* 4:291–302.

Rose, E. J. B., et al. 1969. *Colour and Citizenship: A Report on British Race Relations.* London: Oxford University Press.

Rose, Hannah. 1972. "The Immigration Act 1971: A Case Study in the Work of Parliament." *Parliamentary Affairs* 26:69–96.

———. 1973. "The Politics of Immigration after the 1971 Act." *Political Quarterly* 44:183–96.

Rose, Richard. 1974. *Politics in England.* 2nd ed. Boston: Little, Brown.

———, ed. 1970. *Policy-Making in Britain.* New York: Free Press.

Runnymede Trust. 1978a. *Beyond Tokenism.* London: The Trust.

———. 1978b. *"Sus."* London: The Trust.

———. 1974. "Trade Unions and Immigrant Workers." *New Community* 4:19–36.

Smith, David J. 1976. *The Facts of Racial Disadvantage.* Political and Economic Planning Broadsheet, vol. 42, no. 560. London: Feb.

Studlar, Donley T. 1977. "Social Context and Attitudes towards Coloured Immigrants." *British Journal of Sociology* 28:168–84.

Thornton, A. P. 1968. *The Imperial Idea and Its Enemies.* Garden City, N.Y.: Doubleday Anchor Books.

White, Robin M. 1977. "Does Race Equal Sex?" *New Community* 5:419–25.

Index